From the painting by Lynwood Palmer

THE HON. GEORGE LAMBTON

MEN AND HORSES
I HAVE KNOWN

BY
THE HON.
GEORGE LAMBTON

Foreword by John Hislop

1 LOWER GROSVENOR PLACE, LONDON, S.W.1

British Library Cataloguing in Publication Data

Lambton, George
   Men and horses I have known.
   1. Lambton, George   2. Racehorse owners
   —Great Britain—Biography
   I. Title
   798.4'0092'4   SF336.L2

ISBN 0-85131-419-8

© 1963 J. A. Allen & Company Limited

First published October, 1924
Reprinted October, 1924
Reprinted November, 1924
Reprinted 1963
Reprinted 1986. (This edition being a facsimile reprint of the 1963 edition. The latter was originated from the 1924 original edition with minor amendments to the plates and preliminary pages only.)

No part of this publication may be reproduced, stored in a retrieval system, or transmitted, in any form, or by any means, electronic, mechanical, photocopying, recording, or otherwise, without the prior permission, in writing, of the publishers.

Printed and bound in Great Britain by
Biddles Ltd, Guildford and King's Lynn

It is not my intention in these pages to write the history of my life, except in so far as it brought me into contact with many interesting men and famous horses. I have tried to recall my memories of these and of the great races which it has been my good fortune often to see, hoping they may be of interest at any rate to race-goers of to-day. Much of the material contained in these chapters appeared in a series of articles in the *Weekly Dispatch*, and the success which they met with has encouraged me to put them into more permanent form. I want to thank the editor of the *Weekly Dispatch*, Mr. Frank Griggs, manager to Mr. Clarence Hailey, of Newmarket, Mr. W. A. Rouch, Messrs. Forres, Mr. Lynwood Palmer, Mr. Robinson, and the Sport and General Press Agency for their invaluable help in supplying many of the illustrations.

George Lambton

CONTENTS

	PAGE
CHAPTER I	
EARLY DAYS—MY FIRST RACEHORSE	13
CHAPTER II	
GENTLEMEN RIDERS OF THE 'EIGHTIES—RODDY OWEN, ARTHUR COVENTRY, AND OTHERS	23
CHAPTER III	
MAT DAWSON AND FRED ARCHER	36
CHAPTER IV	
SIR JOHN ASTLEY AND OLD DAYS AT ASCOT	47
CHAPTER V	
ARTHUR YATES—COUNT KINSKY—W. H. P. JENKINS	60
CHAPTER VI	
BURGH BARONY RACES AND TOM GREEN OF BEVERLEY	70
CHAPTER VII	
TRAINING WITH ALFRED SADLER—AN ADVENTURE AT NOTTINGHAM—MY BROTHER HEDWORTH	83
CHAPTER VIII	
SAM LEWIS — A GREAT MONEYLENDER — LORD DURHAM'S GIMCRACK SPEECH	95
CHAPTER IX	
THREE FAMOUS HORSES—ORMONDE, MINTING, AND THE BARD	106
CHAPTER X	
CAROLINE DUCHESS OF MONTROSE AND CAPTAIN MACHELL	121
CHAPTER XI	
JOE CANNON AND HIS STABLE	135
CHAPTER XII	
SOME RIDING EXPERIENCES—TOM CANNON OF DANEBURY	152
CHAPTER XIII	
HE UNLUCKY SAVOYARD—GLENTHORPE AND PARASANG	162

CONTENTS

	PAGE
CHAPTER XIV	
CHARLIE CUNNINGHAM—JOHN CORLETT—ABINGTON BAIRD	177
CHAPTER XV	
LORD RANDOLPH CHURCHILL—JOHN PORTER—THE DUKE OF WESTMINSTER	185
CHAPTER XVI	
HOLLINGTON AND THE GRAND MILITARY—LORD ROSEBERY AND LADAS	197
CHAPTER XVII	
MY START AS A TRAINER—LORD DERBY AND HIS EARLY RACING	212
CHAPTER XVIII	
KING EDWARD — PERSIMMON'S DERBY — MR. LEOPOLD DE ROTHSCHILD	223
CHAPTER XIX	
THE FOUNDATION OF LORD DERBY'S STUD—CANTERBURY PILGRIM—LORD WILLIAM BERESFORD AND TOD SLOAN	233
CHAPTER XX	
SOME AMERICAN OWNERS AND TRAINERS—DOPING—SAVAGE HORSES	250
CHAPTER XXI	
CHAUCER—DANNY MAHER AND ROCK SAND	264
CHAPTER XXII	
THE FIRE AT STANLEY HOUSE—KEYSTONE II—PRETTY POLLY AND THE ASCOT CUP	273
CHAPTER XXIII	
LATER TRAINING DAYS—SWYNFORD'S ST. LEGER	283
CHAPTER XXIV	
STEDFAST AND KING WILLIAM	295
CHAPTER XXV	
DIADEM	302
CHAPTER XXVI	
RACING AND THE WAR—HORATIO BOTTOMLEY	308

ILLUSTRATIONS

	TO FACE PAGE
The Hon. George Lambton	FRONTISPIECE
Lambton Castle	16
Fenton, Northumberland	16
George Frederick, second Earl of Durham	17
Arthur Coventry	32
Bay Middleton	32
Hugh Owen	32
Roddy Owen	32
Mat Dawson	33
Fred Archer	33
Sir John Astley, "The Mate"	33
Count Charles Kinsky on "Zoedone"	64
John Osborne	64
Tom Green	65
Mr. Alfred Sadler	65
Sam Lewis	80
Sir George Chetwynd	80
Minting	81
Mr. Robert C. Vyner	81
Captain Machell	128
Fred Archer on Strathavon	129
Fred Archer at Newmarket going to the post	129
Mr. Joseph Cannon	144
Bellona	144
Robert Peck	145
Tom Cannon	145
The Hon. George Lambton in 1886	176
Mr. Arthur Coventry on his hack when he was starter	177
John Porter	177
Captain the Hon. Charles Lambton, D.S.O., afterwards Brigadier-General	192
Captain the Hon. Hedworth Lambton, afterwards Admiral-of-the-Fleet Sir Hedworth Meux	192
Ladas, winner of the Derby, with the Earl of Rosebery, Mat Dawson and Jack Watts	193
F. Rickaby (Senior)	224
Freddy Rickaby (Junior)	224

ILLUSTRATIONS

	TO FACE PAGE
Jack Watts	224
Harry Barker	224
Mornington Cannon	224
Tod Sloan	224
The Hon. George Lambton at Bedford Lodge	225
Chaucer	225
Chaucer winning the Liverpool Cup	240
Stedfast winning the Coronation Cup from Prince Palatine	240
Stanley House Stables	241
Going out for morning exercise	241
The Earl of Derby, K.G.	256
The late Earl of Derby leading in Keystone II after winning the Oaks	256
Finish of the St. Leger, Swynford winning from Bronzino	257
Lord Derby leading in Swynford after winning the St. Leger— Frank Wootton up	272
Swynford	273
Stedfast	273
The Hon. George Lambton and the lads at Stanley House	288
Diadem, winner of the 1,000 Guineas, with John Lambton, aged 7 years, and R. Osgood	289
Diadem and Stephen Donoghue	289
The Earl of Durham, K.G.	304
Lieut.-General The Hon. Sir William Lambton, K.C.B., D.S.O.	304
The Hon. Mrs. George Lambton and her second son, Edward George	305

INTRODUCTION by MR. E. G. LAMBTON

I was very young when I read for the first time " Men and Horses I Have Known" and I have read it many times since.

Although to most of us, the era which this book describes seems long ago, it is a fascinating description of racing as it was in a possibly happier and more glamorous time.

Horses, trainers, jockeys and people, good and bad, come to life in a way that I have never found in any other book on the sport that I and so many others love, and I am grateful to Mr. Allen for bringing out this new edition.

Teddy Lambton.

KREMLIN HOUSE, NEWMARKET, 1963.

FOREWORD

This delightful book is the most important and valuable mirror of the Turf bridging the 19th and 20th centuries.

It is written with the easy grace distinctive of the era which it depicts, and running through it are the threads of knowledge and experience of one of the greatest masters of the training profession.

Among racing autobiographies it fits that historic description of one of Eclipse's brilliant victories: "First—the rest nowhere."

JOHN HISLOP

NEWBURY, BERKSHIRE, 1963.

CHAPTER I

EARLY DAYS—MY FIRST RACE-HORSE

I THINK the details of anyone's childhood are always tedious, so I shall pass over my early days as briefly as possible.

The first thing that I can remember about myself was my love for horses and dogs. I was the sixth member of a family of thirteen, having eight brothers and four sisters. My mother died when I was eleven years old. My father, Lord Durham, I believe was always a shy, rather reserved man. He never really got over my mother's death, and after it withdrew into his own shell more than ever, and lived chiefly at his places in the North—Lambton, in Co. Durham, and Fenton, in Northumberland. In spite of a very quick temper, he was extraordinarily kind and considerate to his children, and, although we had a wholesome fear of him, we all adored him. He gave us the best of ponies and horses to ride, as suited to our ages, and we each had a dog of our own, and when I was at Eton, fond as I was of cricket and football, in the background my mind was always set on horses and hunting. We made a big party in the holidays when hunting from Lambton with the North Durham, a pack which in those days hunted over a good sporting country, nearly all grass, and which generally carried a fine scent.

Mr. Anthony Maynard, who was then Master, was an enthusiastic sportsman, but believed in getting his hounds well settled down before he let his field go. I well remember when he did give the word his shouting out, " Now then, catch 'em if you can, you won't find hounds run like this in Leicestershire ! "

Mr. Newton Apperley, who was for a long time agent to the late Lord Londonderry, was his right-hand man. A near relative of the famous Nimrod, he knew as much and more than most people about hounds and hunting.

I suppose I took to the game pretty quickly judging from an old account of a run with those hounds which was written by Mr. Apperley and sent me the other day by an old friend in Durham. After describing a preliminary hunt, he says, " The Master then gave orders to trot back to Mr. Gee's plantation, and a fine old fox was soon on foot ; he broke westward and went to ——— wood, and turned short back as if intending Mr. Gee's covert again, but before reaching it he turned to the right and made a circle in the direction of Manor House, when young George Lambton, Lord Durham's fifth son, Mr. Keaner, Lindsay Wood and myself were the only four with the hounds. We had a very nice gallop with heaps of jumping. We were all led by young George Lambton, an Eton boy of about fifteen or sixteen years old, who rode splendidly, and went straight as a bird, mounted on a thoroughbred bay mare. Neither of us could gain on him in the least. I never was so pleased with a lad in my life, the pace was tremendous."

I have no recollection of this hunt myself, but I remember the mare well, my first really good hunter, and my bitter grief when she broke her back with me over some rails later on.

But my happiest days as a boy were spent at Fenton, a place my father had bought in North Northumberland, and my first recollection of hunting was being run away with on my pony near Fenton, and being blooded by that famous old sportsman, Lord Wemyss, at the age of seven. I have the mask and brush which he gave me still.

What a glorious country it was ; you could hunt, shoot or fish every day of the week, and we boys had a splendid time there. Most of my brothers and sisters rode well. We used to ride over in the morning to the River Glen, about five miles from Fenton, taking our lunch with us, and putting the ponies up at a farm. When fishing was over we would gallop home, often jumping the fences instead of going through the gates. I had also a small mixed pack of harriers and beagles which gave me immense pleasure and did not do much damage to the hares.

I can remember Mr. Gladstone running wildly about with his hair streaming in the wind and his coat tails flying when we were hunting rabbits with our terriers. I don't think he was much of a sportsman, but he was so fond of children that he entered into their pleasures.

My family belonged to the Liberal Party, and, though no one could say that politics played a large part in the life at Lambton or Fenton, yet from tradition I looked upon Disraeli, the Tories and the French with hatred and suspicion.

When my father died he left Fenton to my brother Freddy, who was Master, and had hunted the hounds himself for many years. He was a quiet and most patient huntsman. He shewed wonderful sport and could kill a fox as well as any man. When war broke out in 1914, years after he had given up, and at the age of 61, no one else being available in the country, he took hounds again, hunted them himself, and with the assistance of one old Whip, kept the whole thing going for three seasons. He used to say how hard it would be for the young men who were fighting, if they should find their hunting gone when they came back. I spent one winter with him during this time, and in spite of many difficulties we had some good sport.

As I have said, we children had a wonderful time in those old days at Fenton. A large family is a good school, and having four elder brothers and an elder sister as hard as any boy, I soon learnt to take care of myself.

I went first to a private school at Winchester, but

I was only there one term, when I was sent to a school at Brighton. Billy Lee was the Head Master, and a very good coach he must have been for his boys always took good places, and we were taught to play cricket and football, and to swim. He was a great big jovial man, and we all liked him although he was pretty free with his cane. I noticed that the boys who took their gruel well always became his favourites.

I went to Eton rather early, when I was just thirteen, but I was only there about three years. I was at Edmund Warre's House. He was, as everyone knows, a good fellow and became Head Master of Eton. Unfortunately, he and I never got on well together, and that spoilt my life at Eton, so that I was not in the least sorry to leave. Warre was a very obstinate man, and he took it into his head that I could do Latin verses, which I could not, and the consequence was that every week there was trouble for me. Other work I could do easily. It was not an unusual thing for some boys to be let off Latin verses, and put to some other work, and I remember my brother Charlie, who was Captain of the House, telling Warre that I simply could not string two English lines together, let alone Latin ones, but he was adamant. Day after day I would have pupil room after twelve o'clock instead of cricket and football.

The master I liked best was old Mitchell, "Mike" as he was called. He had been a great cricketer in his younger days, and he always coached the Eton Eleven. He had the reputation of being one of the strictest masters at Eton, and so he was in some ways, but you always knew where you were with him. If you played straight either at cricket or at work, he was an easy man to get on with, but the boy who was shifty and told lies had a hard time of it with him.

One Summer half I got into trouble for going to Ascot Races. It was the custom in those days to run over during Ascot week in the afternoons and hope for a lift back on a coach. And on this occasion, nearly a hundred boys, myself among the number, were caught

LAMBTON CASTLE

FENTON, NORTHUMBERLAND

GEORGE FREDERICK, 2ND EARL OF DURHAM

on the way home and reported to the Head Master. He gave us a Georgic to write out, and we had to put in a hundred lines every day at his house. It was no joke having to do this in the Summer half. I happened to be on friendly terms with a certain person in the Head Master's household, who was fond of sport and with whom I used to talk racing. He hinted to me that his master was rather careless about these punishments, and would only take a casual look at the papers, so I thought that I would not put in my next lot and see what happened. As nothing was said I never wrote another line, which was the only time I ever scored over the authorities.

My first real visit to Ascot was in 1878, when I went with my father, and I saw the races from the Trainers' Stand. It is curious how these very early days come back to me, and a race I remember distinctly was the Prince of Wales Stakes won by Mr. Houldsworth's Glengarry ridden by George Fordham. I was standing next James Ryan, the trainer of Glengarry, and I remember that half-way up the hill there were four or five horses fighting out a desperate race. My eyes were glued on the green and gold colours of Mr. Houldsworth, as Ryan had told me that he thought he would win, and I had a bet of £1 on the horse with him. I saw the green and gold jacket drop out. Ryan put his glasses down, saying, "I'm beat," and I thought it was all over. But not a bit of it, for then I saw my horse gradually creeping up again, and one dash close home put his head in front on the winning post. This was my first lesson in the art of race riding, and the first of the many brilliant races I have seen George Fordham ride.

Another thing that impressed itself on my memory was the delight of the other trainers at Ryan's success. When later I came to know him well I understood the reason. He and his master, Mr. J. H. Houldsworth, were two of the best sportsmen in the world. Everyone liked to see them win. Mr. Houldsworth had many

B

good horses, but ill-luck always stuck to him in classic races. I should say the best horse he owned was Springfield. James Ryan was for many years master of the Newmarket Drag, he was a fine horseman, and a good man to hounds.

That same year, 1878, a French horse Verneuil, carried off the Gold Vase, the Ascot Cup, and the Alexandra Plate. He was trained by old Tom Jennings, who was a great trainer of long-distance horses. Tom Jennings gave his jockey, James Goater, orders to jump off in front from the fall of the flag, saying that if he ever allowed any horse to head him he would never ride for him again. I believe Verneuil made every yard of the running in all three races.

When I left Eton, at the age of sixteen, the place not being supposed to agree with me, I went to a tutor in Dorsetshire, and with a good horse and a gun I was ready to get the best of any fun that was going. Bere Regis, where my tutor lived, was another good sporting country, both for hunting, shooting and fishing, and I certainly learnt more about these pursuits than anything else.

I made the acquaintance of Montague Guest, who had a shooting-box there. " Monty," as he was always called, a very tall handsome man with most charming manners, was a great figure in the London world for many years. He was wonderfully kind to me, and gave me as much shooting and fishing as I wanted. He did not care about horses, and said that I would find life more amusing with a rod, a gun and the ladies—and less expensive. I was never much of a fisherman, although there is something very attractive in wandering about a river with pretty scenery and fish to be caught, but it is a lonely pursuit, and I was not happy unless I had a dog with me.

I had then a big fox terrier called " Trap," purchased from the Home for Lost Dogs at Battersea. I really think he must have been a remarkable dog ; anyhow, I thought there was nothing to compare with him in the world. I was fond of going out after dinner to fish, and Trap would come with me. At first he was very much bored, but after a time he became interested in what was going on. It was a difficult river in which to land your fish owing to the weeds, and as I did not have a landing net I often lost a fish when almost on the bank. One night, Trap, seeing the fish struggling at the edge, made a grab at him and threw him clean over his back on to the bank, and from that moment he was as keen as possible on the job. But after he had landed his fish he would not touch it, and looked at it with evident disgust. He was a wonder at catching rabbits, and his name frequently appears in the game-book at Fenton with the number caught by himself when we had been shooting in the Cheviots. How sad it is that a dog's life is so short.

I hunted with the East Dorset, Cattistock, and occasionally with the Blackmore Vale from Bere Regis. The Blackmore Vale was not easy to get at. I had to ride a bicycle from Bere Regis to Wareham, a distance of about ten miles, to catch an early train. I had a hireling at the station nearest the meet, and I had to bicycle home from Wareham at night, all the time in my boots and breeches which I had to clean myself. In those days it was the fashion to wear varnished boots, and, though I started off looking pretty smart, after the bicycle ride my appearance cannot have been up to much. These amusements did not leave much time for work, but somehow or other I managed to scramble into Trinity College, Cambridge.

Shortly after I arrived there, according to the usual custom, I went to pay my respects to my tutor. A very pleasant man he was, and, after a certain amount of the ordinary civilities, he asked me if I had come to Cambridge to work or to amuse myself ; if it was for the former purpose he would put me in the way of getting the best instruction possible, and would himself take interest in me, but, if my wish was for the latter, he could also tell me how to do the smallest amount of work, involving the least possible amount of friction with the authorities. Having unhesitatingly chosen the path of pleasure, so good was his advice that during the whole of that term I never attended a single lecture or did one stroke of work. I became a member of the Beefsteak Club, wore a blue coat with brass buttons, and a yellow waistcoat on Sundays, joined the Athenæum, rode with the Drag, and got no real benefit from Cambridge except for one thing, and that, I think, has been of great service to me in my life.

There was very high gambling in those days at the University, and night after night I and my friends used to sit up till three or four o'clock in the morning trying to win money from each other. I very soon got tired of this, for it not only bored me but it seemed to me a d——d stupid way of gambling. If you won, it generally meant you took the money out of the pocket of your best friend who probably was not able to pay you. I have lived all my life among people whose custom it is to do this, and my early lesson at Cambridge, except on rare occasions, has kept me out of it. Of all the pursuits of amusement and excitement this high gambling amongst friends brings you the least satisfaction or profit.

After my first term my father died. I had been so much with him, and I had such complete confidence in his sympathy and love, that I was never afraid of telling him all my doings, whether good or bad, and for a time I felt I could never enjoy anything again if he was not there to tell it to. Fortunately, young people get over their griefs fairly quickly or the world would be a very sad place.

I had not really cared for Cambridge, for I had gone there in the wrong spirit. Cambridge, if you go there to work, play cricket or football and boat, is a great place, but not having done these things, and finding the hunting indifferent, when my guardian, the late Mr. Charles Barrington, proposed that I should go to a crammer for the Army, I left without regret. So I went, in 1878, to the famous Mr. Faithful, at Storrington, although I had no particular fancy for a soldier's life. Here, again, I am afraid I did little work, and eventually Mr. Faithful, who was a very curious old fellow, told me one day that he would be delighted to see me at Storrington as his guest, but not as his pupil. However, during my stay there I won my first race.

There were seventy or eighty boys at Storrington, most of them had horses, and we used to run what we called the Storrington Derby on the Downs at Michel Grove, where old William Goater trained. When I was at Cambridge my father had given me a thoroughbred horse called St. Julian as a hack. He was not much good, but he won the Storrington Derby from a big field of about twenty, and I took nearly all the money in the place.

During that time I also bought my first race-horse. This was Burgomaster, and he was advertised in the *Exchange and Mart* to be sold for ninety sovereigns. I answered the advertisement and became his owner. He was a great ugly brute, nearly seventeen hands high, and four years old. I sent him to Fred Barrett who trained at Findon, not far from Storrington. Shortly afterwards I bought another horse called The Martyr for £150 from Barrett himself. Not having any money I went up to London and negotiated a bill from some money-lender for £1,000, as may be imagined, at the most exorbitant rate of interest. Burgomaster was not any good, but managed to win some little race, and my first ride in public was on The Martyr at Warwick. I could not run in my own name as there would have been trouble with the authorities in the shape of tutors and guardians, so the horse ran in the name and colours of Lord Douglas Gordon, who was a patron of Barrett's stable. The Martyr and I finished second, and I think I probably rode very badly, as the horse was promptly claimed by Jerry Dalgleish. but as the claiming price was £200, and I got £90 for being second, the transaction worked out fairly satisfactorily from a financial point of view.

My racing career, however, was, for the moment, rather prematurely cut short by the intervention of the aforesaid tutors and guardians, who made it almost impossible for me to continue, but, having had my first taste of riding races, I had firmly made up my mind that my profession would be on the Turf.

CHAPTER II

GENTLEMEN RIDERS OF THE 'EIGHTIES—RODDY OWEN, ARTHUR COVENTRY, AND OTHERS

It was in October, 1880, that I rode my first winner, a mare called Pompeia, at Nottingham, upsetting a three-to-one on chance, ridden by Arthur Coventry, by a neck; the mare belonged to Tom Green of Beverley, who had trained for my father, and was then training for my brother Durham. Tom was a great, burly, sanguine Yorkshireman, a very clever man with horses, and as quaint a character as you could meet. He was enormously strong, and he gave me what he thought was an approving pat on the back as I got off the mare, which nearly knocked me down. After that I had only an occasional ride, and my next winning mount was again on Pompeia, at Winchester, in June, when curiously enough I again beat Arthur Coventry on a hot favourite by a head. This made me think I could ride, but I still did not find people tumbling over each other to put me up.

At the Lincoln Autumn Meeting of the same year a four-year-old called Pudding won a selling hurdle race the first day and was bought by a farmer for 168 guineas. The horse was in a three mile steeplechase the next day, and the farmer was anxious to run him. The course was rather a stiff one, going out into the country over natural fences, and no one was keen to ride as the horse was supposed to have done no schooling, so I offered my valuable services, which were accepted. I was staying with Sir John Astley, at Brigg Hall, for the races, and I remember Sir John, Lord Westmorland, and General Goodlake coming to see me get up on this horse, and their suggestion that I should make a will before I went out, leaving my money to one of them. I had to ride 10 st. 11 lb., which meant a very small saddle. The first fence in the country brought Pudding on to his head, but after that he never put a foot wrong, and going round without another mistake won in a canter at twelve to one.

This performance gave me a start, and after that I began to get mounts more often. When someone was hard up for a jockey they would put me up. Pudding afterwards in his own class was a remarkable horse, and won innumerable races, but I never happened to ride him again

Those who are fond of cross-country sport in these days must find it a much more difficult business to collect a stud of steeplechase horses than when I started in 1880. Then it was quite possible, in fact easy, to go to a race meeting in the Autumn months and buy good sound young horses that were too slow for flat racing for anything between £50 and £300. You would often find three or four big good-looking horses put up after a selling race with practically no reserve on them, and they were sold for no other reason than that they were not speedy enough to win on the flat. At that time there was no foreign market worth speaking of, nor was there so much flat racing, and owners were inclined to cut their losses and get rid of a horse that did not look like paying his way.

In the days of which I write there were hunters' flat races at almost every meeting, Winter and Summer. I have even seen one run at Epsom. These hunters' flat races were the finest nursery for gentlemen riders, and in my opinion a deadly blow was dealt to cross-country sport when they were abolished. Certainly the selling races were contested by a very bad class of horse, but in the other races I have seen some grand types of the British thoroughbred; horses such as Quits, Durham, St. Galmier, The Gunner, Boisterous, and Bloodstone, who made light of fourteen stone, the brilliant Hesper,

Cloister and Why Not, all National winners, made their mark in hunters' flat races.

Durham I particularly remember. He was a brown gelding by Cathedral, the property of Mr. Charles Perkins, and was a grand horse up to 14st. Generally ridden by Tom Spence, or Mr. George Thompson, he certainly won over twenty races, and was the most popular horse in the North. He was a very difficult horse to ride, and wanted a lot of humouring. Once, early in my riding days, I rode him at Newcastle. Tom Spence told me if he was in a sulky humour I must talk to him, and, if politeness did not answer, to call him every bad name I could think of. Evidently my vocabulary was not nearly strong enough, for he laughed at my efforts and did nothing. I remember George Thompson, who only weighed about 7st., winning a race on him carrying 14st. He was quite unable to carry the saddle and weight-cloths back into the weighing room, and they had to send for the Stewards to give permission for someone to help him. These races attracted many young men both rich and poor. The rich man had the opportunity of gratifying his wish to ride winners by spending money freely, and buying the best horses on the market; the poor man had the chance to pick up cheap horses that were good enough to run in the poorer-class races. It also brought many people into racing who would never have come into it without the opportunity to ride themselves. Many who began with hunters' flat races would get bitten with the game, and graduate into the higher form of steeplechasing. Men like Charlie Cunningham, "Bay" Middleton, Wenty Hope Johnstone, and a host of others, would never have been heard of in racing but for these hunters' flat races, their weight being prohibitive.

What really killed this type of race was the slackness with which the authorities looke on the qualifications of amateurs. Many people rode as gentlemen riders who were very far from meriting that distinction. When those sort of people get the chance they will bring discredit on any form of sport. On one occasion I arrived only just in time to weigh out for a hunters' flat race when there were only two runners. My opponent was one of those pseudo-gentlemen with a very bad character. When I got down to the post he quietly said, "How do you want the race run, I am going for you." I told him he could go to the devil, and ride his horse as he liked. My mare being as handy as a cat, I determined to give him the fright of his life, so I never went near him till a hundred yards from home, and then only beat him a neck. He was not only a d——d scoundrel but a very bad rider. Someone said this was the best finish he ever rode because he was not trying and sat quiet.

All the same there were a lot of cheery good fellows riding about that time, both amateurs and professionals, so many that in mentioning their names from memory I fear to miss some.

Among the amateurs, first and foremost came Arthur Coventry, the brothers Roddy and Hugh Owen, W. Bevill, Wenty Hope Johnstone, C. W. Waller, Charlie Cunningham, Bay Middleton, Lord Cholmondeley, Gwyn Davies, Tom Spence, W. Brockton, Willie Moore, E. P. Wilson, Dan Thirlwell, Arthur Brocklehurst, Captain Lee Barber, Mr. Willoughby (now Lord Middleton, and for many years starter to the Jockey Club), Buck Barclay, Mr. Abington, the three Beasley brothers, Mr. Crawshaw, Lord Marcus Beresford, Count Kinsky, Captain Bewicke, Captain "Doggy" Smith, and amongst professionals Jimmy Adams, Tom Skelton, Robert I'Anson, John Jones, Billy Sensier, J. Holman, J. Prince, Childs, Hunt, Jewitt, Dick Marsh.

"Cross Country" riding in those days was the best of fun, but good friends as we all were the rivalry on the race-course was very keen, and you had to look after yourself in a race, but in all the years I rode I only twice personally came across deliberate foul riding, and on neither occasion did it happen in England.

I read in newspapers now that more than half the races under National Hunt rules are cut up, and that jockeys and trainers are out to rob the public and make as much money as they can. I seldom go steeplechasing myself, but I refuse to believe that the world is so changed, and I still think that the majority of people race for love of sport and not for love of money. Black sheep there always are, always have been, and always will be in every walk of life, not only on the Turf.

But even if I were young and keen again I should not care to be a steeplechase jockey in these days. When I used to get up on a horse trained in a good stable, I went out with the feeling that bar an accident my horse would get round the course, and that he would jump over the fences and not through them. One of the chief assets a jockey has, either on the flat or over fences, is confidence, but in these days how can any man have that feeling when he has to ride over the Liverpool course and knows that his horse is accustomed and has been taught to brush through his fences, for that is the case with ninety per cent. of the steeplechase horses nowadays. The jockey may be as brave as you like, but he can have no confidence.

But, to return to some of the jockeys, as I have said before, Arthur Coventry was the best amateur I ever saw. Next to him and perhaps as good on the flat was Mr. George Thompson. He was very light, and could ride 7st. 7lb., and I have seen him hold his own with the best professionals. I remember once at Stockton Lord Zetland giving him the mount on Hardrada in some handicap, his usual jockey, Jim Snowden, standing down. After a tremendous race George beat Fred Archer a head. He got a great ovation on coming back to scale, and as he got off Jim Snowden clapped him on the back, shouting out, "Bravo, George, beat crack jock and all."

I expect my readers, before they get to the end of this book, will be tired of my repeating what a good fellow this man and the other was, but as I look back on my life on the Turf I am astonished myself how many men I have known that you could bet your life on their doing the right thing, and amongst these, if I had to make a choice, I should put Arthur Coventry first.

He was and is a quiet, modest man with charming manners, but, if anyone took a liberty with him, they got a surprise, for he could produce a flow of language that would floor any bargee. What a lot of races he won, often riding in welter races on even terms with the jockeys, and in reputation he was like Cæsar's wife.

Arthur was a nervous, high-strung man, and he often wasted very hard. On these occasions when going out for a race he used to look as white as a sheet, but once he started he was as cool as a cucumber. Many are the good races I have seen him ride, and I can hardly remember ever seeing him ride a bad one, which I could not say of any other jockey, professional or amateur.

He was up to every trick in the trade of jockeyship, and at the same time the fairest rider that ever got into a saddle. I remember on one occasion at Brighton I was riding Oberon for Bill Beresford. Oberon was a smart horse and had won the Lincoln Handicap. The race looked a good thing for him, and Bill had one of his dashes. Jack Watts who used to ride him told me before I got up that the horse would be sure to come badly down the hill. When we got to the turn coming down the hill there were four of us going well, the others were ridden by Arthur Coventry, Mr. Abington, and Harry Escott. I was between Arthur and Mr. Abington. Coming down the hill my horse gradually lost his place and I looked like being squeezed out, but when he felt the rise of the ground he came again; Abington shouted to Coventry, " Keep him out," and Arthur only had to lean to the left to stop me, but he kept his horse as straight as a gun-barrel, and I got up again and won a head, the other pair dead-heated for second place a short head behind.

Over hurdles and on the flat no one could beat him

some people thought he was not too fond of fences. That may have been so in his later days, but I think it was in the first National in which I rode that I remember Arthur sailing past me on Redpath at the last fence but one before the canal turn, sitting as if he were in an arm-chair and whistling some popular music hall tune ; that doesn't look like nerves.

He did not win on Redpath as the horse could never last home. I rode him myself another year, and a glorious ride he was, but the last quarter of a mile beat him. As we were coming to the canal turn, Tom Skelton on Gamecock (who won) was riding him hard; he looked round and saw me apparently full of running, and said, " Great Scott, you will trot in," but in another three hundred yards, one gasp and a sigh, and nothing doing.

As I have said, Arthur was a modest man, and always declared himself that he was the ugliest man in the world, but in my opinion no man with such an honest face can be ugly, and his figure, on a horse or off it, was perfection. He was a great favourite with the ladies of all classes. We always said they were in love with his gaiters and boots, which he took a great deal of trouble over and were the best I ever saw.

When Lord Marcus Beresford gave up being starter, Arthur stepped into his shoes, and as a starter I put him second only to McGeorge. The jockeys were devoted to him, and had the greatest confidence in him, his only fault being that he was too kind to them, although I must say they seldom took advantage of this. He was too anxious to get a bad horse off, but all starters I have ever seen except McGeorge can plead guilty to this latter fault.

Hugh Owen and his brother Roddy were two very attractive men. Hugh was the elder, one of the best men to hounds in England, and a pretty good jockey. He had not the dash and brilliancy of Roddy, but he knew what he was doing, and was good enough if the horse was. He hunted for many years from Market

Harboro', and rode for Mr. Stokes, the celebrated horse dealer. It cast a gloom over the whole of Leicestershire when he was killed jumping quite a small fence, but it was the death he had always prayed for.

Now Roddy was as good a steeplechase rider as I ever saw. He was not such an artist on the flat as Arthur Coventry, but over the fences he was a nailer, always going the shortest way and not very particular how he got there; in a race he was as quick as lightning to take advantage of anything or anybody. He got a lot of riding, and he left no stone unturned to get a ride on a horse he fancied. This was so much the case that at one time he was rather unpopular with the professionals, and on one occasion in a race at Sandown the jockeys openly said that they were going to give him a rough time, and get a bit of their own back. After a race that was rather like a Rugby football match, Roddy emerged from the scrum and won. I went into the weighing room afterwards and found them all laughing and the best of friends, saying that they would not take the Captain on again at the rough game as he could beat the lot at it. Whatever he did, no one could quarrel with Roddy for long.

I knocked him over the rails once in a race when he was persistently trying to come up inside me, and he cut his head very badly, but, when he was brought into the weighing room, he said, " Never mind, it served me d———d well right, I had no right to come where I did."

He had another side to his character in that he was a very keen soldier, and he was very popular in his regiment with both officers and men.

He always told us that when he had won the National he would give up riding and take soldiering seriously. We none of us believed him, but the night after he won on Father O'Flynn he bade us good-bye, and the next week he was off on an expedition to East Africa.

The late Colonel Frank Rhodes told me that later on, when he had greatly distinguished himself as a soldier, he was invited to join the Jameson Raid and to command it. I think if he had been at the head of that ill-fated expedition he would never have landed the country in such a hopeless mess, for he was a clear-sighted, brave man, and as artful as any Boer. As a matter of fact, Roddy was in India at the time, and owing to the distance and imperfect information, he refused to go. He died of cholera in Egypt in 1896 or 1897, just prior to the campaign which Kitchener started to take Dongola, and he was engaged in the preliminary operations connected with it.

When he won the National he had the choice of at least six fancied competitors, and he chose Father O'Flynn, who was the least fancied of the lot, and started at twenty to one.

Once in his riding days, when he was quartered at Aldershot, General Sir Evelyn Wood was in command. Roddy was always away riding. One day the General sent for him to haul him over the coals for neglecting his profession, and opened proceedings by saying, " Captain Owen, I have been here two months and I have not yet had the pleasure of making your acquaintance." " My loss, General, not yours," answered Roddy, with a low bow, and Sir Evelyn Wood instead of giving him a wigging had to laugh, and afterwards he got as much leave as he wanted.

The other day I was reading Sir J. Rennell Rodd's charming book of " Social and Diplomatic Memories." He writes of Roddy as " that consummate horseman and knight errant of adventure," and of his magic gift of charm. Then in alluding to his death he says, " So died a good friend and a very gallant soul. A later recruit to that great band of gentlemen adventurers by whom the Empire has been built up and sustained. Those of his contemporaries who still survive no doubt remember him as the winner of the National of 1892. To me he will always be the Roddy Owen who planted the flag at Wadelai."

Perhaps the best steeplechase rider of my days was E. P. Wilson. He was a short-legged man with a very strong back and shoulders. Although we had no doubt as to his great ability in the saddle, to our idea he had a very ugly seat, for he rode with very short stirrups and took a short hold of his reins. In fact he was the first man I ever saw who rode somewhat after the fashion of the present day.

"Ted," as he was called, was not good-looking but had great charm of manner and a most ingratiating smile, which got him out of many a scrape, for on a horse he was perhaps a rather tricky man to deal with, but off one a good fellow and one of the best-hearted men in the world. Personally, there was no man I was so much afraid of in a race, and it was often my misfortune to be up against him in a close finish. The result was generally against me, so much so that one day, when I came into the weighing room after being beaten a neck, old Tom Gutteridge, the jockeys' valet, said to me, " It's no use your riding against Ted Wilson, for he follows you like a policeman and taps you when he likes."

He won a tremendous lot of races. Roquefort and Voluptuary were his Grand National winners, both rather remarkable horses, and in each case the genius and skill of Wilson were the chief factors in their success.

Voluptuary had never run in a steeplechase before winning and was only six years old. He originally was the property of Lord Rosebery, and had been a horse of a certain amount of class on the Flat. He was then bought by Arthur Cooper, the clever little man who had so much to do with Fred Archer, a straight fellow and a fine gambler. What made him and E. P. Wilson go for the National with a six-year-old that had never run in a steeplechase I do not know, but about three weeks before the race Wilson brought Voluptuary to Upton, where Mr. W. H. P. Jenkins trained, to do a four and a half mile gallop with his National horses. At that time they had the right tackle at Upton to tell anyone " the time of day." I rode myself in the gallop

ARTHUR COVENTRY

BAY MIDDLETON

HUGH OWEN

RODDY OWEN

All photographs by Robinson

From the painting by Allen C. Sealy

MAT DAWSON

FRED ARCHER

By permission of Messrs. Forres

SIR JOHN ASTLEY "THE MATE"

on Satellite, winner of the National Hunt. Count Kinsky was up on Zoedone, winner of the Grand National the previous year, Roddy Owen on Tom Jones, winner of many races, and there were three or four other useful horses. Before we started, Mr. Jenkins cautioned us not to do more than a good exercise gallop, as he did not want Wilson to know all about the form of his horses. We carried out his instructions, but Wilson went so much on the outside at all the turns that I should think he went nearly five miles to our four and a half. Anyhow, he was quite satisfied, and told me after the gallop that he was certain to win the National adding that he had jumped almost every fence in Warwickshire on Voluptuary. But when the horse pulled up the sweat fairly rolled off him and he had to be scraped. Satellite had carried me magnificently in the gallop, and I thought that I should win the National, not Voluptuary.

As it happened I did not ride Satellite, as a bad fall at Four Oaks Park put me out of action for the rest of the season. I did not even see the race, but Voluptuary won in a canter, never having set a foot wrong, and Satellite ran badly. Arthur Cooper won a big stake, and Ted Wilson told me that he himself won enough money to pay all his debts and start afresh. Voluptuary was a brilliant horse, but he was greatly helped to victory by the ground, which was on the hard side. Had the going been heavy there might have been another story.

The following year Ted Wilson again won, this time on Roquefort, and again the " coup " was engineered by Arthur Cooper.

Roquefort was a beautiful short-legged horse by Winslow out of Cream Cheese, half-brother to Miguel, who had been second for the Leger. In his earlier days he was the property of Bobby Fisher, who won several small races with him, but he had the reputation of being ungenerous and very difficult to ride. I remember beating him on a horse of Lord Carmarthen's at Wye, but only because he ran out of the course at the last hurdle when he was winning easily.

This good-looking horse caught Wilson's shrewd eye. He bought him and set his mind on winning a second Grand National, which feat he easily accomplished. Arthur Cooper again won a small fortune, and this time Ted Wilson set himself up for life. It was a fine performance on his part, for Roquefort was a most impetuous, hard-pulling horse, always ready to run out to the left if he got the chance. I can see him now galloping up the Course on the morning of the race hurling the clods of earth behind him like stones out of a catapult (the going was heavy), raking his head from side to side, a veritable steam engine. In the race he hit the third or fourth fence very hard, but being so well balanced he just kept his legs, though Wilson was half off. He told me that it was just a toss-up whether he could get back or not, when Childs, who was riding Albert Cecil, stretched out a hand and gave him a push which just turned the scale. Old Childs said to me afterwards, " Why the h—ll I did it I don't know, for I fancied my horse very much, and I ought to have been glad to see Ted on the floor." The rest of the journey Roquefort fenced splendidly and won in a canter.

The following year with 12st. 8lb. he again ran a great horse, but in a hard struggle up the straight he suddenly swerved and jumped over the rails.

Wilson had many bad falls in his time, and, when the doctors warned him that another fall on his head might have serious consequences, like a wise man, he retired when at the top of his profession.

A fine professional jockey of that period, though a little previous to Wilson, was Bobby I'Anson. He was a very tall man, I should say considerably over six foot, but he had an extraordinary knack of tucking himself up on his horse so that his height looked nothing. No better man over fences and hurdles ever lived, and I think he was the most popular man of his day with the public. There was never a whisper as to his character. We young men worshipped him. He would give us the best advice about riding in the nicest possible way.

His daughter married Bob Colling, so it was not surprising that her sons, Jack and George, quickly made their mark as jockeys. They inherited not only the skill and character of their grandfather, but also, unfortunately, his length of leg and height, so their race-riding days were prematurely cut short.

CHAPTER III

MAT DAWSON AND FRED ARCHER

If I were asked to name the most memorable period in the history of the Turf within my record I should turn to the years between 1880 and 1890—years notable for great horses, great jockeys, great trainers and owners, who were sportsmen in the highest sense of the word.

George Fordham, Fred Archer, Tom Cannon, Charles Wood, John Osborne, Constable, Fred Webb, Jack Watts, Jim Snowden and J. Goater were all riding in the early 'eighties, and without any doubt they were not only good jockeys but splendid horsemen. The parade for a big race was a great sight.

In those days of dandies and swells, jockeys were much more particular about their appearance than they are now. Their breeches were spotless, their boots shone like a mirror. To see Archer, Webb, Tom Cannon or Watts cantering to the post on a big occasion, showing their horses and themselves off to the best advantage, was a sight for the gods. And how many splendid finishes we used to see!

Races then were run in a different style, and at times, no doubt, the practice of waiting and coming with one run was carried to excess. I am not in agreement with those who think our present-day jockeys are bad, but I am afraid they are losing the art of waiting. The present style of seat does not lend itself to this, and the public are so accustomed to see a field charging along in a line that anyone who lies off in a race and then does not win comes in for most unjust criticism.

I am certain if Fordham, John Osborne or Jim

Snowden, who were perhaps the greatest exponents of the art of waiting, were resurrected and began riding again that the public would be howling them down, that certain of the Press would demand their heads from the Stewards ; but equally certain am I that they would win many races and not always on the best horses.

Of present-day jockeys, Carslake, Bullock and Childs often reveal that waiting can even now be practised with great success, but when beaten they are often much criticized.

In 1880, although I was only twenty, I had begun to go racing fairly regularly, and the race that made the most impression on me of that year was the Manchester Cup, won by Isonomy, carrying 9 st. 12 lb., and beating The Abbot, 6 st. 9 lb., a neck. The Abbot had been third in the Two Thousand, beaten less than a length from the winner.

Isonomy was a great public favourite and the best horse in England. He had won the Cambridgeshire as a three-year-old and the Ascot Cup the following year. But in this race the task of giving 3 stone 3 lb. to The Abbot was considered impossible. The latter started favourite, with Isonomy at sixteen to one, but after a splendid race Isonomy, ridden by Tom Cannon, got up in the last hundred yards and won by a neck.

The Manchester crowd went mad with enthusiasm, and it was with the greatest difficulty that Tom Cannon could get his horse to the unsaddling enclosure. The horse stood the mobbing with the utmost unconcern, and Tom Cannon, for once, allowed himself to smile. This scene taught me what splendid sportsmen the British racing public are and how they do love to see a good horse win, even if they have not backed him.

Incidentally, at this Meeting, I first made the acquaintance of Fred Archer. He was not riding in the Cup, and I asked him what I should back. He answered, " The Abbot will probably win, but you put something on the best horse and the best jockey in the race, Isonomy and Tom Cannon." I took 160 to 10.

Then began a friendship which lasted uninterruptedly to the day of his death.

Lord Falmouth, Mat Dawson and Fred Archer were names to conjure with. The combination of owner, trainer and jockey had been extraordinarily successful. Most of their great triumphs were before I went racing regularly. I only knew Lord Falmouth slightly, but enough to know that he had supreme confidence in his trainer and jockey and turned a deaf ear to the malicious rumours which always attack success.

Matthew Dawson trained at Heath House, Newmarket. He did things on a lavish scale, and the principle of "Look after the pennies and the pounds will look after themselves" found no favour with him.

In spite of his strong, fearless character, which would brook no interference from any man in what he thought the duties of his profession, he was the most courteous of men both to his employers and to those who worked for him, and I never met anyone in any rank of life who had not the greatest respect for him, while those who knew him well loved him.

But he had no use for weak men or bad horses. He was never a big bettor, and was continually warning me against the folly of betting beyond one's means, saying that, although he had the good fortune to have trained more good horses than any other man in the world, on the occasions when he had put more money than usual on a horse it had generally been beaten. Apart from this, he had a contempt for money in itself, and used to call Archer, who had an eye to the main chance, "that d——d long-legged, tin-scraping, young devil."

His appearance in the morning at exercise would astonish us in these days; a tall hat, varnished boots, and usually a flower in his buttonhole—for he was almost as good a gardener as he was trainer. Like many people of those times his language was strong, but, as it rolled out of his mouth in broad Scotch, it sounded almost like a benediction.

Shortly before Lord Falmouth gave up racing, the Duke of Portland sent his horses to Dawson, with the same result—he carried all before him. On one occasion, Mat advised the Duke to put a very highly bred filly in a selling race. The Duke said, "Surely, it is a pity to sell one bred like this," and was answered: "Well, she is a d——d bad specimen of a d——d good breed; get out of her, Your Grace." That was his way of dealing with a horse or a man when he found them bad.

In the later years of his life he left Heath House and went to Exning, where he had only a few horses, but his success continued, and he turned out Minting to win the Grand Prix, Ladas and Sir Visto to win the Derby for Lord Rosebery, and Mimi the One Thousand and Oaks for Mr. Noel Fenwick. Mimi was far from a good filly, but trained to the hour; she beat a moderate field for the One Thousand.

At that time there was a Six Thousand Pound race at Leicester in July; Mimi ran for this and started at four to one on. She was second, beaten easily by a French horse called Révèrend. I did not see the race, but the following morning, as I was walking from Newmarket to Exning, I met Mr. Fenwick, her owner, looking very disconsolate and dejected. I condoled with him on the defeat of his mare, and he said, "Yes, that was a nasty blow; but now I am in the devil of a mess. You know Mat Dawson never went to see Mimi run, and there was no doubt she was 'got at,' or that something was very wrong, so I came down early this morning to blow him up about his carelessness. I told him what I thought about it, and, when I had finished, the old gentleman said, 'Look here, Mr. Fenwick, you can take yourself and your horses out of my yard, and take them somewhere where they will not be got at.' I tried to smooth him down, but he would not let me say anything, and only repeated, 'Will you be so good as to get out of my house at once.'"

Mat relented to a certain extent, and consented to train the horses for the remainder of the season, after which they left. Mr. Fenwick was at the head of the list of winning owners that year. I must add that subsequent form showed that Mimi had no chance of beating Révèrend. It must not be thought that this episode left any unpleasant relations between owner and trainer. They were both far too good sportsmen for that. Noel Fenwick although he betted heavily himself was as open as the day about his horses.

In 1896 Mat Dawson's health was failing fast, but he refused to give in, and used to watch his horses working from his brougham. On enquiry as to how he was, "Very well, except for me d——d legs," he would say. He died in July, 1897, a year when the summer was of tropical heat. Shortly before his death he was very anxious to see his secretary, Day, of whom he was very fond. Now Day had just got married and had gone away on his honeymoon. On being told this, " Poor fellow, how d——d hot he will be," was his comment, after which he relapsed into unconsciousness. He had trained five Derby winners, six Oaks winners, and six winners of the St. Leger, and had won all the other big races. He always led a simple life, but where his horses were concerned, " If they want gold they must have it," he would say.

Generous and open-hearted to a degree, with all his long career of uninterrupted success, this greatest of all trainers left only £20,000. One of his favourite expressions, " Damn the Blunt," was truly his motto.

The first time I ever saw Archer (I did not know him till the following year) was on my first visit to Newmarket in 1879. Of course I had read in the papers of his marvellous feats, and I was naturally anxious to see the great jockey. At St. Pancras Station I saw the Duke of Hamilton talking to a quiet, pale-looking young man, dressed in a dark suit with a black tie and a big pearl in it. I asked who it was. " Why, that is Archer," was the answer, much to my surprise, for he was quite unlike what I had pictured him to be.

About 5ft. 10in. in height, with a wonderfully slim

I HAVE KNOWN

and graceful figure, and remarkably small hands and feet, there was even at that time the shadow of melancholy in his face which indicated a side to his nature never far absent even in his brightest days, and which was partly responsible for his tragic death. No one seeing him for the first time would have put him down as a jockey, or suspected that such tremendous energy lurked in that frail body. It was that untiring energy which was the secret of his great success, leaving no stone unturned to achieve the one object of his life, the winning of races.

From the beginning of the racing season to the end, health, leisure and pleasure were sacrificed, walking nearer 11st. than 10st. in the winter he was always ready for Lincoln and Liverpool, riding 8st. 10lb. He had a Turkish bath in his own house, and he used some medicine which went by the name of "Archer's Mixture," prepared by a clever doctor at Newmarket, called Wright. I tried it myself when I was riding races, and from my own experience I should say it was made of dynamite.

Archer ate practically nothing all day, but usually had a good dinner which sometimes would send him up in weight 3lb. to 4lb., but the next morning with the Turkish bath and his mixture that would go. How his constitution stood such treatment for ten years was astonishing, but I have no doubt when he was taken ill with typhoid fever in 1886 his health must have been seriously undermined.

Taking him all round, Fred Archer was the greatest of all jockeys. Apprenticed to Matthew Dawson when he was eleven years old, it was not long before his master discovered that in this long-legged boy he had something out of the common. He was only seventeen when he won the Two Thousand Guineas for Lord Falmouth on Atlantic. From that time to the end of his life, at the age of twenty-nine, he was at the head of the winning jockeys. The number of races he won was astounding. In 1876, 209; 1877, 218; 1878, 229; 1879, 197;

1880, 120; 1881, 220; 1882, 210; 1883, 232; 1884, 241; 1885, 246; 1886 (the year of his death), 170. They included five victories in the Derby, four in the Oaks and six in the St. Leger.

He had many great qualities. To begin with, marvellous hands and seat. I think it was Joe Cannon who once said, " When you give Archer a leg-up he drops into the saddle, and in a moment he and the horse are as one ; no pulling up or lengthening of stirrups, but away they go, complete confidence between man and horse." I have noticed the same thing myself about Stephen Donoghue.

Archer had a wonderful intuition regarding the character of any horse once he had been on his back, and knew how to get the most out of him. He had undaunted nerve and supreme confidence in himself without any atom of conceit. When he was beaten by a neck for a race he generally thought that if he had just done this or not done that he would have won, and that is how a good jockey can make himself into a great one. Nothing escaped his notice during a race. Not only could he tell you all about his own horse, which is more than most jockeys are capable of, but he knew what the others had been doing. He had a great appreciation of other good riders, and he studied their methods. George Fordham he was always afraid of, saying, " In one race George comes and taps me in the last stride on the post. I am determined not to have this happen again, and then in the next race he just gets home and I beat him a stride past the post ; with his clucking and fiddling you never know what the old chap is up to."

Jim Snowden, when in form, he said was a terribly hard man to beat. " You might have him, as you thought, well settled twice in a race, and then he would come at you again ; you never knew when he was done with." Tom Cannon he thought the most beautiful and finished of jockeys. Fred Webb the strongest, Charles Wood, he said, was a wonderful judge of pace and always in a good position in a race.

Effective as he was, you could not call Archer a pretty finisher; he got very forward on his horse, and in the last fifty yards often rode with a loose rein, but horses seldom swerved with him.

There was a tremendous race for the Two Thousand between Galliard and Goldfield, Archer and Cannon riding. It looked much like a dead-heat, but Archer and Galliard had it by a short head. I asked Archer after the race if he thought he had won. "I don't know whether the horse won," he said, "but I know I beat Tom; he sits back when he finishes, and I sit forward, and you know that may just catch the judge's eye."

In those days jockeys were allowed to bet, and Archer, at times, betted heavily, but on such occasions he did not always ride with his usual good judgment, for he said he was in too great a hurry to get home. But I have known him ride some wonderful races against his own money. On one occasion at Windsor, Golding asked him if he would ride a brute of a horse called Westwood, with no mouth and a habit of bolting out into the country. Archer said, "I will if you like, but I don't mind telling you I am going to have £500 on Domino." Golding said that did not matter, as Westwood had no chance. In the race, Archer, riding like a demon, got up and beat Domino by a neck, after having twice nearly gone into the river in two false starts.

He was generally the first man out of the paddock, and, by doing so, was able to get the rails; there was no draw for places then. He was a marvel at the start, never giving trouble to the starter, but always well away. Even with a horse that he was going to wait with he was anxious to get well off, and to be in front for the first furlong. His faults were sometimes being too severe on a horse, and not being too scrupulous in stopping a dangerous opponent.

I remember an interesting race for the Queen's Plate at Newmarket. There were three runners, Lord

Bradford's Chippendale, Mr. Manton's Edelweiss and Mr. R. Vyner's Hagioscope. They were ridden respectively by Archer, Wood, and the north country jockey, Griffiths. So little was Hagioscope fancied by the Talent that I got a thousand to eighty about him, though he eventually started at six and a half to one. Chippendale, a good horse, was favourite ; the race finished on the old Cambridgeshire course. At the red post Archer was on the rails, Griffiths in the middle, between him and Wood. Archer saw that Hagioscope was going too well, so he bumped him on to Edelweiss, and between the two Griffiths looked like having a bad time. But he was equal to the occasion ; he nearly knocked Wood over and then squeezed Archer on to the rails, so that he could not use his whip, kept him there and beat him a head.

Wadlow, who trained Chippendale for Lord Bradford, wanted Archer to object. He replied, " No, I can't, I began it." I met Sanderson, who trained Hagioscope, later and remarked that Griffiths had distinguished himself. " Well," he said, " Griff may not be much of a jock, but when it comes to foul riding I will back him against any jockey breathing." The next week the following appeared in the *Sporting Times*: " Before the Queen's Plate at Newmarket everyone was saying, who the hell is Griffiths ? After the race, Griffiths was saying, who the hell is Archer ? "

Archer had, of course, his enemies and detractors, and rumour and scandal did not spare him ; but I believe the best answer to these charges is the fact that, once a stable, owner or trainer employed him, they continued to do so as long as he lived, and to the end he retained the confidence of the public.

The men he rode for and associated with, whether in a high or low station of life, were always the straight people of the Turf. He, like Mat Dawson, had no use for the bad men, and he avoided them.

So much for Archer as a jockey. In his private life he was in many ways as remarkable. Even when quite a boy he was courted and flattered by every kind of man and woman, and early in life he became the idol of the public. I have seen crowds waiting outside the Queen's Hotel, Manchester, to see him depart for the races, and yet he never suffered from that prevalent and disagreeable complaint " swollen head." I think the shrewd, hard common-sense of Mat Dawson, for whom he had the greatest affection and respect, was a great help to him, and he generally went to him for advice in his difficulties. With his quick brain he was a good judge of human nature and he could manage men as well as horses. He did not make many intimate friends, but to those he had, he was affectionate and loyal and his friendship was lasting.

The early death of his wife, a daughter of the late Mr. John Dawson, was a great shock to him, and for a long time afterwards his devoted friend, Captain Bowling, never left his side, even sleeping in his room, as there was even then a fear that he might take his own life.

His brother Charles was at this time training for Lord Ellesmere. He began life as a jockey. Like Fred, he was a fearless, dashing rider, but weight soon put a stop to that line of life, and he quickly made his mark as a trainer. He was a fine judge of racing; when he fancied a horse it was good enough for anyone to follow. He betted heavily and when he brought off a good thing the Ring knew it.

He and his brother were great friends, but in spite of that on one occasion in a race, when he tried to come up inside Fred, he was promptly put over the rails and nearly broke his neck.

The biggest stake he ever went for was on Lord Ellesmere's Highland Chief whom he trained for the Derby of 1883. Highland Chief was a great, leggy, split up, long striding horse by Hampton. He had started favourite for the Two Thousand and ran moderately, but he improved as the season went on and Charles Archer still had great hopes for the Derby. In his trial before Epsom, he was asked a tremendously stiff question, which, although he was second, he failed to answer. Fred, who rode him in the trial, did not like the horse and told his brother that his hopes of the Derby were forlorn, but Charles did not think so, and at long prices he backed Highland Chief to win a fortune. Undoubtedly he was very unlucky not to land it, for Fred Webb, who rode the horse in the race, waited just too long, and was beaten a neck by St. Blaise.

I saw the race from the Ladies' Stand, being next to Lord Alington and Sir Frederick Johnstone, who were joint owners of St. Blaise. Wood on St. Blaise, a nice handy horse, slipped round Tattenham Corner on the inside, and made the best of his way home, followed by Galliard, Fred Archer's mount, with Highland Chief drawing up in the middle of the course and coming with a tremendous rush in the last hundred and fifty yards. Nearly everyone thought that Highland Chief had just got up and won, but unfortunately for Charles Archer it was two strides past the post that he got his head in front. As the horses flashed past the post, Sir Frederick Johnstone exclaimed, "By G—d, we're done," and when St. Blaise's number went up he was astounded. Galliard was third and Goldfield fourth, thus confirming their Two Thousand form, when they were first and second.

There were the usual suspicious people who said that Fred Archer had gone for Highland Chief and pulled Galliard, whereas in reality he had no fancy for his brother's horse whatever. Webb certainly ought to have won that Derby, and he was the first man to admit it. He made some amends the next day when he got home a neck on Lowland Chief, owned by Lord Ellesmere and trained by Charles Archer, in the Royal Stakes, and by doing so upset a tremendous gamble on Lord Gerard's Sweetbread, hailing from Machell's stable.

Lowland Chief started at 100 to 12. Charles Archer was one of those men who would never be beaten, and he got back all his Derby losses and more besides on the horse.

CHAPTER IV

SIR JOHN ASTLEY AND OLD DAYS AT ASCOT

In 1881 I stayed for the first time at Ascot for the week. That meeting was chiefly memorable for Peter's Hunt Cup. I don't know if it was in this particular year that Peter's gallant owner, Sir John Astley, appeared in the Royal Enclosure in a short coat without any tails to it. The Prince of Wales took exception to this and told him he should come properly dressed. So the " Mate," as he was always called, got a pair of large buttons and wore them sewn on to the back of his coat next day. He showed himself to the Prince, saying that he hoped His Royal Highness was satisfied. The latter was too much amused to be angry.

Sir John was about the most popular racing man of the day with the public. He had a large string of horses, and there was no mystery about them. He betted heavily, and, although he won a great many races, I am afraid the account was generally on the wrong side.

However, in 1881, both financially and physically, matters were not going very well with him, but game as a fighting cock the old man would not be beaten, and, having won some money on his mare Windsor when she won the Chester Cup, he determined to buy a brilliant horse called Peter, which he had long coveted, thinking by this means to restore his fallen fortunes. Even then, so hard up was he, that he had to borrow £2,500 to complete the £6,300 which he gave for the horse.

Peter was a big chestnut horse, five years old. He could go like the devil, but he had a queer temper and was not an easy horse to ride, and Sir John thought he had been mismanaged and badly trained. Charles Wood was Sir John's jockey. He had ridden Peter in the Lincoln Handicap and the City and Surburban, and he had not got on well with him. Sir John entered him in the Manchester Cup, a big betting race in those days, and he backed him to win a small fortune.

One day Archer came to him and said, "If you let me ride Peter you will win the Cup and as much money as you like, and, if I ride, Captain Machell will not run Valour," he added. "You know Peter won't go for Wood."

Sir John was the most loyal of men to anyone he employed, but he was sorely tempted. I dined alone one night with him at Newmarket and he told me that he had backed the horse for a big sum, enough to get him out of all his troubles. He wanted Archer to ride, but he hated the idea of taking his own jockey off.

When we went to bed I still thought there was a chance of seeing Archer on Peter, but in the morning when I met Sir John he curtly said, "Wood rides." I remember also meeting Archer that day and his saying to me, "It is a pity about this; Sir John wants a turn badly, and I am afraid he won't get it now. I shall ride Valour for the Captain, and he is very dangerous on that course."

I went to Manchester with Sir John and we stayed at the Queen's Hotel. Peter started second favourite for the Cup at nine to two and Valour at twenty-five to one. After a good race, in which Archer completely outrode Wood, Valour beat Peter a neck. What a sportsman the old "Mate" was; neither by word nor expression, as he patted Wood on the back after the race, did he show a sign of the severe blow to his fortunes.

The following week was Ascot, where Peter was engaged in the Gold Vase. By now it was common property that Wood and Peter did not hit it off. There were only three runners for the Vase, and Sir John's friends begged him to put up Archer, who was without a mount.

No, he would be d——d if he would take his jockey off just when the horse had an easy job. The horse started at three to one on. Result : he ran out at the top turn and did not complete the course.

The following day Peter was in the Hunt Cup with 9st. 3lbs. Wood had a prior retainer and Sir John put up Archer. In the race, after going about two furlongs the horse stopped to kick. Archer gave him one pat on the neck, he took hold of his bit again and won in gallant style by three parts of a length ; a remarkable performance on the part of horse and jockey.

On Friday he was in the Hardwicke Stakes. Archer again rode him, and on this occasion showed his brains and resource. In the Ascot Vase Peter had run out just where they start for the Hardwicke Stakes, so Archer got weighed out early and walked and trotted the horse all round the reverse way of the course, so that he should think he was galloping back to his stables. He won by eight lengths, but, alas ! these successes did not make up for the expensive defeat at Manchester. Virtue is not always rewarded.

Before the days of Wood and Archer, Fordham often rode for Sir John, who considered him the finest jockey in the world. He once told me this story about him : Sir John was running a horse in the Lewes Handicap and Fordham was riding it. In the race there ran a horse belonging to a widow called Mrs. Drewett.

Now Fordham had been brought up as a boy by the Drewetts, and he was always very grateful for the kindness he had received at their hands ; and Mrs. Drewett was very hard-up at that time. In the race he was beaten a head by the widow's horse. Sir John had been quite satisfied with the way his jockey had ridden, but after the race Fordham came to him and said, " You know, Sir John, I ought to have won that race for you." " Nonsense," said Sir John, " I could see nothing wrong." " Well, you know, Sir John, Mrs. Drewett has not been able to pay her rent, and all through that race I could not help thinking of that d——d rent, and, you know, I ought just to have won."

I should say this was the only occasion in his life on which Fordham might have been accused of " not doing his best." The Bank of England would not have bought him.

Sir John was typical of the gallant bluff Englishman ; outspoken and hating humbug and cant, always ready to go out of his way to do anyone a good turn. About a year or so before his death he was being laughed at by some of his friends for having been taken in by a begging impostor. Someone said, " Hang it all, you're old enough to know better." Sir John replied, " Thank God, I have never been a suspicious man, and I have had a happy life ; I hope I shall die before I lose my faith in humanity."

But to return to that Ascot of 1881, a good horse, Robert the Devil, won both the Ascot Cup and the Alexandra Plate. The previous year, as a three-year-old, he had been beaten a head for the Derby by Bend Or. But he was a fine stayer and took his revenge on his Epsom conqueror by easily winning the St. Leger from him.

Bend Or did not put in an appearance at Ascot as a four-year-old, but he had won the City and Suburban easily with 9 stone, beating Foxall (6 st. 8 lb.) and a big field of useful horses. Foxall's next appearance was in the Grand Prix, in which, ridden by Fordham, he won a head from that good horse, Tristan, with Archer in the saddle. I should like to have seen that race.

On the Friday of the Epsom Summer Meeting, 1881, Bend Or and Robert the Devil ran their great match over a mile and a half for the Epsom Cup, a sight I shall never forget. When the two horses came on to the course there was almost a hush. Betting stopped and everyone gazed at these two champions. Robert the Devil was ridden by Tom Cannon in place of his old jockey, Rossiter. He was a great slashing bay horse slightly on the leg. In the parade he was somewhat on his toes and anxious to get to his work, while Bend Or, a beautiful chestnut, walked sedately along with Archer on his back. The reins were loose on his neck, and when he passed the stands he actually turned his head round and yawned, as much as to say, " What is all this fuss about?" What a gentleman he looked. The odds were six to four on Robert the Devil. From the fall of the flag Cannon did all he could to cut his opponent down, but two hundred yards from home Archer brought the golden chestnut alongside and won almost easily by a neck.

The jockeys of those days had marvellous confidence. In a match of the greatest importance, opposed to an artist like Cannon, Archer was content to win by a neck when he could certainly have made it a length or more.

Bend Or, though he had beaten Robert the Devil at Epsom, did not oppose him for the Ascot Cup. If he had he would most assuredly have been beaten, for he could not stay that severe course.

Ascot is a course where good jockeys and good horses shine. In those days the two-year-old course was 200 yards over the five furlongs, so that any horse that won on it was sure to be a stout one. But at times, when two good two-year-olds opposed each other, the struggle home would be very severe and left its mark, so that the course was altered to the present one. It is now easier and in consequence not nearly such a good test. As the start is down hill the speedy horses get such an advantage that they are sometimes never caught. I thought at the time the change was made that it was a good one, but I am sure now that I was wrong. A good horse if he does not strike off quickly has not sufficient time to make up his ground without a very great effort. The result is he may get an even more severe race than was the case before.

In the evenings after the races, in those early days of which I have been writing, everyone foregathered at the stables of the Royal Hotel to see the horses. There you would meet all " the swells," as they were called, usually in company with their trainers. I can picture in my mind many remarkable figures of those days. There were the two partners, Lord Alington and Sir Frederick Johnstone, both of them full of fun and wit, but with the keenness of a sword under it where racing matters were concerned. They used to train with William Day, and afterwards joined the Kingsclere Stable, owning many good horses, among them St. Blaise, Common and Matchmaker. Lord and Lady Bradford, with Tom Wadlow from the North, always had a good string for Ascot. Lord Bradford's best horses in my day numbered amongst them that great stayer, Chippendale, Sir Hugo, who won the Derby, and Retreat. With the Bradfords there was generally dear old Colonel Henry Forester, " the Lad," as he was always called. He was the frailest, most delicate-looking man in the world, but one of the shrewdest that ever went racing, and he was supposed to be one of the only gentlemen who ever made money by betting.

Colonel Forester was a wonderful old man, and I have seen him go well to hounds when he was so weak that he could hardly sit on a horse. He worked hard at racing and kept his own handicap book, which he made up carefully after each day. When he said a horse was a good thing in a handicap, it generally won. He gave me much good advice in his time, some of which I took and some I unfortunately did not.

There you would also find Lord and Lady Cadogan, Lord Lascelles, the Castlereaghs, Lord Hastings, the Duke of Portland, with Mat and George Dawson, and Sir George Chetwynd, Lord Lurgan, General Owen Williams, Harry Hungerford, with Sherrard from Newmarket, a trainer who turned out his horses with a most wonderful polish. Sherrard's was a big betting stable, and for a time most successful, but it did not last long.

Lady Cadogan and Lady Castlereagh (afterwards

Lady Londonderry) both knew as much and more about a horse than most men.

W. G. Craven, one of the best-looking men I ever saw, would come with William Goater from Findon. He was also a fine judge of racing, but never very lucky. Some people said he was too fortunate in other matters, for he was a great man with the ladies. But his trainer, Goater, brought off some big handicap coups, notably Don Juan's victory in the Cesarewitch. Fordham was the stable jockey, and the story goes that when the boy who was riding Don Juan in the race went out to get up on him Fordham took his whip, a new one, from him, saying, " Dear me, what a pretty whip this is, my boy, but what a pity it is these pretty things lose so many races ; don't you think you had better leave it behind," and, putting it in his pocket, he walked off with it.

Also at the stables you would see the North Country lot, Sir Robert Jardine, Lord Zetland, Mr. James Lowther, my brothers Lord Durham and Freddy Lambton, the Vyners, Johnny Cookson, Charles Perkins, and with them the big, burly North Country trainers, Fred Bates and William I'Anson, Joe Enoch, and sometimes Tom Green. Horses from the North had to be reckoned with at Ascot in those days.

Mr. and Mrs. Rothschild would come with the Arthur Sassoons. They and their trainer, Hayhoe, always had a good string of horses. If he could find time from his political duties Lord Hartington was sure to be there. In later years, when he became Duke of Devonshire, he and the Duchess were great lovers of racing. The Duchess took the greatest delight in betting, and would back three or four horses in one race for small sums. She had an extraordinary knack of picking out long-priced winners. I remember once having to back four horses for her. I forgot one of them and it turned up at thirty-three to one.

Prince Soltykoff, who trained with Tom Jennings, always had useful stayers in his stable. He won the

Cup one year with Gold, a great, big, burly chestnut horse. Gold took a lot of riding, and Fred Webb, a magnificent horseman, was given the mount.

When the horse came in there was a raw place on each side of him where Fred had been squeezing him with his knees. It was a fact that he could nearly squeeze the life out of any horse.

Another successful stable much in evidence was Captain Machell's, and with him there were to be seen Lord Calthorpe, Harry McCalmont, Lord Gerard, Mr. "Bunny" Leigh, and Sir John Willoughby. The Captain and his trainer, Jewitt, always laid themselves out for Ascot. The Hunt Cup was their favourite race. They won it twice for Lord Gerard with Elzevir and Sweetbread, and also with Suspender and Knight of the Thistle. Captain Machell's handicap winners were nearly all good-class horses with plenty of weight. He did not win with horses that had shown no form, and were thrown in at the bottom, but he was a past master in throwing dust in the handicappers' eyes in a legitimate manner.

Then there was the Duke of Westminster, with the Grosvenors, who had a splendid lot of horses trained by John Porter, old Alec Taylor, with Caroline Duchess of Montrose, that most courtly of gentlemen, the late Duke of Beaufort, Lord and Lady Coventry, and many others.

Altogether, those Ascot evenings are good to look back upon.

Owners in those days had the time and the leisure to manage their own horses. They had their own handicap books, and made a study of racing. This took a great responsibility off the shoulders of their trainers. Nowadays, most of the big owners are so busy with one thing or another that they not only have no time for this, but often they are not even able to see their horses run.

This year, 1881, was remarkable for the debut of six very beautiful and good fillies, Kermesse, Dutch Oven, Geheimness, Nellie, St. Marguerite and Shotover.

I HAVE KNOWN

Dutch Oven, the property of Lord Falmouth, was a great slashing brown filly by Dutch Skater out of the flying Cantiniere. She won nine good races as a two-year-old, ending up with the Dewhurst Plate. She had a glorious bang tail, which she carried very high; when she galloped it floated behind her like the flag of a ship.

Nellie, a chestnut filly by Hermit out of Hippia, belonging to Mr. Leopold de Rothschild, was one of the most beautiful mares I ever saw. She and Dutch Oven were continually up against each other. Always ridden by the same jockeys, Archer and Fordham, it was wonderful how true they ran. In the Prince of Wales Stakes at York, Nellie receiving 7lb. from Dutch Oven won by three parts of a length, and then at even weights Dutch Oven was second to Kermesse with Nellie third in the Champagne Stakes. In the Rous Memorial again at even weights Dutch Oven beat Nellie a neck, and, in the Clearwell the following week, she gave her 3lb. and won by a head. I think this consistency is a great tribute to horses, jockeys and trainers.

Kermesse, a brown filly by Cremorne out of Hazeldean, was probably the best of the lot. A long, low filly, full of quality, so dark a brown as to be almost black, she was the property of Lord Rosebery, and was trained by Joe Cannon. She won five good races, including the Middle Park Plate. She was only beaten once, when she and St. Marguerite dead-heated for second place in the Richmond Stakes at Goodwood, behind Dutch Oven, Kermesse giving away 4lb.

Geheimness, a brown filly by Rosicrucian out of Nameless, owned by Lord Stamford, and trained by John Porter, was a magnificent mare, a trifle on the leg, with beautiful action. She won all her seven races in a canter.

St. Marguerite, a chestnut filly by Hermit out of Devotion, the property of " Mr. Manton," a beautiful filly and royally bred, won four good races, and

Shotover, another magnificent-looking chestnut filly by Hermit, owned by the Duke of Westminster, and also trained by John Porter, ran three times without distinguishing herself.

Neither I nor any other man have ever seen six such fillies in one year. Between them they won the Two Thousand Guineas, the One Thousand Guineas, the Derby, the Oaks and the St. Leger.

Before the Two Thousand Guineas (1882) we heard that Shotover was greatly improved and was to run against the colts. As we all knew that Porter did not imagine his geese to be swans, she was well backed and started at ten to one. In a big field, ridden by Tom Cannon, she won easily by two lengths. On the Friday she came out again for the One Thousand, starting at four to one on, and was beaten a neck by St. Marguerite, with Nellie third, only a neck behind.

I did not see the race as I had gone to ride at Ludlow. I know that I left a commission to put a thousand pounds on Shotover, and my pleasure in riding two winners at Ludlow was considerably marred when I heard the result. But the next day, greatly to my relief, I had a letter to say the money had not been put on, as my commissioner did not like the look of the mare before the race.

Dutch Oven did not run in the One Thousand Guineas as she had not been doing too well during the Spring. She was held in reserve for the Derby.

The colts of that year were not good, and Bruce, by See Saw out of Carine, stood out as the best. He had won all his four races as a two-year-old and had been the winter favourite for the Derby. Reputed to have wintered well and to have won a good trial, he made his first appearance in the Derby, starting favourite at nine to four, with Shotover at eleven to two. Sammy Mordan had ridden Bruce in all his two-year-old races. He was anything but a good jockey, and in the Derby he rode even worse than usual. Shotover, beautifully ridden by Tom Cannon, won somewhat easily from Lord Bradford's Quick Lime ; Dutch Oven was unplaced.

I HAVE KNOWN

I expect Bruce was a good horse. He afterwards won the Grand Prix with Archer up, and then I fancy leg troubles practically put an end to his career.

Shotover was not pulled out for the Oaks, and it was left to her stable companion, Geheimness, to do duty for Kingsclere. Starting at six to four on, Tom Cannon brought off the double event, beating St. Marguerite and Nellie easily by two lengths.

My readers will be wondering what had become of Kermesse, who, in my opinion, would have been the best of the lot. Unfortunately for Lord Rosebery and Joe Cannon she split both pasterns early in the spring, and she never ran till the second October Meeting, where in the Select Stakes she met Nellie and Shotover, the latter giving away 9 lb. After a great race, Kermesse and Nellie ran a dead-heat, with Shotover beaten a length. On this form, considering the split pasterns and the long rest that was necessary, I think that there are good reasons for saying that Kermesse was the best of these good fillies.

After Epsom, Shotover went to Ascot, where she won the Ascot Derby and another race. She was then put by for the St. Leger. Geheimness also went to Ascot, and started in the Fern Hill Stakes, five furlongs, at the odds of eight to one on, but the transition from mile-and-a-half work to five furlongs being too much for her, she was beaten a head by the two-year-old, Narcissa.

Dutch Oven so far had not reproduced her two-year-old form, but she was supposed to be at her best when she came out again at Goodwood for the Sussex Stakes. The race was on the Wednesday. On that morning I saw Dutch Oven go a canter with Mat Dawson's other horses, and again later I saw her come a good mile gallop. Archer was beside me and nearly dropped off his hack with horror. He rode up to Mat Dawson, saying, " Why, the mare's race is to-day." The old man took out his book and replied, " By God, so it is. I was thinking it was on Thursday." Notwithstanding this, Dutch Oven started at even money, but only finished a bad third. Archer told me the next day that I ought to back her for the Leger, as the race was all wrong owing to the morning's work having taken too much out of her. I told a friend of mine, Mr. Algy Bourke, this story, and he backed her to win him a good stake.

At York August Meeting there was the usual interest and talk about St. Leger. The public fancies were Geheimness, Shotover and Dutch Oven. On the Tuesday, Dutch Oven won the Yorkshire Oaks in a canter, and was pulled out again for the Great Yorkshire Stakes on the Thursday. This time she blotted her copybook badly, being only a moderate third to Peppermint and Nellie. Peppermint, ridden by John Osborne, set a tremendous gallop from the fall of the flag, and showed up Dutch Oven as an apparent non-stayer. She went out to forty to one for the St. Leger.

As it was well known that Geheimness was better than Shotover she became a raging hot favourite for the race. Fred Archer, thinking that Dutch Oven had no chance, asked Lord Falmouth to let him off riding her, as he had been offered the mount on Geheimness. I believe Lord Falmouth was quite willing to do this, but Mat Dawson would not hear of it, and Archer had to ride Dutch Oven.

Before the start of the race, they betted eleven to eight on Geheimness, a hundred to fifteen Shotover, and forty to one Dutch Oven. I remember seeing my friend, Algy Bourke, just as he was going up into the stand to watch the race, the most dejected of men, for not only had he a lot of money on Dutch Oven, which he could not get out of, but he had also laid heavily against Geheimness. If she won he was a ruined man.

I have not a clear recollection of the early stages of this race, but I know that Dutch Oven was away behind at first. Two hundred yards from home Geheimness had taken the measure of her field, appearing to be an easy winner. Then Archer, on Dutch Oven, apparently dropping from the clouds, swept past her and won in a canter to the great astonishment of everybody. I shall never forget seeing a radiant Algy Bourke bounding down the steps of the Stand, and for the rest of the afternoon he did not know whether he was standing on his heels or his head. As usual, there were people who said Archer must have pulled Dutch Oven at Goodwood and at York. I have written what occurred at Goodwood, of how Archer had told me to back her for the St. Leger and of how after York he was greatly disappointed with her, declared she had not a thousand to one chance, and did his best to get off riding her.

I should imagine this was the only occasion on which fillies had filled the first three positions in the St. Leger, and the most curious part of it all was that not one of the three could really stay.

CHAPTER V

ARTHUR YATES—COUNT KINSKY—W. H. P. JENKINS

A GREAT personality of the 'eighties was dear old Arthur Yates, of Alresford. He had been a fine steeplechase rider in his day, but that was before my time. He had a big stable of horses of every description. They were kept very rough, with no clothing, and in every sort of tumbledown place, but in spite of this they won a tremendous lot of races, and it had to be a very bad horse that Arthur could not get through some sort of a race.

He was a great believer in really efficient schooling, and it was very seldom that his horses fell. He had at that time three very good jockeys in Billy Sensier, Childs and Dollery to help him.

Sensier was an accomplished jockey, and was of great assistance to him in training his horses. Dollery and Childs were two bold, rough fellows, and a horse had to go over or through a fence when they were on top.

Arthur's horses looked anything but prepossessing in the paddock. They were light and rough in their coats, but they could go. Someone said, " I wonder what Arthur feeds his horses on." Marcus Beresford answered, " It must be orange-peel, because that makes you slip along so."

You would often see three of his horses in different ownership running in the same race. He would have a couple of sovereigns on the one he fancied most, and he usually won with the outsider of the party. Even if some people were annoyed, Arthur was always beaming as long as the winner came from his stable and was ridden by one of his "boys." But I shudder to think what would be said in these days about his stable, although it was run on the straightest lines regardless of betting.

He trained many good horses, Cloister, Gamecock, Midshipmite amongst them. The two former won the National, and Midshipmite was a great horse up to three miles.

Anybody who wanted to ride schooling always found a ready welcome at Alresford, and it was a kind of headquarters for many young soldiers. Arthur would put them on anything, and send eight or nine horses together, with Billy Sensier or Dollery to lead them. Falls were plentiful, but no one ever seemed to get hurt there.

Another gentleman trainer of that time was Mr. W. H. P. Jenkins, such a good fellow and a very fine trainer of steeplechase horses. Hurdle races and flat races he rather despised.

Like Arthur Yates, he kept open house for young men who were fond of riding. I and my friends, particularly Charles Kinsky and Roddy Owen, were often there. Old "Jenks," as we called him, was the most hospitable man. Strong as a bull himself, he wanted anyone who rode for him to go in for the most rigorous training. After a hard morning's work he thought nothing of a twelve miles' walk with sweaters on in the afternoon. Personally I never had the strength for much of that sort of thing, and he soon settled me. After that, to the disgust of the others, I was let off lightly.

When Charles, Roddy and myself arrived to stay with him he used to say, "You fellows don't look half fit, so I shall give you some work while you are here, and we shall go to bed at ten o'clock." But "Jenks," when he started talking after dinner and puffing away at his pipe, hated going to bed, and it always ended with, "By

God, why it's 11.30; this will never do, you ought to be in bed at ten if you want to ride." In the morning, as soon as it was light, he would be up with a pipe in his mouth shaking us out of bed. Then away we would go to the stables. There was no getting up at the last moment on a horse just before he galloped, but you were on him when he left the stable. We would generally trot and walk up a steep hill near by to stretch the horses' legs. That was all right, but sometimes coming down that hill was not so pleasant on a bucking, kicking four-year-old. Then the serious business would begin. Jenks was a man who made his horses go through the mill and there was no slovenly jumping at Upton after they had been there any length of time. The first fence we had to jump was a naked flight of hurdles, not ordinary sheep hurdles, but deer hurdles, four bars, and you could not knock them down.

The general practice is for the first fence to be easy and rather weak, but I am sure Mr. Jenkins's plan was better, for if a horse gives his shins a good rap over the first fence it will make him careful, and he will attend to his business.

One very cold morning, Roddy, Charles Kinsky and I were going down to ride a school on three young horses. As we got near the starting place Roddy, who never missed anything, said, "By Jove, the old man is the other side of the hill, let's miss this d——d hurdle." So off we started the wrong side of the hurdle. At the end of the gallop Jenks said, "How did the young ones get over that hurdle?" While Charles and I were thinking what to say, Roddy replied without a moment's hesitation, "Oh, George and Charles sailed over it, my horse only got half-way up it, but recovered himself, he will do better next time."

I rode Cloister his first school when he was a four-year-old, after he came over from Ireland. Irish horses are never very good at timber, and Jenks said, "Be careful at that hurdle; get a good hold of him, and get him to jump off his hind legs." The first thing that happened was that Cloister gave a tremendous kick as we started, got his head right down on the ground, and went at the hurdle anyhow, completely out of hand, with Jenks swearing at me for not pulling his head up. In spite of this he flew the hurdle like a bird, and what a ride he was, although he always liked to carry his head very low, and to be ridden with a long rein. I am not certain, but I don't think he ever fell. He certainly was a much better horse at Liverpool than on any other course, it was no effort to him to jump those fences.

Dear old Jenks, what a good fellow he was, simple as a child, he trusted everyone and could not believe that all men were not as honest as himself. His wife, Lady Caroline, was a great contrast to the rough, burly man, a very delicate frail little woman, but she always gave us a ready welcome to Upton, and we were very fond of her.

Many good horses were trained at Upton, amongst them Zoedone, who won the National. I think, perhaps, this race gave Jenks the greatest joy of his life.

The first time I saw Zoedone, she was in Mr. Edward Clayton's hunting stable at Oakham. I was staying with Mr. Clayton that winter for hunting, and he trained his flat race-horses in Exton Park.

"Uncle" Clayton is well known to the present generation, and only the other day I heard that he was still hunting, and could gallop as well as ever. He is over 80. There was no better judge of a horse, and he had always a very high opinion of Zoedone, who was a beautiful short-legged chestnut mare, about 15-3, by New Oswestry. I don't think it was possible to find a fault with her make and shape.

After doing some hunting with her, and running her in one or two small races, Mr. Clayton sent her to Jenkins to train for the National. So well did she do that she was thought to be a good thing, but an attack of coughing interfered with her preparation, and she was short of work when she ran. She was ridden by that grand horseman, Captain Doggie Smith, the very best man to hounds I have ever seen.

Extraordinarily well did she run, never set a foot wrong and finished third. Doggie Smith was confident that she had the race won till want of condition told.

Count Charles Kinsky, as he then was, a young man in the Austrian Embassy in London, bought her, and said she was to be kept for the National the following year, and that he would ride her himself.

I was introduced to him at Newmarket, and he asked me where I should advise him to have her trained. I said, " Leave her where she is with Jenkins."

Charles Kinsky's first experience of London society was rather amusing. He had been asked to dinner by Horace Farquhar (afterwards Lord Farquhar) who entertained a great deal at his house in Berkeley Street. Charles went with some trepidation, as his English was not very fluent, and Horace generally collected all the smartest people in London. His cabman was drunk, and drove him to the wrong house, and then all over London; consequently, by the time he arrived, dinner was half over. His place was next the late Lady Londonderry, then Lady Castlereagh, and at the height of her beauty. He explained why he was so late, and someone said, " I suppose you were very angry with your cabman ? " " Oh, yes," said Charles, " I did give him the hell of a rowing, he drove me all round London," and waving his arms to express himself he knocked the plate of soup which was being handed to him right into Lady Castlereagh's lap. Charles always said she took this unfortunate accident with perfect good-humour, and continued her conversation with him as if nothing had happened.

Charles Kinsky was a splendid horseman, brave to recklessness with hounds, but he did not know much about race riding. Having made up his mind to ride his mare in the National, he also resolved that he would

By permission of Messrs. Forres

COUNT CHARLES KINSKY ON "ZOEDONE"

Photo: Clarence Hailey

JOHN OSBORNE

TOM GREEN

Photo: W. A. Rouch

MR. ALFRED SADLER

Photo: W. A. Rouch

be fit for the job, and he never missed a chance of riding her at work. He trained himself, and turned up at Liverpool as fit as a prize-fighter. In the race he made nearly all the running, went round the course without the semblance of a mistake, and won by ten lengths. It was a great performance for a foreigner, and a young man without much experience of racing. I did not see the race as I was laid up, but Charles soon afterwards became my best and dearest friend.

He loved England and the English, and always spent more than half the year in this country. I said good-bye to him at the end of Goodwood week in July, 1914, when he left to go and fight for his own country, and on the side of the Germans, a nation he had always hated.

He volunteered for service on the Russian Front so that he should avoid having to fight against the English and the French, and for two years he was with the Austrian cavalry at the age of 58, or more.

He died in 1919, and if ever a man died of a broken heart Charles Kinsky did; his own country ruined and done for, and he himself debarred from coming to the country he loved, and where his friends were.

But to return to his early career: after he won the National he became a very capable cross-country rider, and rode a lot of winners. He had some good horses, Kilworth for one, who ought to have won the Paris Steeplechase in 1885. Charles was not riding himself, but the stable jockey, Sly.

Kilworth was a very difficult horse to ride, and used to run out at his fences, but Sly understood him well, and, although he started at fifty to one, he was well fancied and backed by Charles to win a big stake. I rode Lioness for Harry Hungerford in the race, a charming little mare that I had already ridden in the National of that year. She was running well throughout but it was one of Kilworth's good days, and he was dominating the field after he had gone two miles. Coming to the last fence but one I was just behind him, and he had the two horses alongside of him stone cold, when for some extraordinary reason Sly, with the Auteuil stand, and thousands of yelling people on it, straight in front of him, went up the wrong course and threw away the race, and a small fortune in bets besides.

Charles Kinsky loved hunting better than anything. He always had good horses, and at one time he was a desperate hard man. On one occasion I remember a check in a good gallop with the Quorn, when the first whip, looking very scared, came up to Polly Carew (General Sir Reginald Pole Carew) and myself, and said, "The Count's had an awful fall, I think he's killed." At that moment away went hounds again in full cry, and I am ashamed to say Polly and I pursued.

At the finish, to our surprise, and relief, a battered Charles appeared ; Polly Carew went up to the Whip, saying, "What the d–v–l do you mean telling us the Count was killed?" "Well, if he aint dead now, by G—d he soon will be," was the answer.

For three years before the War he and I hunted together from Market Harboro', and, although he was not so rash in those days, his nerve was as good as ever. When he left England for Austria, his horses, as fine a stud of hunters as ever any man had, were taken for the Army.

A report was spread that he had given orders to have them shot or poisoned. Who started this malicious and totally untrue story I do not know but I always thought it must have come from some friends of Germany, for Charles had always been a great friend of King Edward's, and was greatly liked in Court circles. As a matter of fact, before he left for Austria, he asked me, if possible, to get his horses distributed amongst his many friends in the English Army. I am glad to say that, to a certain extent, this did happen, for General Kavanagh and General Bruce Hamilton each had two of his best horses. I managed to get this news conveyed to him in the early days of the War, and that did much to soften the pain and indignation he felt at the malicious report that was circulated about him. I contradicted it in the papers, and whenever I could, but the story would crop up again. There is no doubt that the friendly feeling that existed between Austria and England at the beginning of the War caused considerable uneasiness in Germany, and that this story was originally an invention of German agents.

The Austrians behaved wonderfully well during the War to the English colony that was living in and around Vienna. They were allowed to carry on their lives and go about their business just as usual, and those that were in bad circumstances were helped and looked after. Mr. John Reeves, the great trainer over there, spoke in the highest terms of the way he and his compatriots had been treated. The good Austrian is a sportsman, and a friend to England.

A great friend of Charles and myself in our riding days was that fine Irishman, Garrett Moore. I should say that he and his brother Willie were the two biggest men I have ever seen who were really first-class steeplechase jockeys, both of them being well over six foot, and Garrett, when he was not wasting, must have walked well over 12 stone. He was a typical Irishman of the best sort, a reckless, careless man, full of ready wit, who always made a joke of everything.

His best riding days were before my time, but I remember so well the day I first made his acquaintance. It was at Four Oaks Park, in 1882. After the races on the first day, a party of us, of whom Garrett was one, set off to walk back to Birmingham. He was riding a horse called Turco the next day, and, although the weight was 12st. 7lb., Garrett had sweaters on. He kept us amused all the way with his stories and jokes. At the first chemist's shop he came to in the town, he stopped and asked for a glass of water and a box of Cockle's pills. The chemist looked in amazement, and said, " Good Heavens, what can your inside be made of," when

Garrett opened the box and emptied about half of it into his hand, swallowing the lot.

The next day I saw him on a horse for the first time, and I should not forget it if I lived for a hundred years. When he jumped the preliminary fence on his great good-looking horse there was a combination of skill, strength and elegance which I have never seen equalled. He did not win the race, but did enough to show me the truth of what I had been told, that he was the finest horseman in the world. As I have said before, I did not see him ride often, and it was more as a trainer that I knew him so well. He had a great knowledge and love of horses, but nothing could make this somewhat careless, pleasure-loving Irishman into a business man, and he was sometimes the despair of his owners, some of whom were big betting men. I remember Oliver Jones telling me how Garrett brought a horse to Manchester for him to bet on ; he had his maximum on, the horse was beaten to blazes, and after the race he was walking into the paddock feeling annoyed and disconsolate. Garrett came up to him, hit him a thump on the back, saying, " D——n it all, *look* as if you liked it anyhow ! "

That was the way he took everything. In spite of these faults, which in themselves were lovable, he turned out a lot of winners, and was a past-master at getting the better of a bad-tempered horse.

Old John Hubert Moore, Garrett's father, was a wonderful old fellow, a great, rugged, tall man about 6 ft. 4 in., with a most irascible temper, but on a horse as gentle as a woman. There was nothing he liked so much as taking in hand an unruly horse and teaching him manners. His great axiom for steeplechasing was this, " You can do what you like with a horse until fifty yards from a fence, but after that you must leave him alone." How true this is, but how difficult to follow !

Riding was in the blood of the Moores. Garrett and his brother Willie, and then their nephews, Frank and Hubert Hartigan. Frank was after my time, but I have seen him ride. He was a beautiful horseman and about the best jockey of his day, and even now schools his own steeplechase horses.

Hubert, who is built much like his grandfather, only on a smaller scale, is a champion over big fences.

CHAPTER VI

BURGH BARONY RACES AND TOM GREEN OF BEVERLEY

A FRIEND of mine who did most of my betting for me when I was riding was Lord Lurgan, then a very prominent figure on a race-course. He betted very high himself and did many commissions. Billy Lurgan had an extraordinary knack of getting information. With his attractive manner and quick brain he could extract the truth from an oyster, so much so that he went by the name of the " Aristocratic Tout." He knew men better than horses, and was wonderfully clever in sifting the wheat and the chaff from the mass of information he acquired. We went racing a great deal together, and great fun did we have. When he did my commissions I always got the top of the market.

There is a curious custom in Westmorland that on the succession of each Earl of Lonsdale a race meeting is held at Burgh Barony, a place close to Lowther, when the principal race is for a Cup given by the new Earl. On the succession of the present Lord Lonsdale, Billy Lurgan, Harry Hungerford, Sir Charles Hartopp (then Mr. Hartopp, a young man in the Guards) and I were amongst a large party at Lowther.

Lord Lonsdale, who even in those early days had a marvellous power of organization, had taken considerable trouble to make the races a success. He had not only got decent-class horses to run, but, as the men I have mentioned were all big betting men, he had induced several influential members of the Ring to be there to accommodate them. It was a most curious little course where the races were held; as far as I can remember not much bigger than Chester, but it was a most amusing Meeting.

My old friend, Tom Green of Beverley, had brought quite a string of horses and expected to do well. He had a royal time and won five races. The bookmakers

"THE ARISTOCRATIC TOUT."
[*Caricature by Colonel Montgomery.*]

said they hoped Lord Lonsdale would live for ever, as they never wanted to see Burgh Barony again. But the last race of the Meeting was a tragedy.

That famous old horse, Durham, was to run for it, and, ridden by Tom Spence, looked a real good thing. A well-known Scottish sportsman, old Johnny Martin, had won the fourth race of the day, a mile handicap, with a horse called Rosemount, and at the last moment he decided to pull him out again. Seeing me in the weighing room without a mount in the race, he asked me to ride. I said I would be delighted to, but that I had asked Lord Lurgan to back Durham to win me a considerable amount of money, and that it was too late to stop him. "That won't make any difference," said Johnny Martin, "you ride my horse." There were only five runners, and two to one was laid on Durham, Rosemount starting at four to one against. After we had gone a mile and a half the other three were beaten. I could see old Durham was in a sulky mood, so I dropped in behind him, much to the disgust of Tom Spence, who could not induce him to do anything, in spite of the picturesque language he used both to his horse and to me, and I just sailed past him in the last hundred yards and won easily. Tom, when he got off his horse, was in an awful rage. He threw his saddle into the corner of the weighing room, exclaiming, "If it was good enough for you to have £1,000 on why the hell couldn't you make running," and Billy, who showed no outward sign except for being rather flushed in the face, remarked, "I wish you rode as well for your own money." This reverse took some of the gilt off the gingerbread at the Meeting from a financial point of view, but what did it matter, I had a certainty to bet on at Derby the next day.

We left by the night train for the South after the races. When we arrived at Carlisle station we found quite a crowd of people, and, on investigating the cause, there was Tom Green the centre and hero of it. As I have said, he had a glorious time at Burgh Barony, and no one had appreciated Lord Lonsdale's lavish hospitality more than he, but also he must have been having a royal time of it at Carlisle and have been treating half the town. Anyhow, after saluting two ladies on the platform, he stepped into his reserved carriage amidst cheers from the crowd, the station-master and porters all attending him, as if he was a royal personage. Such was old Tom Green when the world went well with him. But when we got to Derby, as I was going off with Harry Hungerford, Tom came up to me, took me aside and said, " Mr. George, it's all very well for the trainer to enjoy himself, but it won't do for a jockey, and for goodness' sake remember you are riding Polariscope to-morrow, and take care that Mr. Hungerford doesn't lead you into trouble ; they tell me he is the devil of a fellow at night."

Polariscope was a four-year-old by Speculum, which I had bought for £50, after he had run unplaced in a selling race. We had tried him well, and for this race at Derby he was the greatest certainty I have ever had in my life. There was only a small field of four, but the others were all useful horses with good recent form, which made a good market for me. I had the dash of my life. The horse started at even money, but my commission averaged six to four against.

Going down to the post, Captain Lee Barber, who was riding the second favourite, remarked that I was looking very pale and ill. The fact was I had so much money on my horse that I was in the devil of a funk and shaking with fright, but that did not last long as in the race I soon went to the front and won by five lengths.

Captain Lee Barber was a gallant little fellow and a real good jockey. He was at one time the Fred Archer of the soldiers at the Grand Military Meeting at Sandown and won many races. He was always the life and soul of any dinner party, but his fondness for the pleasures of life prevented him from being as great a jockey as he should have been. He was generally better to back the first day of the Grand Military Meeting than the second, although he was as hard as nails. Once at Sandown he got a horrible-looking fall on the far side of the course, and lay there without a sign of life. I was running down to see what could be done for him when I came upon his old father walking leisurely along. I breathlessly said, " I'm afraid the Shaver (his nickname) is very badly hurt." He replied, " Don't you worry, he'll be all right; you couldn't kill the boy with a sledge-hammer," and he was not far wrong. The old man was tremendously proud of his son, and always backed his mounts heavily, but, in spite of many winners, I am afraid the account was often on the wrong side, and he had to pay the Shaver's losses as well as his own.

When I think of the Shaver's life as a jockey I am tempted to launch out against what I think is a pernicious practice amongst some of the jockeys of to-day.

In the last few years, on the Friday night of the Manchester November Meeting, it has become a custom for the jockeys to have a dinner. I am sure they have a very merry evening, and that is all right, but I know that many of them do not get to bed till 3 o'clock in the morning, if then. Last year I read an account in some paper of Donoghue's Derby dinner, when many of the guests appear to have been up all night. Now, even Steve, fit, hard, plucky little chap as he is, cannot possibly be at his best next day, when he has been eating eggs and bacon at six o'clock in the morning after revels which have lasted till daybreak, although I expect he can stand it better than many of them. I think it is ridiculous that owners of race-horses who pay jockeys high salaries and fees, and the Stewards of the Jockey Club, who have control over the licences of riders, should tolerate such proceedings for one moment. Jockeys may not like what I say, but they are servants, and well-paid ones, and when they sit up all night in the middle of a race week they are grossly neglecting their duties to their employers. They have all the winter to enjoy themselves in that way if they want to, and if, which is quite natural, at the end of the season they wish to have a " jolly " together they should wait till Saturday night or later when the racing is over. Fred Archer used to give a ball at Newmarket, but always in the winter.

A celebrated trainer once told me an amusing story of a race at Manchester on the last day of the Meeting. He was running a horse in the first race. He and the owner had a lot of money on at starting price. As he did not want to be placed in the position of either having to tell lies or give the business away, he did not arrive at Manchester till six in the morning. After having been to the stables to see if the horse was all right, he went to a quiet little hotel and stayed there till it was time for the races. He then went, not to the weighing room or the paddock, but on to the course outside, but when the time came for the jockeys to get up he could not refrain from going into the paddock just to see that the horse was properly saddled, and to have a last word with his jockey (one of the best that ever got on a horse). To his horror he found him so drunk that when he gave him a leg up he nearly fell off on the other side. It was too late to do anything, his money was on and he looked upon it as already lost. But, to his immense relief, the horse proved good enough to carry his jockey first past the post, though the latter was not able to ride again that day.

This was some years ago, and one cannot imagine anything of the sort taking place in the paddock to-day. All classes of people are much more sober than they used to be. But fitness, judgment and nerve are essential qualities for good riding, and I am sure there is no jockey of the present day who in his heart will not agree with me about these late nights.

Writing of Burgh Barony Races reminds me of the many great stables and trainers there were in the North of England in those days, also there were some great North Country jockeys. Although for many years I have lived and trained in the South, even now there is something about North Country racing which appeals to me. When I go North and get on to a race-course, although so many of my old friends have retired or are dead, I get into an atmosphere of sport and good fellowship which is somehow less conspicuous in the South. In the old days there were among the trainers, besides my old friend Tom Green, the brothers Osborne, Fred Bates, William I'Anson, Harry Hall, Charles Lund and

Sanderson; and of the jockeys John Osborne, Jim Snowden, Fagan, Bruckshaw and Weldon were all in the front rank. And what a host of good sportsmen as owners, Lord Zetland, Lord Durham, Mr. James Lowther, Mr. F. W. Lambton, the two brothers Clare and Bob Vyner, Charles Perkins, J. B. Cookson, Dudley Milner, the Duke of Montrose, Lord Lascelles and many others. One looks back with pleasure to those days when sport was the first thing and money the second consideration, although it was not by any means despised. And these old North Country trainers, perhaps they did things which would not quite have pleased the authorities in these days, but when they did have a good thing they wanted all their friends to be " on."

The rivalry between North and South Country jockeys and trainers was great. In 1883 I won a selling race at Gosforth Park with a horse of mine, Echo, ridden by Tom Bruckshaw and trained by Charles Lund. I had a dash on him and the chief danger to him, a horse called Chesterfield, was left. Having bought him in, I entered him again the next day. Chesterfield was also entered, and Archer was asked to ride him. Always keen on a winning ride, he came to me and said, " You had better let me ride Echo, otherwise I shall ride Chesterfield and probably beat you." I would not take Bruckshaw off, and in the race Echo started at six to four and Chesterfield at two to one. They were a long time at the post, and, eventually getting a flying start, Echo scrambled home from Chesterfield. Everyone knew that Archer had wanted the mount, and Bruckshaw might have won the Derby for the reception his North Country friends gave him when he rode in. In the weighing room there was a lot of chaff, and Fred Archer said to Jim Snowden, who had ridden in the race, " What was the matter with you and your horse at the post ? " " Well," said Jim, " you're generally a bit too quick at getting off, and I didn't want you to beat Tom and Mr. George, so I shouted ' No, no ' until I saw Tom would get away better than you."

Snowden was a great character, and when at his best a great jockey, but unfortunately he was rather.too fond of the ladies and the bottle. He was a wonder at coming with one long run and getting up in the last stride, and he knew to an inch where the winning post was. I remember his winning a selling race for Tom Green at Doncaster, when after apparently being out of the race he got up and won by a head. Charlie Merry, a very shrewd man and fond of a good plater, was determined to have the winner and out-bid old Tom Green, who was somewhat annoyed at losing his horse. When he was knocked down to Mr. Merry, Tom said, " Well, you have bought the horse, but you can't have his jockey, for he won't ride him for you." Merry replied, " Never mind about that, if Snowden hadn't waited so long he would have won in a canter." Ten days after, at the Newmarket First October Meeting, the horse was entered in another selling race. To my surprise I found Tom Green at the races, and on my asking what he was there for he replied, " Why, to get my horse back again, for he will be beaten to-day ; no one but Snowden can ride him."

The horse started favourite, with Jack Watts up, got a good start, looked all over a winner, and then faded out of the picture. Tom, who was a most popular man, found no difficulty in getting him claimed, and went back chuckling to Yorkshire.

Once at Catterick Bridge Jim was riding a good old plater called Aragon, also the property of Tom Green, who was not present at the Meeting. By the time he came into the paddock to get up he had been doing himself pretty well. He looked at the horse walking round, and said to the boy leading him, " Take those blinkers off." The boy said that the horse always ran in them. " I tell you," said Snowden, " take those blinkers off, it's bad enough to have a blind jockey without having a blind horse as well." But in spite of his condition he won the race. Another time at Thirsk, early in the day, he had been engaged to ride a horse in the last race.

The owner had said to him, "Now, Jim, this is a real good thing, but I don't want you to show the horse up, so don't win more than a neck or half a length. You know how to do that." When the race was run, being at the Autumn Meeting, it was dark and foggy, and as the horses emerged from the gloom Snowden was seen to be out by himself, and he won by ten lengths. As he came back to scale the owner said to him, " I think you might have remembered what I told you and not shown my horse up like that." "You were d——d lucky to win at all," replied Snowden, who was blind to the world, "for I never saw a post from start to finish." In spite of these failings he was a good and loyal servant, and Jim in the white and red spots of Lord Zetland was a favourite figure in the North.

Quite a different character was dear old John Osborne. Like Archer in the South, Johnny was the idol of the North, and, when these two jockeys opposed each other, excitement was great, and the North to a man would stick to Johnny. I can call to mind some thrilling struggles. In short races I have no doubt that Archer was quicker, but in a long race no one could beat "the old pusher," as he was called. He had not a pretty seat, and rode, for those days, very short. He was a wonderful judge of pace, and, although his favourite race was a waiting one, he could fairly excel himself when he wanted to make running.

I don't know whether these stories of races ridden by old jockeys will weary my readers, but I must risk it. To me the riding of jockeys is almost as interesting as the running of horses.

As an instance of how true horses will run when ridden by two first-class jockeys I will quote the case of Privateer and Passaic at Goodwood in 1881. In the Drawing Room Stakes of a mile and a quarter on the Wednesday, Privateer, ridden by John Osborne, beat Passaic, Archer up, by a head. The winner, an unknown quantity at that time, started at a hundred to seven and Passaic five to four on. The following day the horses met again at the same weights over the old mile in the Racing Stakes.

I have said before that Archer, when he was beaten a head, always thought he might have won, and he thought so on this occasion, with the result that Passaic at their second meeting started at two to one and Privateer at five to two, but after another splendid race Privateer won by exactly the same distance as before, a head.

Another time at Goodwood, Johnny was riding Reveller for Sir Robert Jardine, father of the present Baronet, in the Goodwood Stakes. Fred Bates, who trained him, told me that it was a good thing and advised me to have a good bet. Having the greatest respect for Fred's judgment I had £1,000 on. After a very pretty race Reveller was beaten a head by Fortissimo with Fordham up. Many people thought that Johnny had waited too long, and Fred Bates said, " For once Johnny has made a mistake, but you can get your money back, as the two horses meet again in the Queen's Plate on Friday, and mine will win." I had a talk with Johnny about this. He would not have it, and even said that he rather thought Fordham had a bit up his sleeve.

The race came off; Fred Bates stuck to his guns and betted heavily again, and, although Reveller was giving 3 lb. in spite of the head beating, the ring betted even money about the pair, which showed that the public had the same opinion as Bates. Coming to the distance, it looked like being a good race, then Fordham produced that bit, which Johnny had suspected of being up his sleeve, and won in a canter. After the race Fred Bates, in forcible language, declared he ought to be kicked from Sussex to Yorkshire for thinking that he knew better than Johnny.

Talking of riding with Johnny, he told me that he had often been greatly praised for winning a race by a head or a neck when he had really ridden badly, and often when he had ridden a good race and been beaten a head he had been greatly blamed. I think that some of the young and old critics of present-day jockeys might take these words to heart.

Sir Robert Jardine had a very powerful stable, and he and Fred Bates were always to be feared in long-distance races. Bates trained at Middleham. He was a most genial man, who did himself very well. He used to entertain some of the South Country trainers for North Country Meetings. They generally came back rather the worse for wear, declaring that a week of Fred's hospitality would kill any South Country man.

Another North Country trainer of the same type was William I'Anson, who trained at Malton for Mr. Charles Perkins and Mr. J. B. Cookson, and had a fine stable of horses, winning a number of big races. He also was a great trainer of long-distance horses, and one of his greatest feats was winning the Cesarewitch with Mintagon. He bought the horse very cheaply at Mr. Whitney's sale, and when he said that the Cesarewitch was his objective we all smiled, for Mintagon was a flashy chestnut, with bad legs and back at the knee. He gave the horse a tremendous preparation, brought him to Newmarket fit to run for his life and told everyone that he was a certainty, and so it proved, for he had his field beaten three-quarters of a mile from home. William was about the best judge of a yearling I ever came across. He had not an enemy in the world, and there was no more popular man on the Turf. He was of a very sanguine temperament and was never so happy as when he brought off a good thing with all his friends well on.

These North Country trainers made it a custom to dine together every year at Stockton Races. On one occasion, just as they were all going to sit down, Tom Green addressed the company, saying, "Gentlemen, there is one man here who is a d——d thief, and I refuse to sit at the same table with him." He pointed to one of the guests, whom we will call Mr. X, and it was at once decided that the two must fight it out ; so the room was cleared and they set to. Both were very big men, but Tom had a fist and an arm that would

SAM LEWIS

SIR GEORGE
CHETWYND

From the painting by Emil Adam

MINTING

MR. ROBERT C. VYNER

Photo: W. A. Rouch

fell an ox, and in the second round Mr. X was knocked out. He bore the scar across his cheek for the rest of his life. After this interlude they sat down to dinner.

Tom Green was a remarkable man, a wizard with unsound horses, and always kept a lot of useful platers, betting on them as much and more than he could afford. He trained for my father, also for all my brothers and myself. He would have been a great trainer, but he had the same failings as his favourite jockey, Jim Snowden.

He never had the luck to train really good horses, but at the plating game he was hard to beat, in fact he was called the " King of the Platers." On the rare occasions when he did have a good horse he did the best possible with him.

I remember him bringing a horse to Goodwood called Binfield for the Stewards' Cup. He told me how he had tried him, and the race looked a certainty. On the morning of the race, the late Mr. Tom Corns, a well-known commission agent and owner, asked me what I fancied, and I said, Binfield. " Not a hundred to one chance," said Tom. " You would not say that," I replied, " if you knew the trial." " I tell you the horse won't win," he repeated, " Tom Green and his party are all stone broke, and that will stop him."

In the race Binfield looked a certain winner, four lengths in front two hundred yards from home, when suddenly he bolted straight across the course from the far side to the stands, and was beaten a short head.

Tom Green never said a word in answer to the many condolences he received, for everyone would have liked to have seen him win, till he had put the clothing on his horse, then, taking off his great broad-brimmed hat, he said, " Thank you, gentlemen, I am now going back to England." He did not consider any county south of the Trent could be dignified by that name.

Tom brought off many little gambles for me, and if I had stuck to him, and followed his advice, I should have done well, but like all young men I had to buy my experience.

Charles Lund who trained at Malton was a charming man, also of a sanguine nature, but, unlike Tom Green, he hated betting. He trained a mare called Irma for me, and I rode her in a race at Derby. When he put me up I asked him if the mare was all right, and he assured me she could not be better. "Well," said I, "that's a good thing, as I have got £2,000 on her." Charles nearly fell down with horror, went into the weighing room and sat with his head in his hands, saying, "Oh, how I hate this gambling," until after the race was over. I won it by six lengths.

CHAPTER VII

TRAINING WITH ALFRED SADLER—AN ADVENTURE AT NOTTINGHAM—MY BROTHER HEDWORTH

My association with Tom Green had been pleasant, instructive and lucrative, but North Country racing was too far from London to suit my tastes for long.

In 1882 I heard of a mare for sale called Claribel, in Alfred Sadler's stable near Winchester, so one morning I set out early from London to go down to see her. I had not let Sadler know that I was coming, and he was rather surprised at the visit of a young man with whom he was not even acquainted, but not more surprised than he was at the amount of bread and cheese I ate after buying the mare. I could eat in those days, and I can still remember that new bread, good butter and cheese.

I left the mare with Sadler, and the week after Goodwood we produced her for a hunters' race at Brighton.

That year I joined a small party for Goodwood consisting of George Chetwynd, Lord and Lady de Clifford, and Mr. and Mrs. Hwfa Williams. On the Monday evening it transpired that we were all more or less in financial difficulties, but were looking forward to Goodwood to rectify this. On the Friday morning, however, our position was lamentable ; George Chetwynd had lost £10,000, Ned de Clifford £6,000, I myself £3,000, and Hwfa Williams, who was not a betting man, £800. Ned and the latter said they would bet no more. I comforted myself with the thought that it was the Sussex fortnight, consequently there was no need to settle on Monday, and one might get home at Brighton and Lewes the following week.

My new purchase, Claribel, was engaged at Brighton, and Sadler was quietly confident that she would win, so I decided to wait for that.

It came off all right, and I got half-way home, and was delighted with the mare and her trainer. I had no other bet at Brighton, but the first day at Lewes Harry Morgan was riding a mare in the de Warrenne Handicap, called Eastern Empress, belonging to the eccentric bookmaker, Gregory. Vibration, a horse of the Duke of Hamilton's, was a hot favourite. He had been second in the Stewards' Cup. Morgan was a North Country jockey, and I asked him what had brought him so far South. He replied that he had come to win this race, so I took eleven hundred to one about the mare. It was the devil of a race, and I thought Vibration had won, but the right number for me went up. Then on the last day of the meeting two very good horses met in a sprint race; Mowerina (the dam of Donovan) and Martini. The betting was very close. I laid £1,100 to £1,000 on Mowerina, who, with Fordham up, won in a canter, and I went back to London feeling a millionaire because I had got home. I remember before this last race Captain Machell tried to persuade me to back Martini instead of the mare. Fortunately, I thought I knew better, but in reality he was quite right; subsequent events proved Martini to be the better horse.

That same year, Sadler ran a two-year-old called Dexterity in a Nursery at Derby. He told me to back her, and she ran a good second. I bought her after the race for £500. We sent her on to Warwick where she won a Nursery and got me back my money, and plenty more besides.

I remember asking Sir John Astley what he thought of Sadler as a trainer, and he replied, "He is one of the nicest young fellows I know; his horses always look well, and he knows when to back them."

It was then that my friendship with Alfred Sadler

began, and if ever anyone had a better friend he was devilish lucky. Shortly after this Sadler migrated from Winchester to Stockbridge House, Newmarket. I got several of my friends, including Harry Hungerford and Charles Kinsky, to send some horses to be trained by him, and for years there was never a happier combination. Our horses were not good, but we won a lot of races, and should all have been full of money if we had not lost it on other people's horses, for when Sadler had his " pony " on, and fancied a horse, it was hard to beat.

The horses we had, much as they interested us, were not of the class to interest my readers, with the exception of one mare belonging to Harry Hungerford, with which he nearly brought off a gigantic coup.

Harry was one of the best fellows I have ever met, clever, and a good judge of horses and racing ; he backed his opinion heavily, and at times won a great deal of money. But he had one failing which hurt no one but himself. He always wanted to be thought cleverer than anyone else. I remember Tom Cannon saying, as Harry was walking away after talking over some race, " It is a pity, but I am afraid Mr. Hungerford's opinions will cost him a lot " ; a prophecy which came true.

The mare I am writing of was an Irish one called Xema, by Ben Battle. When she came to Sadler's she was weak and in poor condition, but he soon altered that, and eventually put her in the Manchester Summer Cup, where she was nicely handicapped. Sadler said she was just about good enough to win, and, as she was practically a " dark horse," Harry was able to back her to win about £30,000 at nice prices.

I went to Manchester with Harry the day previous to the race ; when we arrived we found that Xema had gone out in the betting, and was quoted at fifty to one. This disturbed Harry, and he went to find his trainer, who said, " The mare is as well as I could wish, and I still think she will win." In the course of that evening

Harry backed her to win another £20,000 which only brought her to thirty-three to one.

She was ridden by Sadler's good apprentice, Fred Rickaby (afterwards my jockey for many years). All through the race the boy stuck to the rails, a practice he kept to all his life, and he had a good place, but, coming round the bend, Fred Barrett, on the favourite Borneo, got alongside of him, and after a great race beat him a length, the rest of the field a long way off. That night Archer, who had ridden in the race, told us that Rickaby was the best boy he had ever seen in his life, for, said he, "we pinned him on the rails and tried to frighten the life out of him, and he never gave way an inch."

Harry, as usual, took his defeat smiling, and said to Sadler, "Now we must win the Cesarewitch." When the weights came out for the Autumn Handicaps, Xema had 7st. 2lb., the same boy, Rickaby, was to ride, and that night Harry and I discussed the race and what we should do with the money when she had won.

As the time approached, the mare was really in fine condition, and Sadler said, which was a great deal for him, "I do not fear anything in the race except the French mare, Plaisanterie, for I don't know anything about her, and I hear she is a good one." Now Harry and I used to frequent a gambling place in London, owned by a man called Seaton, who, besides keeping this gambling hell, did a great many commissions. He was not half a bad fellow, and was always ready to do anyone a good turn. When Harry asked him if there was any money for Plaisanterie, he said that there was plenty of it, but that the people who had backed her would lose. He did not think she would win, and had laid heavily against her himself, for he had reliable information from France that the race she was going to win was the Cambridgeshire, and not the Cesarewitch. This was rather reassuring. On the morning of the race I was with Sadler by the Ditch when Xema did her last canter. For a light-framed mare she really looked marvellous. Sadler, who was always the most modest of men, allowed that she was near perfection, and that this was the day of her life.

At the time of the races the rain came down in torrents. Harry Hungerford went about looking as happy as a sandboy, full of fun and jokes, as if he had £50 on instead of standing to win a fortune. I was much too excited to do anything except gallop about on my hack in spite of the rain. Plaisanterie was not saddled in the Birdcage, and I rode off to try to find her. When I saw her come out of the old stables by the Ditch, my heart sank, for she was a most beautiful mare and trained to the hour. I started off to go and save on her, but then, remembering what Seaton had told us, and also something I had heard from a well-known French commission agent called Morris, I pulled up, and decided that some of my winnings would go on Plaisanterie for the Cambridgeshire.

In the race, as the horses came from the T.Y.C. Post, there was Xema in the front rank going well. She soon took up the running, and I turned round to gallop home with her, with the race, as I thought, won; but then to my horror out came Plaisanterie, and desperately as young Rickaby rode, gallantly as the mare answered, she was beaten cleverly, if not easily, by two lengths.

Sadler never again could get Xema within a stone of the form she showed that day; it was the effort of her life. Seaton and the Frenchman, Morris, were both ruined, and Harry Hungerford, though still full of jokes and fun, had a blow which would have knocked out most men.

Plaisanterie, a fortnight later, won the Cambridgeshire with a penalty. There has seldom been a better field for the famous handicap. The Derby winner, St. Gatien, then a four-year-old, ridden by Charles Wood, was a hot favourite, and that fine judge, Jack Hammond, his owner, was said to have his betting boots on. The horse had won the only three races he started for that year, including the Ascot Cup. Then there was the great Bendigo, with Fred Archer up, who in his only two races that season had won the Lincoln Handicap and the Hardwicke Stakes ; Eastern Emperor, the winner of the Hunt Cup ; the beautiful Thebais, and many other good horses. But the Cesarewitch winner with 8st. 12lb. on her three-year-old back won in a canter by two lengths from Bendigo. It is not to be wondered at that she should be the grandam of such a great horse as Tracery, the sire of the Derby winner, Papyrus. The result of this race showed what Harry Hungerford and Xema were up against.

When I first knew Sadler, Mr. R. H. Coombe was his principal patron. He was one of those real lovers of racing who never betted a shilling, was tremendously fond of horses, and the most sanguine man I ever met. His horses might go down time after time, but he always came up smiling, and was as confident as ever about the next one.

After a few years at Newmarket, Sadler became private trainer to my brother Durham, and I and my friends, to our great regret, had to look for fresh quarters. We were fortunate in finding an equally good fellow in Joe Cannon. The names of Sadler and Cannon have been famous in Turf history for years, and the sons of these two men are now keeping up the family tradition.

I am afraid the horses Sadler had to train for me were about as bad as they could be, but he always managed to get them through a race of some sort. There was one he was particularly successful with and on which I won a lot of money. This was a great big bay horse called Roundshot, by Toxophilite, and was given to me by the Duke of Portland. He was a grand-looking horse, but roared like a bull. I generally exploited him in selling races, for, owing to his wind infirmity, he was easy to buy in. He only let me down once, and that was not his fault.

It was in a selling race at Newmarket, and Tom Cannon was riding. Before the race, Fred Archer, who knew the horse well, came to me and said, " You had better warn Tom not to ride one of his ' pretty ' races on your horse; if he does he will probably get beaten." I did not like to give advice to Tom myself, but I got Arthur Coventry to drop him a hint. However, coming into the dip, Tom was having an arm-chair ride, and, as someone said, looking at his boots to see how well they were polished, when Roundshot suddenly dropped his bit, lost a length or two, and could never recover it.

Lord Cardross bought the winner and we tried the two horses at the end of the week, Roundshot winning easily, which showed how wrong the form was.

Jack Watts once did me a real good turn with this horse. He rode him for me at Shrewsbury in a selling race for which he started favourite. I had a lot of money on him, and he only scrambled home a neck from a very moderate field. So I decided to part with him. But, as Jack Watts got off, he said quietly, "Don't let him go, I ought to have won in a canter," and I bought him in. Afterwards Watts told me he had lost both his stirrups as they jumped off, and never got them again till a furlong from home, adding, "Put him in that seller at Derby, and let me ride him for you, he will be sure to win." I told him I would, but that I could not give him the ride as I had already asked Archer. The good thing came off. Watts kept his mouth shut; in fact, he did more than refrain from talking. When one very big Professional Backer asked him if he had any excuse for the horse at Shrewsbury, he answered, "I could not have won another inch," which was strictly true as it happened.

Roundshot started at four to one, which was a wonderful price for anything ridden by Archer, and won by four lengths. I had £1,000 on. But I only got half my bets, as I had asked Lord Lurgan to put on £500, and another man £500, and the latter did not weigh in. Lord Lurgan, who betted heavily himself, after putting my money on, also had a dash. After the race when he went to the ring one of the bookmakers said to him, "Roundshot, indeed! Why you've given us a regular broadside, my lord!" The following year

Roundshot ran in a selling race at the Liverpool Spring Meeting. It was the year I should have ridden Satellite in the National, but instead I was in bed after a bad fall at Four Oaks Park. I had written to ask Archer to ride my horse, and told him I was going to have £500 on starting price.

Just before he got up on him, the Prince of Wales, who was staying at Croxteth, came up with a party of friends and asked Archer if he was going to win. Here was a predicament. If he said "Yes," what was going to happen to my starting price? So Fred answered, "I believe all Sadler's two-year-olds have beaten the old horse, and I expect he is out of form." The result was that in a small field he started at three to one, and won in a canter; but after the race Fred was not at all popular with what he called the "swells."

At that time my brother Hedworth (now Admiral of the Fleet Sir Hedworth Meux, and then a lieutenant in the Navy) had some horses in training with Tom Green. One night he was chaffing me, saying what rotten horses I had got, and that not one of them could stay more than five furlongs, so I challenged him to a match over one and a half miles, weight for age, and owners up, Roundshot against any horse in his stable.

He promptly accepted and the match came off at Catterick Bridge. Hedworth ran a three-year-old called Glenhill, and as his lowest riding weight was 11 st. 10 lb. I had to carry 13 stone on Roundshot, who was a four-year-old. Tom Green was sanguine to a degree, and told his jockey to jump off and come as hard as he could, declaring that then "he would have Mr. George on his roarer stone-cold half a mile from home." Now, Hedworth could ride a bit, and had won many pony races at Malta, but he was not accustomed to race-horses, and when he thought he was going a good gallop he was really only cantering, so he never got Roundshot on the stretch, and I won in a canter by three parts of a length.

Most Lambtons like horses, but I know no man who loves racing and his horses more than my brother

Hedworth. Early in life, when a midshipman in the Navy, he started owning horses, and for many years Tom Green trained some very useful ones for him, though nothing really in the first class, and he has continued in the ranks of owners without a break till now. After Tom Green's death and before he settled down with Atty Persse at Stockbridge, he had one or two trainers, myself among the number, but I was not very successful for him. He was inclined to compare my methods in the stable with the way in which he conducted matters on his ship. But he had, and still has, only one fault as an owner, from a trainer's point of view : so fond is he of his horses that he refuses to get rid of them even when he knows himself, and has been told by his trainer, that they are no good. He still keeps them for years and years. This is, indeed, a fault on the right side, but rather an expensive one for the owner. But, in spite of this amiable weakness regarding his own horses, he is a rattling good judge of racing, breeding and all matters connected with the Turf. If he had not been, he would not have kept his stable going for so many years when comparatively a poor man.

The match he made with Roundshot recalls another one to my mind. On one occasion, coming home on leave, he brought with him a grey Barb pony called Cetewayo, on which he had won the Malta Derby and other pony races. He told us this was the best pony in the world, and he certainly was a beauty.

Now at that time the Duke of Portland had a bay pony of which he held the same opinion. One night after dinner, when they had been arguing about the respective merits of these ponies, a match was arranged at even weights, with owners up, at Newmarket, over five furlongs. The match took place on Sir Blundell Maple's private training-ground close to the Limekilns, one morning before racing. The whole of Newmarket turned out to see it, but Hedworth started with a severe handicap, for, not only did he have to carry 3 stone dead weight, but Fred Archer, the Duke's jockey, and Mat

Dawson, the Duke's trainer, acted respectively as starter and judge. No one doubted the integrity of the judge, but we had our doubts about the starter, and sure enough Archer let off the Duke with nearly a length the best of it.

A most thrilling race ensued, Hedworth making up his ground inch by inch. The Duke must have been the first man I ever saw who rode in the present style, for he got well forward on his horse's neck, and as he neared the post we wondered which would get there first, the jockey or the horse. Whereas Hedworth adhered to the old style and got farther and farther back in his saddle. But both methods were effective, for the ponies ran as straight as a gun-barrel. The grey could never quite recover his loss of start, and the verdict went to the Duke by a head.

Writing about my brother Hedworth reminds me of rather an unpleasant, but at the same time humorous adventure which happened to me at Nottingham. The old race-course there was narrow and egg-shaped, with two nasty turns. One day I was riding a horse called Westwood in a two-mile race. He was trained by Golding at Newmarket, and, before going out on him, Archer, who always rode for Golding, told me that the horse would be sure to try and bolt out at the turns unless I kept him behind. He was, in fact, the same horse on which Archer had ridden such a wonderful race at Windsor against his own money. There were only three runners, so as soon as we started I dropped him in behind, and all went well till a furlong from home when I sailed past the other two. No sooner did Westwood get his head in front than he bolted straight for some iron railings with spikes on them, which bounded the course from the road. I was more busily employed in keeping him from going over them than in winning the race and got beaten. As I rode back to the paddock a great big fat brute started hurling abuse at me. I wasn't feeling too pleased with things, and jumping off my horse I gave him two cuts across the face with my whip. In a second there was a pandemonium, and all the roughs on the course seemed to join in the fight. Things were beginning to look very disagreeable for me when I suddenly saw some of my opponents going down like ninepins. This was the work of Jim Carney, a well-known prizefighter, ex-champion of England, who had come to my rescue, and when he hit his man, down he went. By this time Marcus Beresford, my brother Hedworth, and some others had also joined in the fray. The first thing Hedworth did was to hit Carney as hard as he could, but the only notice the latter took of this was to say, "All right, Captain, I'm on your side." Fred Archer, who could box better than some people, went for one very big man when he wasn't looking. He got one in behind the ear and another under the chin, and then he sprinted for the weighing room, leaving his friend, the late Mr. Joe Davis, behind, who was promptly knocked down by the man as he recovered himself. Eventually surrounded by my friends, we fought our way back to the weighing room. The Clerk of the Course, the late Mr. William Ford, was there wringing his hands and in a terrible state of mind. "Gentlemen," he said, "there is a back way out of the Stand, let me beg of you to go out by it or there will be a riot." "Back way, be d——d," said Hedworth; "we won't do anything of the sort." So out we sallied from the Grand Stand entrance, where an ugly-looking crowd was awaiting us. But Marcus Beresford, Hedworth, Percy Cooper (whom I was staying with for the races) and Jim Carney were tough customers to tackle, and the crowd, not liking the look of them, we got into our carriage, where a very gallant lady, Mrs. Cooper, who had refused to leave without us, was waiting, and we drove off amidst a shower of stones which were hurled at us. The "Nottingham Lambs," as they were called, were a rough lot, and the next day Mr. Ford begged me not to ride a horse which I was engaged for, belonging to Mr. W. H. Manser, as he feared a repetition of the riot. But we were not going to stand that, and I rode the horse, which was called Ismail Pasha, and won the race, starting at a hundred to eight, and upsetting a hot favourite in Roquefort, with Ted Wilson up. Instead of the riot, I might have won the Derby, such a reception did I get, and from the very people who wanted to kill me the day before.

W. H. Manser, who trained at Newmarket, was a real good fellow, but very eccentric. When Sadler's stable first broke up on his becoming private trainer to Lord Durham, Harry Hungerford sent his jumpers to Manser. Now, both Harry and his new trainer were given to exaggeration, in fact Manser went by the name of " Romancer," and between the two it was impossible to know where you were. They did not get on for long. One day at Kempton in a hurdle race, I nearly popped up on a twenty to one chance of Manser's. The mare was no good and it was really one of those curious flukes which occasionally occur in racing and which are impossible to understand. I am sure Manser was quite as surprised as other people, but he could not refrain from going about saying that he had backed the mare to win him thousands, when really I don't think he had a shilling on. Harry hearing this was furious, and said he had kept his good thing to himself, so the horses left and went to Joe Cannon. I was very sorry for Manser, who was the most generous of men, and when he really did have a good thing wanted the whole world to be on.

CHAPTER VIII

SAM LEWIS, A GREAT MONEYLENDER—LORD DURHAM'S GIMCRACK SPEECH

HAVING started life with rather less than £800 a year, it did not take me long to find out that such an income would not go far in keeping race-horses and a stud of hunters. In consequence visits to the family lawyer became pretty frequent, and as the result of these visits my income became smaller and smaller. I never could get over the feeling that I was a boy at school up before the head master when I entered the lawyer's office, so after a disastrous week at Manchester instead of facing my lawyer I found myself on Monday morning knocking at the door of the great money-lender, Mr. Lewis, of Cork Street.

Sam Lewis was really a very remarkable man, the best and straightest money-lender of all time. He was a man of little education, who had, I believe, started life in a very small way. But at the time I knew him he was quite a personality in the fashionable world, and had a big business.

When I was shown into his room I saw a little fat man with a bald head sitting at a desk smoking a big cigar. As I was proceeding to explain who I was he said, "Never mind about that, I know all about you, young man; you have been betting very high and have got no money. I have been expecting you here for some time. What can I do for you?" Here was the right sort of man for me. I no longer felt like a schoolboy, but was quite at my ease, so I did not beat about the bush but said, " I want a thousand pounds this morning."

He asked me what security I had, to which I replied that I thought I had about £10,000 in the hands of my lawyer, giving his name. " Well, why on earth don't you go to him and get the money instead of coming here ? " was his question, so I frankly told him that I was really ashamed to show my face in the office. " Don't be a fool," said Lewis. " Get into a cab, go to him at once, and you can get the money at 5 per cent." But I was a fool and an obstinate one, and eventually Sam wrote out a cheque for £1,000, and I signed a bill for three months ; and so ended the first of many similar interviews between myself and Sam Lewis. But as I was going away his manner changed from that of the pleasant, easy-going man to the hard business one. " Remember," said he, " I expect my bills to be met when they become due." I walked out of his house treading upon air, thinking how splendid this was, that life would be quite simple, as I could get £1,000 as easily as picking a gooseberry off a bush.

Sam had a merry, quick wit, and was a wonderful judge of character, and, curious as it may seem, the majority of his clients were also his friends. Often when there was nothing to do in the afternoon we would say, " Let's go and see old Sam," and if he was not busy one would be certain to have an amusing half-hour and hear all the news of the political, racing and social world. He certainly was a great gossip, but when it was necessary he could be as silent as the grave, and I think he knew more secrets than any man in London.

His great pride was in being above all a man of his word, and when you dealt with him you knew exactly where you were. He naturally drove a hard bargain, otherwise he would not have been a successful money-lender, but in all his dealings he was as straight as a die, and he expected the same treatment from his clients. It was a bad day for anyone who tried the other game with Sam, for he could then be a tiger. I could tell many stories of his good nature and kindness to men who were really down. He was a man of simple tastes himself, with no extravagant habits.

I once asked him if he was really a very rich man. He replied, " Well, my boy " (his favourite expression), " it depends what you call a rich man, but I can tell you this, that I have a great deal more money than I want, and if it was not for Monte Carlo and Ostend, where I always lose heavily, I don't know how I should get rid of it."

On one occasion at Monte Carlo an impecunious friend of mine, who had lost all his ready money, asked Sam to lend him £200. " Certainly, my boy," said Sam, pulling the notes out of his pocket. " But what are you going to charge for it," asked my friend. Back into his pocket went the notes and Sam walked off in a fury, saying, " You ought to know by this time I never do business out of London." Afterwards, when he cooled down, he insisted on my friend taking the money, but simply from one man to another.

He was very fond of Monte Carlo, but one winter he deserted it for Rome. That city did not suit him for long, and he soon returned to the Riviera, and, when my brother Durham, who had extolled the glories of Rome, asked him how he had enjoyed himself, he replied, " Oh, you may 'ave Rome, give me Monte Carlo."

He had a large and rather handsome wife, of whom he was very fond, and she always had a box at the opera and a pair of the best carriage horses in London, which was saying a good deal in those days.

This reminds me of a story typical of Sam's good nature and shrewdness. There was a certain great lady noted for her beauty who had the best turned-out carriage in London. Being very extravagant she was often in need of money ; on one occasion, being especially hard up, and knowing that I often had dealings with Sam Lewis, she asked me if I thought he would give her £600 for her pair of horses (a large sum in those days), as he was supposed to be looking out for some for his wife. So I went to Sam, who at once said he would buy them. The next morning I had a note asking me to come and see him, and to my surprise he said, " I can't buy those horses." I said, " But I have already told the lady that you would." He shook his head and said, " It is impossible, for I have found out that she is head over ears in debt, and if Mrs. Lewis is seen driving her horses everyone will think she is in my hands, every tradesman in London will be down on her, and there will be a crash, but you can tell her that, although I will not have her horses, I will lend her £600 on her note of hand." The lady sent him her most grateful thanks, but did not accept his generous offer.

There is no doubt that several prominent owners of race-horses were at that time in the hands of Sam Lewis, but never did he use this power to his own advantage, and I believe it is a fact that Kisber would not have run in the Derby, which he won, if it had not been for his intervention. Kisber's owners, the brothers Baltazzi, were in the hands of other money-lenders, who threatened to stop the horse running and seize him unless they were paid. Sam stepped into the breach and settled the debt.

He played a very important part in my life, as one action of his probably altered the whole course of it. At last the time had come when I was stone-broke with no money left. No man was ever so fortunate in an elder brother as I was, but there was a limit even to his endurance, and, after having saved me many times in my financial difficulties, he arranged that I should go out to Canada, where my uncle, Lord Lansdowne, was Governor-General, as a member of his staff, so that my affairs could be straightened out and myself settled down to a more useful life. On the afternoon of my departure for Liverpool to join the boat, I was arrested and taken to Holloway Gaol on the suit of Mr. Lewis, who was my principal creditor, under a writ of " Ne exeat regno." After twenty-four hours I was released on giving my word that I would not leave England, so my Canadian trip was knocked on the head. At the time I was greatly surprised at Lewis's action, and thought he had behaved badly, and it was not till two years later that he told me the true history of the affair. It was this. On hearing the rumour that I was being sent to Canada, he went to Marcus Beresford, who was a great friend of mine, and asked him if it was true, and also if I really wanted to go myself. Marcus said yes, I had to go, but that I hated the idea of leaving England, and that in his opinion I was quite unsuited to the life that I was intended to lead there, so Sam said, " Well I shall stop him going, but it must be a secret between us two," and, until Sam told me himself, Marcus never breathed a word to me.

So far as I know, Lewis only once came into the Law Courts over a money transaction. It was a famous and painful case, which ended in a heavy sentence for a well-known man in Society. The case was tried by the late Lord Russell of Killowen, then Lord Chief Justice of England. Lewis was the plaintiff. The counsel for the defendant tried to represent to the jury that he was a dishonest, blood-sucking money-lender. Lord Russell would not allow this and addressed the jury in words similar to these : " Although the plaintiff has carried on the business of a money-lender for many years he has conducted his affairs in an honest and straightforward manner, and his word is as much to be credited as that of any other honest man of business." Sam was highly delighted about this, for he said that never in the history of the world had such a thing been said in a Court of Justice about a member of his profession.

On his death, which was somewhat sudden, there was consternation in the West End and genuine sorrow. In his vocation there never has been and never will be a man like him. He died worth, I believe, a very large sum. His executors had orders to collect money owing to him, but to give all reasonable time to those that needed it; instructions which they faithfully carried out.

Mrs. Lewis was left a rich woman, and I have the authority of Lord Farquhar for saying that she contributed £10,000 a year up to the day of her death to London hospitals.

Frequently to be seen at Cork Street was Sir George Chetwynd, who at that time was perhaps more talked of, more envied and in some quarters more disliked than any man of the fashionable world.

A tall, slight, distinguished-looking figure, with, when he chose to exert it, a considerable charm of manner, but when success was at flood-tide inclined to be somewhat overbearing. I don't think Sir George had ever been a rich man; he certainly was not one when I knew him, but he was determined to live as if money was no object, and in many ways he was the most extravagant man I have ever met. He was an extraordinarily fine judge of racing, and it was well known that the Turf had to supply the money to support his style of life.

He trained with R. Sherrard at Newmarket, the fashionable stable of that time. Besides Sir George, the other patrons of the stable all betted high, and consequently their horses generally started at short prices when fancied.

Sherrard the trainer was a very nice man who simply loved his horses and thought of nothing else. He never left them for a moment. He was the most particular man about every little detail and kept his stables very hot, as was the custom in those days. I don't think I have ever seen horses turned out looking so beautiful.

Although he won the Cesarewitch for " Mr. Manton" with that good mare, Corrie Roy, I think he was a better trainer over short distances than long. I remember seeing the mare one morning shortly before the race looking more as though she were trained for the Stewards' Cup than the Cesarewitch, and Sherrard told me that, being a natural stayer, he had only trained her over a mile. On that preparation she was good enough to win and win easily, but that is the only case I have known of that race being won without the horse being really put through the mill. I have myself trained some good stayers descended from Corrie Roy in Glacis, Queen's Journal and Silurian.

Good as Sherrard was in the stable and on the training ground, about the form of horses and racing he knew little. But with George Chetwynd and his jockey, Charles Wood, this did not matter much, for what these two did not know was not worth knowing. Although Sir George did not have any horse of outstanding merit, he won a tremendous lot of races both big and small, but a large stable and an extravagant life wants the devil of a lot of money to keep it going, and, clever as he was, I fancy it was a continual struggle, which, like so many others, ended in the road to Cork Street. Sam Lewis had a tremendous admiration for Sir George, and I think he would have done more for him than for anyone in the world. I know that when the crash came he was terribly upset and moved heaven and earth to try and avert it.

Many of my readers may remember the painful incidents of the libel case brought by Sir George Chetwynd against my brother, Lord Durham.

During the season of 1887 there had been a great deal of talk about the running of horses from Sherrard's stable. I remember one evening at the Jockey Club rooms, after a horse belonging to that fine old man, Mr. Redfern, had won the last race of the day, starting at a hundred to six, and upsetting some hot favourite, Sir George said to Mr. Redfern, " Thank God, horses in my stable don't start at a hundred to six and break all the backers." The old man replied, " No, George, that's true, but your horses often start at a hundred to six and *don't* win." The law actions which followed on the famous speech made by my brother at the Gimcrack Club dinner were long and protracted, and ended in the downfall of Sir George Chetwynd and his jockey.

Personally I had never been very intimate with the former, nor had I ever really liked him, for perhaps he was not a sympathetic personality to those younger than himself. But, after watching him for days engaged in a struggle which practically meant life or death to him,

MR. REDFERN.
[*Caricature by Colonel Montgomery.*

his coolness, his pluck and the staunch way in which he stuck to his jockey compelled my admiration. When it was over he accepted the inevitable and retired from the Turf.

In after years, when the hatchet was buried, I often used to meet him. He still took the greatest interest in racing, and it was quite extraordinary the grasp he had of the subject. From the way he talked, and his knowledge of the form of horses, one would have thought that he still lived on a race-course and amongst the surroundings that he loved so much.

There was one incident which it always gives me pleasure to look back upon.

Mr. Leopold de Rothschild asked me if I thought it was possible to bring about a reconciliation between Sir George and my brother, as he knew that the former was anxious for it. My brother, who is the quickest of men to relent when the fight is over, at once agreed to a meeting, which took place at Newmarket. Sir George died at Monte Carlo in the winter of 1917.

The result of the case broke up Sherrard's stable, although the other owners were in no way implicated.

After some years of retirement, Charles Wood had his licence given back to him by the Jockey Club. Lord Durham, to show that, when a man is forgiven, his past should be completely buried, gave him his first mount on one of his own horses. He soon showed that he had not lost his skill as a jockey, and won the Derby for Mr. Gubbins on Galtee More.

Lord Russell, then Sir Charles, was counsel for my brother in his case against Sir George, in conjunction with the famous solicitor, the late Sir George Lewis. At the numerous consultations in Sir George Lewis's chambers, there was a marked contrast between these two men. When things were going badly—and so badly did they go at one time that we looked like losing the case Russell was despondent. He begged my brother to plead mitigation, but the latter replied that he intended to fight it out at all costs. Little Sir George, with his fiery keen eye, so like that of the game-cock which he greatly resembled, was still full of confidence, and never lost heart for one moment. But when Russell got into court he was the finest and most skilful fighter I have ever seen, and having once found an opening in his adversary's defences he carried all before him.

There is no doubt that Lord Durham's action had a

far-reaching effect on the Turf and did an immense amount of good. The case created great interest, not only in Turf circles, but in the fashionable world. There was a very strong and influential clique behind Sir George, and before the trial began it was evident that my brother would get little support from many of the people who had most thoroughly agreed with what he had said at the Gimcrack dinner.

But there was one man, the late Lord Marcus Beresford, who stuck to him most loyally, in spite of the great pressure which was put upon him to go over to the opposite camp. The evidence and opinion of such an expert carried great weight, but Lord Marcus was very unpopular in certain quarters afterwards.

An equally staunch partisan, but on Sir George's side, was that charming and versatile gentleman, Mr. H. V. Higgins.

Harry Higgins was a notable personality on the Turf at one time, and had been keenly interested in racing. He was a good judge, betted freely, and was very popular with everybody. A big fine figure of a man, he took up a good deal of room at the rails when he wanted to get his money on, and one day someone said as he was approaching, " Look out, here comes the Great Eastern " (the biggest ship of the period), and the name stuck to him for a long time.

I am certain that Harry firmly believed in Sir George, and in the early days of the trial his face plainly showed his delight and confidence, but when Sir Charles Russell once got through the defence, which then fell like a house of cards, his surprise and consternation were equally evident. I don't think I have ever seen him on a race-course since that time.

The late Duke of Beaufort was another firm believer in Sir George and Wood, and he would hardly speak to anyone on the other side. General Owen Williams was also of their party. The General was at that time very ill, and extraordinarily thin, also it was well known that he had got through most of his money.

I remember Russell in his winding-up speech saying, "The Turf is much changed from the old days, when the jockey was the servant, and the owner the master. Now you see the jockey getting fatter and richer" (Wood was always very prosperous-looking) "and," pointing to the General, "the owners thinner and poorer."

CHAPTER IX

THREE FAMOUS HORSES—ORMONDE, MINTING, AND THE BARD

I WAS looking through Sir John Astley's book on his life the other day, and I read that if Peter had won the Manchester Cup, instead of being second to Valour, Sir John would have bought that great horse Barcaldine. This intensifies his cruel bad luck, for Barcaldine was one of the best horses that I have ever seen, and would probably have put the " Mate " on his legs again.

Barcaldine belonged to an Irishman, and had never been beaten in Ireland as a two-year-old. His owner, having got into trouble with the Stewards of the Jockey Club, the circumstances of which I never knew, was forced to sell the horse, and he became the property of Robert Peck.

He was a grand-looking horse, nearly seventeen hands high. His first appearance on a race-course in England was something of a tragedy. He ran in the Westminster Cup, a weight-for-age race at Kempton, on May 4th, 1883. There were only four runners, Barcaldine, Tristan, Wallenstein and Lucerne. Barcaldine looked very much on the big side, and Robert Peck said that he was not half fit, consequently, even in this small field, he started at ten to one. But in spite of this he beat that good horse, Tristan, in a canter by a length, Robert Peck not having a shilling on him. The fat was in the fire. He next won a handicap at Epsom with 9st. 4lb., a race at Ascot, and the Northumberland Plate with 9st. 10lb. He came home from Ascot very sore, and there were great doubts of getting him to the post for the Northumberland Plate. I believe it to be a fact that he did nothing but walking exercise, and had his leg constantly in a bucket of ice between Ascot and Newcastle, and his only gallop was on the evening before the race. In consequence of this he started at eleven to two. Archer, who was riding him, told me that he would win, saying that in spite of his 9st. 10lb. his speed was so great that he would have his field settled before they got into the straight. Sure enough, Archer let him stride to the front a mile from home, and he had them all beat coming into the straight, and won without an effort. But he pulled up very sore. He was then put by till the Autumn and entered in the Cambridgeshire, and I think his weight was 10st.

One morning at exercise I met Robert Peck, and he said, " I am going to try Barcaldine, come and see it." He was tried with a smart horse, Fulmen, who had won the Lincoln Handicap. Peck told me the weights, which I have forgotten, but he said, " If he can just win this trial, he will win the Cambridgeshire." I can see it now. They were tried up the Cambridgeshire Course, and, at the Red Post, Barcaldine, with Archer riding, left the others as though they were rocking-horses, and came home alone, except for Robert Peck who was galloping alongside of him on his hack, cheering him on with his hat in his hand like a huntsman with his hounds. Fulmen was second, many lengths in front of the others. It was some trial, and Peck was bubbling over with excitement, saying that there had never been such a horse, and that the Cambridgeshire was a certainty. Alas! for his hopes, the gallop found out the weak spot, and Barcaldine never ran again.

He was what some people call a very high-couraged horse, but what I call a bad-tempered one, and I have noticed that when you have Barcaldine in a pedigree you often have temper.

The year before Barcaldine's Northumberland Plate, I remember Peck producing a four-year-old mare, called Hackness in a hunters' flat race at the February Meeting at Sandown. Starting at six to four and ridden by Hugh

Owen, she was beaten a head. That same year she started favourite for the Cambridgeshire and won it. The following year she was second to Don Juan for the Cesarewitch.

Running her in this hunters' flat race, for which he backed her heavily, was a clever move on the part of Robert Peck, for, even if she had won, what handicapper would have feared danger in the Cambridgeshire from the winner of a hunters' flat race. Peck probably had that race or some other handicap in view when he produced her for the hunters' race. There was a remarkable incident in this Cambridgeshire won by Hackness. Owing to a terriffic hurricane of wind and rain, the race had to be put off till the next day. On the original day of the race a storm had been blowing all the morning, and when the horses had gone to the post it had increased to a hurricane. Hats were flying in all directions, and even three or four cabs were blown over. McGeorge, the starter, sent word to the Stewards that it was impossible to start the horses. His messenger was instructed to go back to tell McGeorge that the race was postponed till the following day. He found he could not make his horse face the gale that was blowing up the course, so that gallant old gentleman, Mr. Edward Weatherby, started off on his hack to do this job. He had not gone far when he was literally blown off his horse. Then Arthur Coventry and I got our hacks, and after a great struggle we got down to the post, where pandemonium prevailed, the horses careering all over the place.

When we gave McGeorge the message, one of the only horses near the starting post was Hackness, with her coat up and her tail between her legs; she looked more like a wretched cab horse than the favourite for the Cambridgeshire. Arthur and I came to the conclusion that whatever won the Cambridgeshire the next day it would not be Hackness, but she did so, and Peck landed a big stake.

What a clever man Robert Peck was; he had

practically given up training before I knew him, but he was extraordinarily quick and sure in his judgment of horses, full of vitality, and lived every hour of his life.

When I was training Canterbury Pilgrim as a two-year-old, I was very disappointed with her as she could not stay four furlongs, although she had very great speed. I told him about it at Doncaster one morning, as he took a great fancy to her seeing her at work. She ran in the Champagne Stakes, and for half a mile led the field. He came to see me after the race and said, " Don't be downhearted about your mare, she will be a stayer, and will probably win the Oaks."

But for these encouraging words I don't think I should ever have set my mind on training her as a three-year-old for the Oaks, and setting aside all other races.

. . . . . .

I have heard many discussions as to which is the best horse that has been seen in the last fifty years ; all such comparisons appear to me to be futile, but for what it is worth I should certainly give St. Simon the first place. Perhaps he had not such great horses to oppose him as had Ormonde and others, but no matter what his opponents, whether good or bad, when his jockey let him out to win his race they appeared like common selling-platers.

In 1883 this wonderful horse electrified the public by his astounding performances as a two-year-old. His history is too well known to need much comment.

Originally the property of Prince Batthyany, and bred by him, St. Simon came up for sale at Newmarket after the Prince's death in 1882. He was then trained by John Dawson, whose brother Matthew went to see the horse before the sale ; both his hocks had been dressed.

A story is told, which I cannot vouch for, that the old gentleman looked carefully over the horse, licked his fingers and then rubbed them over the dressing, smiled and went away murmuring something about " me brother, John." When the horse came up for sale he was bought by Matthew Dawson for £1,600 for the Duke of Portland, assuredly the cheapest horse that was ever sold.

Everyone knows that St. Simon was never beaten and was as great a stallion as he was a race-horse. He laid the foundation of the great Welbeck Stud and the wonderful success of the Duke of Portland on the Turf.

The last time I saw the horse remains in my memory. I was staying at Welbeck. A Hungarian, Count Potocki, who had come purposely to see St. Simon, was there. The Count was an extraordinarily handsome man, and a great lover of horses. When we were shown into St. Simon's box he stood and looked and looked, but not a word did he say. Eventually he took off his hat and made a low bow to the horse; St. Simon looked somewhat astonished, and as the man and the horse stood looking at each other they presented a wonderful picture of the equine and human thoroughbred.

St. Simon did not run after 1884. He had educated the public as to what a high-class race-horse should be, and the two-year-olds of 1885 nobly lived up to that standard—Ormonde, Minting, The Bard.

I doubt if there were ever three such good horses of one year. Besides these three there were Saraband, Mephisto, Gay Hermit, St. Mirin, Loved One, Fullerton, Oberon, The Cob, Carlton, Miss Jummy, Modwena. Nearly all these horses made Turf history at some period of their career by winning great races.

The flying little Modwena, the property of the Duke of Portland, won nine good races as a two-year-old, but this was not surprising seeing how she was bred, by Galopin out of Mowerina. I remember so well the mare starting at six to five on for the Post Sweepstakes at the Second October Meeting at Newmarket.

There was a rumour that John Porter was running a good horse belonging to the Duke of Westminster, and everyone was on the qui vive in the paddock. The general verdict was that Porter's youngster was a great, fine horse, but had not the best of shoulders, and was not likely to beat such a filly as Modwena.

In the race, ridden by Fred Archer, the big colt won without an effort, although the verdict was only a length. This two-year-old was the redoubtable Ormonde, who never suffered defeat.

Ten days later Ormonde came out for the Criterion Stakes at the Houghton Meeting, which he won in a canter by three lengths. On the following Wednesday he started at six to four on for the Dewhurst Plate, and again won easily by four lengths. That completed his labours for the year 1885.

Ormonde as a two-year-old, and even as a three-year-old, was very low in front of the saddle, and in his slow paces was not a taking mover. Archer told me himself that until the horse was extended he always felt himself to be sitting on his neck. This no doubt gave rise to the idea that Ormonde had not the best of shoulders. He retired into winter quarters, in the opinion of many people the probable Derby winner of the following year.

Now The Bard, the joint property of General Owen Williams and Mr. Robert Peck, and trained by Martin Gurry, was an exactly opposite type of race-horse. He was a beautifully made little chestnut horse, ticked with white, in shape and conformation impossible to fault.

He made his first appearance in the Brocklesby Stakes at Lincoln, which he won easily by two lengths. He won sixteen races without knowing defeat, a wonderful record for a two-year-old, and he was never properly extended in any of these races. His last race that year was for the Tattersall Sale Stakes at Doncaster, and he then retired for the season, his half-owner, General Williams, declaring that he would not run again before the Derby, and that no horse in the world would ever beat him, and there were many people who agreed with him.

Minting, owned by Mr. R. C. Vyner, like Ormonde, was a great big colt of enormous power and substance, but in spite of that Matthew Dawson managed to bring him out in June for the Seaton Delaval Plate at Newcastle, when, ridden by Jack Watts, and starting favourite, he won in a canter by six lengths.

He followed this up by a victory in the Prince of Wales Stakes at Goodwood, again ridden by Watts and winning by five lengths, Jacobite, a nice colt belonging to Mr. Bowes, being second on each occasion. He then won the Champagne Stakes, this time his jockey being Archer, and he beat Gay Hermit and others easily by a length and a half.

After that he beat two bad horses in a Triennial Stakes at Newmarket, and then came the Middle Park Plate, a race which gave rise to an immense amount of discussion both before and after.

Robert Peck had at this time retired from active training, and had put Humphreys in charge of his own horses and stable, but he still held the reins and kept the closest supervision over the establishment.

Minting's chief opponent was Saraband, a beautiful chestnut colt belonging to Sir John Blundell Maple (who then raced under the name of Mr. Childwick) and trained by Humphreys. He had won six races out of seven, and it was known that his trainer entertained the highest opinion of him.

Even in those days rumour was busy with the names of the leading jockeys, though, thank heaven, not to the same extent as it is at the present moment, and there was no doubt that Archer, Minting's jockey, and Robert Peck were great friends.

Archer rode for Peck whenever he could, he dined with him, he hunted with him, and that was quite sufficient to make the suspicious and " know all " brigade say that Archer was in Peck's pocket. Therefore, previous to the Middle Park Plate, there was a prevalent " canard " that Saraband would win the race and not Minting.

I remember the race vividly. It was run in very heavy going, and, coming down Bushes Hill, Braw Lass, trained by John Dawson and ridden by a " pillar to post " jockey called Giles, held a useful lead from Wood on Saraband, Archer on Minting waiting on the pair.

Everyone expected Braw Lass to stop as she breasted the hill, but instead of this, slipping through the mud, she increased her lead. There was a roar from the ring as Archer and Wood were seen to call seriously on their horses. Minting rolled badly as he came into the Dip. In a desperate race home it was always doubtful if Saraband would catch Braw Lass. Two hundred yards from the post Archer, having balanced Minting, put in one of those superhuman efforts which had gained him the name of "The Demon," and got up in the last twenty strides to win a neck from the mare, amid immense excitement, Saraband being beaten a neck for second place.

After the race gossip was rife, the aforesaid "clever brigade" saying, "What did we tell you ? If Saraband had been good enough to win, Archer would never have got up on Minting." A story went round the clubs that Mat Dawson had said, " If it had not been for me brother John coming down like an angel from Heaven wi' his Braw Lass, Minting would not have won the Middle Park Plate."

I very much doubt if the old gentleman ever made this remark, as I am convinced he never for one moment questioned the integrity of his jockey.

At that time, and always, I had a great admiration for Matthew Dawson, and many are the pleasant afternoons I have spent in his company, listening to his words of wisdom on horses, men and jockeys. Knowing my love of racing, and being a great raconteur, he never seemed tired of imparting his great store of knowledge to me.

At Exning, a fortnight after the Middle Park Plate, I was having a cup of tea with Mat while he partook of whisky, when in strolled Archer. They began talking about the race : " You nearly threw that race away, Fred," said the old man.

Archer admitted that he had held Braw Lass too cheaply, thinking he had only one horse to beat in Saraband, and that he had called on his horse too suddenly coming into the Dip, with the result that Minting was completely unbalanced, and it was a hundred yards before he could get him going again. "But," said he, "the horse does not act well downhill, and he will not suit the Epsom course."

After Archer had left I asked Mat what he thought about this with reference to the following year's Derby. The old man scratched his head and said, in his usual broad Scotch, "I'm no saying he's not right; I've had doubts meself, and the young divil, when he's ridden a horse, seems to know more about him than I do."

Thus at the end of the season 1885 we have three unbeaten two-year-olds, all engaged in the Derby of the following year, owned by great sportsmen, trained by three of the best trainers of the day, and sure to be ridden by high-class jockeys. The Bard was not engaged in the Two Thousand Guineas.

During the winter and spring of 1885-86, I was more interested in hunting and steeplechasing, and I had not been flat-racing except at Liverpool before the Two Thousand week. But up to that time none of the crack three-year-olds had been seen in public.

Reports as to their progress were most flattering. John Porter was supposed to have said that Ormonde was the best horse he had ever trained; Mat Dawson vowed Minting was a smasher; and Peck averred that The Bard was better than ever under the skilful training of Gurry, and also that he would give the two cracks a dusting-up with Saraband in the Two Thousand, as he was very forward and greatly improved.

The week before the First Spring Meeting I was staying at Exning and went to see Mat Dawson. He showed me Minting, who was looking a picture, having gone through one of Mat's severe preparations with every satisfaction; and there was no mistake about it, a horse had to work for his living when Mat set about him. Often three canters before a gallop, and out nearly three hours every morning.

I wonder how the horses of these days would stand it? Perhaps they would do better on it than we think. But at the same time Mat liked his horse to go out for a race full of confidence, and, as he put it, " thinking he could lick creation."

Before going away I asked him what he thought about Ormonde. He replied, " When John Porter says he has a good horse, you may be certain that he has a d———d good one, but he does not know what I have got," adding, " when it comes to a matter of talking, Ormonde wins the Two Thousand, but, when it comes to a matter of racing, Minting will win."

On the day of the race confidence in Minting was unbounded. Ridden by Watts, he started at eleven to ten, Saraband, with Archer, three to one, and Ormonde, George Barrett up, seven to two, any price the rest. George Barrett was a dashing young jockey just coming to the front, much like Archer in style, but inclined to be in a hurry.

The race was disappointing to watch. From the fall of the flag Ormonde and Minting raced right away from the field, both jockeys trying to cut the other down. Half-way up the hill it was all over, and Ormonde won cleverly, if not easily, by two lengths, nothing else near.

As I saw Minting again roll and change his legs coming into the Dip, I remembered Archer's words to Mat Dawson after the Middle Park Plate, but unfortunately for my pocket I had forgotten them before the race.

Naturally the disappointment of Mr. Vyner and Mat Dawson was great, and old Mat retired from view for two days, but never again from that moment did he have any illusions as to which was the better horse.

Archer's view of the Two Thousand is interesting. I was much disappointed at what I thought rather a tame display on the part of Minting, arguing that he must be quite 10 lb. behind Ormonde. Archer would not have this, saying that when you get two smashing good horses trying to cut each other down over the Rowley Mile the pressure is so great that one or the other is sure to crack some way from home ; it may be just a toss up which gives way first, but the one who does has no struggle left. He said, " Minting will never beat Ormonde, but Ormonde will never again beat Minting two lengths in a properly run race."

I have experienced the truth of this theory many times in my racing career, and there is no better illustration than when Diadem, the best mare that I have ever trained, and that great sprinter, Tetratema, met at Goodwood over six furlongs. They raced together for five furlongs at terrific speed, Tetratema eventually winning a length and a half. Carslake, who rode Tetratema, told me afterwards that he did not have an ounce in hand at the moment when the mare cracked.

Ormonde and Minting never met again till Ascot of the following year, when Minting was again beaten, this time by a neck, with the great Bendigo three lengths off.

It was decided soon after the Two Thousand, that if Ormonde kept well, Minting should not run in the Derby, but should be kept for the Grand Prix. So Ormonde had nothing to beat but The Bard, who had not yet run that year, although he had satisfied Peck in his home work that he was good enough to win ninety-nine Derbies out of a hundred.

But the public would have nothing but Ormonde, and with Archer up, the Duke of Westminster's horse started at nine to four on, and The Bard (Wood) nine to two against. As in the Two Thousand, the two good horses came right away from the others, Ormonde winning, as I thought, easily by a length and a half.

I believe that Robert Peck, and I know that General Williams and Gurry, thought that Wood rode a bad race in not making enough use of his horse, but I don't think there was anything in it—good as he was, The Bard could not beat Ormonde.

Three weeks after the Derby, The Bard put up a great performance in the Manchester Cup, when he ran second to Riversdale, a very smart horse, giving him no less than 31 lb. After this he was never beaten again.

Minting was sent over to run for the Grand Prix, his old pilot, Archer, to ride. I went over to Paris for the week. At that time the feeling between England and France was not at all friendly, and the authorities were nervous lest there should be a riot if the English horse won. Besides Minting, the Duke of Hamilton's Miss Jummy, winner of the Oaks and the One Thousand, was in the field, ridden by J. Watts.

The race before the Grand Prix was a handicap with a biggish field. Archer got a mount, as he wanted to have a ride round the course before the big race, but said he, "I am not going to take any risks; they are a rough lot riding, and if they want to put me over the rails they will have to do it on the outside, for that is where I am going this time." I felt rather sorry for the owner.

In the Grand Prix they went off as usual at a cracking pace; it was a very wet day, and the going was heavy, and half a mile from home Minting was some way behind the leaders, but, coming through quickly, he won in a canter by two lengths.

Archer, having been warned of the danger of a riot, pulled his horse up short, on the post, was into the unsaddling enclosure and off his horse before anyone had time to leave the stands; as smart a performance as I have ever seen.

At that time there was a Yorkshire solicitor named Fernandez, who for a short period had some influence with Mr. Vyner; he was a shrewd judge of racing, but a most disagreeable man, and thought the worst of everyone. He told Mr. Vyner that Archer was going for Miss Jummy, and that he had backed her to win him a lot of money.

I told Fernandez that Archer had advised me to bet on Minting as much as I could afford. "Oh," says he "he will put you in the cart like everyone else." I laughed and offered to bet him £500 to £200 on Minting beating Miss Jummy. After the race I saw him looking as sour as a green apple. "What about it now?" said I. "The d——d thief," he replied; "he never let Minting go till Miss Jummy was beat." It is impossible to convince such people, nor are they worth the argument.

Bob Vyner and his brother, Clare, were both extraordinarily kind to me when I was a boy.

Clare was a most attractive man with a wonderful charm of manner, but when I knew him he had very bad health, and did not take any active part in racing.

Bob was more robust, and liked to pretend he was a hard man, but he really had the kindest heart in the world.

Clare owned many good horses, but that was before my time. I believe he was a first-class judge and betted fearlessly when he fancied a horse. He and his brother always employed a fine old fellow, Harry Bragge, to do their commissions. He was one of those rugged Yorkshiremen, as honest as the day. On one occasion, having tried Lily Agnes, the dam of Ormonde, a certainty for the Ebor Handicap, which in those days (1875) was a great betting race, Clare Vyner wired to Bragge to back the mare for the race, but omitted to say what sum he was to invest. Bragge wired back asking how much he wanted "on." The answer was, "Go on betting till I tell you to stop." The mare won the race.

Bob Vyner was about the most successful owner in the North, and won an enormous number of races. Minting was, of course, the best horse he ever owned, but he also won the St. Leger with The Lambkin, the One Thousand with Minthe, and the Ascot Cup with that beautiful and brilliant horse Marcian. The majority of his horses were trained in the North, but he would pick out a few of the best and send them to Mat Dawson at Newmarket.

Minting very nearly remained in the North. Before

sending his yearlings away, he had them trained in the park at Newby, his place in Yorkshire. He told me that Mr. George Thompson, who was one of the best Gentleman Riders in England—in fact, I should put him on a par with Arthur Coventry—rode the horse, and said he was a heavy-shouldered beast that would never win a race. Besides being a fine rider, George Thompson was a great judge of a horse, but, fortunately, Bob did not agree with him on this occasion, and the horse went to Newmarket.

Bob was a shrewd, hard-headed Yorkshireman, true as steel, greatly loved by his friends and servants, but anyone who did not play the game, or tried to " do " him, would come off second best, and he never forgave him.

To continue the story of the season 1886, Ormonde won the St. Leger and every other race he ran for, always without an effort, and The Bard, after his defeat at Manchester, was also unbeaten.

The Eclipse Stakes of £10,000 at Sandown was run for the first time that year, and was won by that great horse Bendigo, who beat a good field including St. Gatien. Minting was in the race, but his leg filled a few days before, and he did not run. I have little doubt that he would have won had he gone to the post fit and well.

Bendigo was the property of a good sportsman, Mr. H. T. Barclay, " Buck " Barclay as he has always been called by his friends, the right sort of man to own a good horse; a fine rider to hounds, a fair jockey, riding his own horses in welter races, and as straight as a gun-barrel. He is well known to present-day race-goers, as for the last ten years he officiated as judge at many meetings, a position which he filled with great ability.

Bendigo, the winner of the first Eclipse Stakes, deserves a word of notice. He was a magnificent brown colt by Ben Battle, bred in Ireland. As a three-year-old he ran so well in the Cesarewitch that he was marked down by clever judges as the likely winner of the Cambridgeshire. Unfortunately he started coughing badly after the Cesarewitch, but, throwing it off a few days before the race, Mr. Barclay decided to start him, and let him take his chance, and ridden by Luke he beat Tonans by a head.

Tonans was trained by Tom Brown, and backed to win a fortune. Luke, who rode Bendigo, was a very excitable little man and often lost his head in a race. On this occasion he went all over the course and finished by himself on the stand side. After the race he said to Joe Cannon : " Well, I pulled that race out of the fire." " Did you," said Joe, " then the fire must have been all over the course."

The following year Bendigo, like most Irish horses, improved greatly, and won the Lincoln Handicap and the Hardwicke Stakes, but his greatest performance was in the Cambridgeshire again, when, ridden by Archer, and carrying 9st. 8lb., he was second to Plaisanterie (8st. 12lb.).

Bendigo, in the Eclipse Stakes and Cambridgeshire, beat the Derby winner, St. Gatien, practically at level weights, and he affords an eloquent testimony to the great qualities of Ormonde and Minting, for in that memorable race at Ascot in 1887 he was a moderate third to these two champions, although that same year he had won the Jubilee with 9st. 7lb., had been second for the Cesarewitch with 9st. 7lb., and again second for the Cambridgeshire with 9st. 13lb., being beaten only half a length.

CHAPTER X

CAROLINE DUCHESS OF MONTROSE AND CAPTAIN MACHELL

THE performances of Ormonde, Minting and The Bard had made the year 1886 a remarkable one, and the Cambridgeshire of that year was also a memorable race in more ways than one.

Many people thought that the severe wasting which Archer had undergone, in order to ride St. Mirin at 8 st. 7 lb., was the cause of his early death. St. Mirin was trained by old Alec Taylor (father of the present master of Manton). He trained for the Duke of Beaufort, Mr. Manton (the Duchess of Montrose), and many others.

He was a most independent man and did not care a d———n for anyone. His language was strong, as, for instance, when the Duchess of Montrose asked him what he thought the chief danger to one of her horses. " D———ned to H—ll if I know, Your Grace," was his reply.

Taylor was a great trainer, and was always especially to be feared in the back-end handicaps. There was one class of man with whom he would have nothing to do, and that was a commission agent, and he never employed one to back any horse that was his own property.

Several times he came to me with a cheque for a hundred pounds in his hand, saying, " Put this on my horse." When I told him that I was not clever at getting a good price, he said, " Never mind ; do the best you can."

After the Cesarewitch of that year he advised me to back St. Mirin for the Cambridgeshire, telling me that Archer was going to ride and that the horse was at a good price. I followed his advice and took 25/1 to fifty pounds.

Four or five days before the race Carlton, an unknown three-year-old in the same stable, suddenly became a strong favourite. Rumour said he had won a great trial. Carlton belonged to Lord Edward Somerset, son of the Duke of Beaufort, who raced under the name of " Mr. Somers."

In those days racing at Newmarket began on the Monday, and on that morning I met Alec Taylor going out to exercise. He said, " Come and see my horses work." I did so, though I was feeling a little sore at having been put on apparently the wrong one in St. Mirin. After the work was over I asked old Alec, " What about this Carlton, and do you remember you told me to back St. Mirin." " Well," said he, " do you see this stick ? " (he always rode with a very short stick) " there is not more than the length of it between the two horses, and the Long'un (Archer) rides St. Mirin."

I was delighted at this, and later on, when I saw Archer, I asked him what he thought about it. He said that no doubt Carlton was a good horse, but would be a handful for even as good a boy as Woodburn, who would ride ; he had not himself ridden in the trial, and believed that Carlton had not beaten St. Mirin far, adding that he thought he could get a great deal more out of St. Mirin than the boy who rode him in the gallop.

The Cambridgeshire was then run on the old course, finishing at the Old Stand almost at the top of the town. It was the finest course in the world, but the stands and enclosures were so placed that it was impossible to get a good view of the race from them. Arthur Coventry and I were on our hacks below the red post, and I can see the race as if it was yesterday. Coming to that historic landmark, Carlton, who had always been in the front rank, was going as well as anything with Tom Cannon on Melton and Archer on St. Mirin drawing rapidly up,

Melton looking especially dangerous. In a moment Woodburn flew to his whip, upon which the horse in two strides was rocking like a ship ; Archer dashes out St. Mirin and rides desperately for home, something on the far side of the course catching him fast. I thought St. Mirin had just got home, but the outsider, Sailor Prince, beat him on the post by a head, Carlton being a bad third. Archer afterwards said that Melton cost him the race ; he was going so well that he brought St. Mirin out too soon.

Sailor Prince, trained by that most patient of men, W. G. Stevens, brought off a big coup. I used to ride occasionally for Stevens in welter and hurdle races, and some weeks before the race his commissioner came to me and said he had taken £1,000 to £25 for me about a horse in Stevens's stable for the Cambridgeshire. I had forgotten all about it, and it was quite an hour after the race when I realized that I was on the winner.

I have already written of how Alec Taylor told me that there was only the length of a short stick between Carlton and St. Mirin ; yet Carlton, with Woodburn up, starts at four to one, and St. Mirin, with Archer up, at twenty to one ; such is the glamour of a private trial and a mystery horse, and, when St. Mirin beats Carlton, the supporters of the latter look about for the reasons of his defeat, and eventually the story gets about that Archer had squared Woodburn.

About a month afterwards I heard a man at my club saying that he knew for a fact this was the case. I said that I did not believe it, and repeated what Alec Taylor had told me before the race. " Well," said my friend, " Lord Edward Somerset himself told me that he had positive proof of Archer having paid money to Woodburn." At that moment in walks Lord Edward, so my friend says, " You tell George Lambton about Archer and Woodburn, because he won't believe me." So Lord Edward proceeds with his story : firstly, they had tried Carlton a certainty for the race ; secondly, Archer had told him the day before the race that he would beat

Carlton on St. Mirin ; and, thirdly, he knew Archer had given Woodburn a large sum of money.

This last statement, if true, settled everything, but on asking him how he knew, and what the sum was, then everything fell to pieces. He did not know how much, but still, "everyone knew Archer had given a large sum," but he could give no name to that ubiquitous "everyone," and he had no evidence whatever of any payment made by Archer to Woodburn. In short, he knew nothing whatever beyond the fact that his good horse, Carlton, did not run up to his private form.

Lord Edward was a most good-natured and kindly man, without much strength of character, and these sort of people can talk, or be talked into believing anything, and I am sure that more than half the stories of wrong-doing on the Turf are based on similar foundations.

The performances of Carlton in the following year showed two good reasons for his defeat in the Cambridgeshire ; one being that the course was too short for him, and the other that the boy could not ride him. He started a hot favourite for the City and Suburban, carrying 6 st. 12 lb., ridden by a good light-weight jockey, Calder, and was second, beaten by a length.

He then proceeded to win six races off the reel, including the Chester Cup, the Manchester Cup, the Goodwood Stakes, and the Doncaster Cup, in all of which he was ridden by a strong jockey in George Barrett, and he finished the season by winning the Manchester November Handicap, with 9 st. 12 lb. on his back.

St. Mirin was the property of "Mr. Manton," the assumed name of Caroline Duchess of Montrose, who, on the death of her second husband, Mr. Crawford, carried on his great racing stud. At the time of which I write she was well over sixty.

She was blessed with a soft and most charming voice, and when things were going right was the best company in the world ; but she was hot-tempered and changeable, and was easily put out if she did not get her own way. When at Newmarket she lived at Sefton Lodge, and just on the opposite side of the road was the great Captain Machell, of Bedford Lodge.

Two such strong personalities at such close quarters were bound to clash ; at times they were devoted friends, at times most bitter enemies. The Duchess used to tell the most amusing stories about her friends, and had a very lively imagination ; once she had told a story she was then firmly persuaded it was true.

One night, coming home from dinner, Captain Machell, in his fly, unfortunately drove over and killed her favourite dog. At the moment they happened to be enemies, and the Duchess, when she told the story, declared that the Captain lifted himself up and came down with a heavy bump on the seat of the fly, so as to make certain of killing her dog.

At that time Reggie Mainwaring was one of the handicappers, and the Duchess, like many owners, always thought her horses were unfairly treated. She took a great dislike to Mainwaring, who was one of the kindest and most amiable of men. He was a tall, dark man, rather like Othello, with an habitual scowl on his face. The Duchess used to refer to him as " the man who murdered his mother." So far from this being the case, he had an old mother in Wales to whom he was absolutely devoted, and when I told her of this she said, " Well, I can't help it, he ought not to look like that."

The Duchess built and endowed the little church of St. Agnes at Newmarket, next door to her house. One very wet summer, when the prospects of the harvest were very bad all over the country, she had a horse in the St. Leger particularly suited to the heavy going.

One Sunday, the Rev. Colville Wallis put up a special prayer for fine weather. The Duchess rose from her pew and walked out of church. She sent for Wallis and said, " How dare you pray for fine weather in my church when you know perfectly well it will ruin my horse's chance, and I shall not allow you to preach in my church again." Mr. Wallis, who knew the old lady well, and had a great affection for her, did not argue the matter, and holds the living to this day.

The Duchess had a big stud-farm at Newmarket, where the Stanley House Stables and Lord Derby's Stud Farm are now situated.

At the dispersal of her stud in 1894, the year of her death, Pilgrimage, carrying Jeddah, winner of the Derby; her daughter Canterbury Pilgrim, winner of the Oaks, and dam of Chaucer and Swynford; and Roquebrune, winner of the New Stakes at Ascot, and dam of Rock Sand, winner of the Derby, were sold. In fact, she owned some of the best blood in England, and she bred and raced many good horses, but their management left much to be desired, and her success was not what it should have been.

She led her trainers an anxious life, with the exception of Alec Taylor, and he was supposed to be the only man she was afraid of. She was very capricious and changeable with regard to her jockeys—a failing not unusual in her sex.

Huxtable used to ride for her when the weights were light at one time. On one occasion, when he was beaten, she was furious, and said to him, "Why on earth didn't you do as I told you and come along with the horse?" "I am sorry, Your Grace, but I should have had to come along without the horse," was the reply.

Huxtable was a quaint little man. Once at Manchester on a very foggy day a certain jockey of rather unsavoury reputation was beaten on a very hot favourite, and, when riding him back to the paddock, kept looking down at his horse's legs, as if he was lame or sore. Huxtable shouted out, "Don't look at his legs; I think his jaw is broken."

With all her peculiarities, the Duchess was a great lady, and a good sportswoman. She loved her horses and was a good judge of racing and a great figure on the Turf. She was always wonderfully kind to me and I was very fond of her.

The early life of Machell must have been full of adventure and excitement. Beginning as an impecunious subaltern in the Army, he became one of the greatest powers in the racing world. When I first knew him, he was already a broken man in health, having, as I imagine, burnt the candle at both ends, but he was as keen as ever on racing.

He suffered terribly from gout. A most pleasant and entertaining companion when he was well, but often attacked by moods of great depression and gloom. He was famous for having engineered many great handicap " coups," and was reputed to have won a great deal of money. He managed a large stable of horses at Newmarket and had, at the time of which I write, a very clever young trainer in J. Jewitt.

Some of his great successes on the flat and steeplechasing were before my time, but many great triumphs were to come, notably those of Isinglass, perhaps the best horse he ever had to do with.

It was the fashion of the day for the " young bloods," as they were called, to put their horses under his charge, and invariably they won big races, but, at the same time, the careers of these young men were short. Many people put this down to the fault of Machell, but I do not think it was so; it was an age when young men betted furiously, and whatever the advice, and whatever the successes, there is only one end to that.

Take, for instance, the case of Lord Rodney. In 1887 he had a wonderful year, winning many races, including the St. Leger with Kilwarlin, and the Cesarewitch with Humewood, yet at the end of the racing season he was " broke." However much he won on his own horses he was sure to lose it, and more besides, on other people's.

Many of the early triumphs of Machell were achieved with steeplechase horses, and I always thought he was an even better judge of 'chasers than of flat race-horses. One year he had over £20,000 to spend on yearlings, which in those days was an enormous sum, and he told me that out of the lot not one reached even second-class form.

I do not say this proves him not to have been a good judge, for such a thing may easily happen to anyone, and there is no such lottery as buying yearlings.

I have said that he was supposed to have won a great deal of money, but when I knew him he was by no means a rich man. He kept open house, was the most hospitable of men, very careless about money matters, and was often short of ready money. If he took a fancy to a horse he would buy it, even if the price was beyond its value, and on occasions he was unable to find the money after he had completed the deal. I know that Fred Archer was part owner of several of his horses—jockeys were allowed to own horses then, neither was there any rule about declaring partnerships. Valour, a horse I have written about, was certainly partly owned by Archer.

Without question Machell was a very clever man concerning horses. He and his trainer, Jewitt, used to have tremendous rows, both being hot-tempered, high-strung men, and their opinions sometimes differed.

When Isinglass was being trained for the Two Thousand, the going was very hard, and after every good gallop he was sore. Jewitt wanted to strike him out, and said it was impossible to have him fit enough to win. The Captain said, "If you train him as I tell you it can be done." He had the horse out twice a day and cantered him up a short bit of hill on the Bury Tan time after time. Jewitt said a horse could not win a Two Thousand on such a preparation. "Isinglass can," replied Machell, "because he is certainly at least a stone better than any horse in the race." It came off all right, for although Isinglass, running in very slovenly fashion, looked like being beaten, he eventually struggled home from Ravensbury.

All through his three-year-old career, Isinglass was handicapped by hard ground and the impossibility of training him properly, but he was a great enough horse just to pull through in all his classic races, winning the Two Thousand, the Derby, and the St. Leger, but he

CAPTAIN MACHELL

FRED ARCHER ON STRATHAVON

From the drawing by Finch Mason
FRED ARCHER AT NEWMARKET GOING TO THE POST

I HAVE KNOWN

was beaten for the Lancashire Plate at Manchester by the Duke of Portland's Raeburn, the race being only a mile, not far enough to bring out his great staying qualities.

I can remember Isinglass as a four-year-old just scrambling home from Bullingdon, in the Princess of Wales Stakes at Newmarket, again having been trained on the tan, owing to the hard ground. That night it poured with rain, and this continued more or less up to the day of the Eclipse Stakes at Sandown.

Jewitt said to me on the morning of that race, " You will see what Isinglass will do with his horses to-day ; it is the first time I have been able to gallop and train him properly." He was right. Instead of frightening his backers to death and struggling home after being apparently well beaten, as he had done in most of his races, Isinglass commanded his field, which included Ladas, the winner of the Derby, from start to finish, and won in a canter, proving Machell's words, that he was a stone better than any horse in England to be correct.

To go back to Machell's earlier career, Hermit was in his stable when he won the Derby for the then Mr. Henry Chaplin. Mr. Chaplin won a small fortune, and the Captain was always supposed to have done the same, but Mr. George Herring, who was one of the biggest commission agents of that time, and did Machell's business, told me the following story, after Machell's death.

He had been telling me how he had seen Machell fight against a man two stone heavier than himself, Major Hope Johnstone, in a small room in some hotel in London ; the smallness of the room prevented Machell from making use of his superior quickness and activity, but he put up a splendid fight, and, although beaten, never gave in until nearly battered to death. As Mr. Herring said, " The gamest exhibition I ever saw ; but," he added, " I saw him once show even greater pluck. I had backed Hermit to win him £60,000 in the Derby.

I

As all students of turf history know, Hermit broke a blood vessel shortly before the race; it was so bad a case that Machell thought his chance hopeless, and told me to try and get out of the money, which I was able to do, and, when Hermit passed the post a gallant winner, Machell had next to nothing on, but he received the congratulations of his friends, who all imagined him to have won a fortune, with a smile and without a sign of chagrin on his face, though no man wanted the money more, and not a soul except myself knew the real state of affairs."

I saw a lot of Machell during the last years of his life. One could not say that he was a popular man; in fact, he was more feared than liked, and in common with all very successful men he made enemies as well as friends. There were two sides to his nature, one cold, hard, calculating and suspicious, the other generous, affectionate, simple as a child's; the contrast was so violent that it was almost impossible to believe him the same man. He once told me that suspicion had been the curse of his life, and had made him an unhappy man. The following story is an illustration of this:

He had a great opinion of Fordham's riding and before the days of Archer put him up whenever he could get him. On one occasion, Fordham was going to ride a horse for him in a selling race; Machell thought it would win, and told Fordham that he was going to back him heavily.

Fordham did not fancy the horse and tried to persuade him not to bet, without avail. The horse went badly in the betting, and in the race was beaten. Fordham said when he came in, "I told you so," but Machell, in his disgust, accused the jockey of not trying. Fordham never forgave him, and never rode one of his horses again. "The d——d horse," said Machell afterwards, "was no good, and I lost the best jockey in the world." There it is, when people lose a lot of money on a race, they are apt to suspect everyone of wrong-doing except the horse, who in most cases is the culprit.

The Houghton Meeting at Newmarket of 1886, when St. Mirin was beaten in the Cambridgeshire, had been a very bad one for backers, especially for the numerous followers of Fred Archer. On the Friday morning, at exercise on the Heath, Archer rode up to me, saying, " I suppose you have had a very bad week." I answered that I had. " Well," he said, " you can get out on Queen Bee " (a mare of Robert Peck's) ; " she can't be beat, but I have only told you and the Captain, and I know you will give Peck time to get his money on ; he also has had a very bad week, so don't say anything to a soul."

When the race came off, Queen Bee was beaten the shortest of heads by Wood on Draycot, no one knowing which had won till the number went up. Machell was standing next a friend of his, Mrs. Chaine, always an ardent supporter of Archer, and who, as the numbers appeared in the frame, exclaimed, " Thank God ! " Machell turned to her saying that he thought she always backed Archer. " So I do," she replied, " but he told me not to this time." The Captain threw up his hands saying, " God save me from my friends."

When he passed Archer in the paddock he cut him dead. Archer came to me after the races, looking worn to a shadow, saying that he had ridden the mare into the ground, so anxious was he to win. He was cut to the heart by Machell's behaviour to him. " I had to put all those touting people off," he said, " and the Captain thinks I put him wrong."

Ten days after Archer was dead. For a long time Machell was a miserable man ; this episode preyed on his mind, and he could never forgive himself for his treatment of one who had been such a good friend and servant. " Could you believe it possible," he said to me, "that, after seeing a horse beaten a short head in a desperate finish, I should think Archer was not trying, and yet I allowed myself to think so, and I am haunted by the look on his face when I refused to speak to him after the race."

There is no doubt that Archer, when he rode this race, was already sickening for the illness which was the cause of his death.

The following week was Brighton and Lewes. Archer went to Brighton, which was one of his favourite courses, where he rode several well-fancied horses without success. On the Thursday, at Lewes, I saw him just before he was getting up on Tommy Tittlemouse (the last horse he ever rode), an eleven-to-eight-on chance. He looked very ill, and said, " My horse ought to win, but I am dead out of luck and can't win a race." He was unplaced, and after the race said he would not ride any more that week, but was going home to Newmarket. Just before he left he said " good-bye " to me. He was walking away when he turned back and said, " If you see a two-year-old called Eunuch in a mile selling race to-morrow you ought to back him ; I got beat on him in a five furlong race, but he is a certain stayer."

Sure enough Eunuch, the property of the American sportsman, Mr. Ten Broeck, was entered, and won easily at five to one ; so, curiously enough, on my first acquaintance with Archer, he put me on a good winner in Isonomy, and the last words he ever spoke to me were to back this Eunuch.

On his arrival at Newmarket he was found to be seriously ill with what turned out to be typhoid fever. Unfortunately, he always kept a loaded revolver in his bedroom, and this had not been taken away. He had overcome the crisis of his illness, and was a little better, when his sister, who was nursing him, left his room for a moment, and he jumped out of bed and shot himself.

I was at Liverpool when the news of his tragic death came. It was a terrible blow to me and many others. As Lord Marcus Beresford said, when he heard the news, " Backers have lost the best friend they have ever had." He certainly was the most attractive figure that I have ever come across on a race-course, and, apart from my admiration for him as a jockey, I was very fond of him as a man.

As I have said, Archer's death was a great shock to Captain Machell, and it is a curious thing that in later years he, also, made two attempts to take his own life.

Writing of Machell and Hermit, one's mind naturally travels to Hermit's owner, the late Lord Chaplin. Till just before his last illness, Lord Chaplin took the keenest interest in horses and racing.

It was only about two years ago that I met him in London, on his way down to Newmarket to see Polemarch, the property of his son-in-law, Lord Londonderry. He had just recovered from a long spell of illness, but in spite of that, and bitterly cold weather, he was as keen as a boy.

In the days of Hermit he lived at Blankney, and was known as "The Squire." He was, I believe, a most dashing bettor, and there was no finer judge of horses and racing.

He had more or less retired when I started racing, so of his many successes and triumphs on the Turf I cannot write, but when I first went to Leicestershire he was still hunting. What his weight was I do not know, but anything from 18st. to 20st. Moreover, he was not like most welter weights, who are content with seeing as much sport as they can from the background, but as long as his horse lasted he was there in the front rank.

To see him thundering down at a fence on one of his great horses was a fine sight. I remember on one occasion we were all held up in a field close to Melton, the only way out being where a young sapling had been planted in the fence surrounded by an iron cage, which stood about 4 ft. 6 in., the thin tree growing up several feet above it.

There were shouts for a chopper or a knife, when down came the Squire, forty miles an hour, with his eyeglass in his eye, seeing nothing but the opening in the fence. There was no stopping h'm, neither did the young tree do so, for his weight and that of his horse broke it off as clean as you would break a thin stick, and away he went without an idea that the tree had ever been there. A magnificent horseman, what he did not know about hunting was not worth knowing.

I was hunting with the Pytchley the year before the war, and he and another veteran, General Brabazon, had a house at Brixworth. The Squire's pluck was marvellous, for it was with the greatest difficulty that he could be got on or off his horse, but once in the saddle he was as happy as a sand-boy.

One night, Count Kinsky, my wife and I went to dine with these two old warriors. The Count and I, after the slipshod fashion of the present day, had on short coats and black ties, and we felt quite ashamed when we found these two old men, after a hard day's hunting, beautifully turned out in evening coats, white waistcoats and ties.

Men of the old school—they may have had their faults, but in many ways they put the present generation to shame.

CHAPTER XI

JOE CANNON AND HIS STABLE

IT was about this time (1886) that my friends and I sent our horses to Joe Cannon, my brother Durham having, as I have said, taken Alfred Sadler for his private trainer. For half a century the name of Cannon has been famous on the Turf, and well has this reputation been deserved. I have known Joe Cannon, who still lives at Lordship Farm, Newmarket, intimately for over thirty years. In fair weather or foul, you could not put him wrong, and he is the best friend I have ever had racing.

Joe, before I knew him, had been a splendid cross-country jockey. He rode and trained Regal when he won the Grand National for Captain Machell, who told me that Joe was the bravest man he ever saw on a horse, but very nervous before a race. Once in the saddle he was cool and determined, and Machell was so impressed by this that in his later days, when he (Machell) had given up steeplechasing, he would go round the paddock before the National to find a jockey who looked pale and nervous, saying, " If I like his horse I shall back him, for I know that man is going to do his best."

Joe Cannon left Captain Machell to become private trainer to Lord Rosebery, a connection which lasted for some years. He afterwards set up at Grafton House, Newmarket, where he quickly got together a most miscellaneous collection of horses and owners, among the latter myself and my friends, Charles Kinsky, the two brothers Chris and Frankie Murrietta, Mr. Hartopp and Baron Max de Tuyll. None of us had any ready money ;

we were often slow in paying our training bills, and how poor Joe carried on I do not know. They were merry times, although, as I look back on them, the owners seem to me perhaps more interesting than the horses they owned.

Charles Kinsky I have already written much about. The Murriettas came of a Spanish family which had settled down in England. They were very wealthy to start with, but became involved in a famous City failure. I have always heard that they might have escaped great financial loss, but chose honour before riches. Chris was the typical Don—a tall, distinguished-looking man, rather eccentric, with a hasty temper. As long as his money lasted he lived like the great gentleman that he was. The best of everything was just good enough for himself and his friends, especially the latter, so long as it was in his power to give it to them. Frankie was different—a dear little fellow in his way, clever, with an eye to the main chance, and with a great show of being a hard, shrewd man of business, but, *au fond*, he was one of the best and kindest-hearted men in the world.

I remember Captain Machell, after he had been staying in some house with him, saying, " I like that little Murrietta : a clever fellow, and a bit of a rogue, too." That was the impression Frankie wanted to leave, but in reality he was as straight as a die.

The two brothers owned horses together ; they never had anything of much class, but at the end of each year Chris was a little poorer and Frankie a little better off.

One horse I bought for them had a curious career. This was a great big brown gelding called The Lown, by Lowlander, and Frankie won a lot of money with him. I had seen the horse running all over the country in every sort of race—over fences, over hurdles and on the flat. He won many of them, carrying very big weights. He was owned by Colonel Clitheroe, and trained by Tom Leader, father of the three Leader brothers now training, members of one of those families who have made the English Turf what it is.

One day I was riding a very fast horse against The Lown, in a steeplechase, and he showed such a turn of speed when my horse was still full of running that I bought him for Frankie for £500, thinking he would probably win a good hurdle race. When we took him home and tried him he was winning easily at one and half miles, but did not stay it out.

He was a great big heavy horse, and I could never ride him properly myself, although I won a hurdle race on him at Four Oaks Park, where he showed again such a dash of speed that I felt confident he would win a nice race on the flat. So, although he was seven or eight years old, and had been running all his life over a country, Joe Cannon turned his attention to flat racing. He soon found that what I said was right, and that his real course was six to seven furlongs. Frankie put on his most cunning look and said, " Now you must leave this to me ; I shall manage the horse myself, and win a lot of money."

I don't recollect the details of the " coup," but I do remember the horse running for a handicap at Epsom in Derby week and winning in a canter. I also remember Frankie being very angry with Chris for having given the good thing away at a supper party the night before. And then again this gallant old horse won a seven furlong handicap at Doncaster from a big field. In those days there was a very awkward bend in the course, but so great was his speed that, although he drew on the outside, before they had gone a furlong he was on the rails and was never headed again.

I shall always think it was a marvellous thing that a horse which had all his life been trained for jumping races, and carried welter weights, should have retained his speed when he was eight years old.

Old Alec Taylor took a fancy to Frankie, who worked several good commissions for him, and so quiet was he about it that no one ever suspected that he was the agent of that powerful stable.

I first learnt to beware of a horse with prick ears when I trained with Joe Cannon. As I have said, I and my friends were men without much ready money, and the only way we could get our horses together was when we bought one cheaply from some owner who was disappointed with him. When we went round the stable, it was remarkable what a good-looking collection of prick-eared scoundrels we had. Bad as this characteristic is for flat racing, many a horse of this sort makes a good jumper. To begin with, they are too cunning to fall, and then the fact of having to jump a fence every furlong takes their attention off the business of racing.

The biggest rogue that ever stepped was Pan, who was second in the Grand National. He had a chequered career. I bought him as a three-year-old from the late Mr. W. H. Manser, of Newmarket, after I had ridden him a gallop up the Limekilns one July meeting. He was a great big leathering horse, with the best of legs and feet. As an instance of Captain Machell's quick eye for a steeplechase horse, I was having breakfast at the Jockey Club rooms the morning I had bought Pan, when "Bunny" Leigh, who trained with the Captain, asked me what the horse was that I had been riding on the Limekilns, and when I told him that it was one I had bought for £150, he offered me £50 profit, which I refused. Later in the day he offered me a hundred, and seemed prepared to go on, so it struck me that he might be the Captain's agent. This he did not deny when I asked him, saying, "Machell saw you riding the horse up the Limekilns, and told me to find out what it was, and buy him, as he looked like winning a National." I would not sell, as I thought if it was good enough for the Captain it was good enough for me, and sure enough Pan did run second for the National, and if he had been honest would probably one day have won it.

We had a lot of trouble to teach him to jump, and he showed so much temper that I took him out of training and put him into my hunting stable, where we fairly set about him, but I don't think I should ever have conquered him if I had not starved him and kept him short of water. However, in the end he became a glorious horse over any sort of fence. I then sold him to Mr. Hartopp. We brought him out for the first time in a hurdle race at Sandown. Having tried him a good horse " Topps " betted freely, and I, leaving nothing to chance, took the lead at once, and by the time we got to the pay-gate, was two hundred yards in front, and nothing ever got near him. He next ran in the North at Malton. In that race, coming to the last hurdle I was having it all my own way, but not out by myself as at Sandown, when suddenly up went his head and he fairly stuck his toes in the ground. By the mercy of Providence, the horse that was beating me tried to run out and jumped the wing of the last hurdle. He was disqualified and I got the race. From that day, Pan was the most incorrigible thief I ever came across. Time after time he would allow himself to be beaten when he had a race at his mercy. Eventually he was sold to Teddy Woodlands, who ran him all over the country in the worst possible company, but in spite of that he was continually second. For instance, the week before Liverpool, he was second in some selling race, and then, with Halsey riding him, he ran second to Ilex for the Grand National. I was standing next " Topps " on the Stand when this race was run, and, when Pan jumped on to the race-course alongside of Ilex, he exclaimed, " My God ! there is Pan going to win the National." He dropped his glasses out of his hand (I often wondered if they hurt anyone below), and nearly fell off the Stand himself.

The career of Pan taught me something. If you have to resort to tactics of starvation to conquer a horse, when you have succeeded you have probably also broken his heart.

I must say Joe worked wonders with many of these

horses and his patience with them was admirable. But there was one glorious exception in the stable, a great raking, brown mare called Bellona, with the grandest head you could ever wish to see.

I was her owner, and came by her in the following manner. Some time in September, 1886, Mat Dawson wrote and told me he had a mare which would suit me for jumping, so I went out one morning to see her. The old gentleman was not out himself, but there was the mare ridden by a dark, slim young man, who told me that " the guv'nor " had said I could get on her and do what I liked with her. After being on her back for a few moments I knew she was a mare after my own heart. When I got off her, I asked the lad a few questions, and he said " Don't make any mistake, buy her ; she is a good one." Incidentally, this was my first acquaintance with that great trainer, George Blackwell, who always says that he owes his success to the lessons he learnt from his old master, for he was the young man riding the mare.

Mat had made no mention of price when he wrote to me, so that same evening I went over to see him, and told him that I liked the mare and would buy her if I could give the money. " You can have her for £300," said the old man, " and d—d cheap she is." So I thought ; but unfortunately, at the moment, I had not three hundred shillings. When I made him acquainted with this unpleasant fact : " D—n the blunt ; you take her and pay for her when you can," was the answer. So she went to Joe Cannon's and was at once put to jumping. I rode her myself, and she took to the game like a duck to water.

In those days, at the November Meeting at Croydon, there was a race called the Grand National Hurdle Race, and you could win some money on it. So well did the mare shape that we decided to go for this big race at the first attempt. Rather a curious thing happened when we tried her. We had a jumping ground just beyond the Limekilns, on the other side of the railway.

As both Joe Cannon and I were rather hard up, we were naturally very anxious to win some money on Bellona before she was exposed, so we asked her a big question in the gallop, thinking that, if she put up a good show without actually winning, it would be good enough to bet on. I remember the morning was very foggy when we tried her, and very little could be seen. Two hurdles from the finish I had got the trial horses beat to the world. There was no doubt about it, so I pulled her up, and, much to Joe Cannon's disgust, came in a bad third. After the horses' rugs had been put on, I was talking to Joe as we were standing by the hedge close to the road. I told him what had happened and that I could have won in a canter, and no sooner were the words out of my mouth than to my horror I saw a man lying in the ditch on the other side of the hedge, and I realized that he must have heard every word I had said. I took the bull by the horns and told him that if he kept his mouth shut I would give him a good present when the mare won. He was a real good sort, and said he would not spoil our market for worlds, and he was as good as his word, for, though she started for the race at a hundred to thirty, I got seven to one to my money. She did her part gallantly, too, strolling home ten lengths in front, and the race put me on my legs for a short time.

That day at Croydon was a good one for me, as I also won the big steeplechase for Sir William Throckmorton on Phantom, carrying 12st. 7lb., and starting at five to one. Phantom was a great horse over hurdles, but this was his first effort over fences, and so well was he schooled that he never put a foot wrong. I rode him the next day in a hurdle race with 13st. in heavy ground, and was easily second best.

Having landed our "coup" with Bellona, we became very ambitious. Such a grand fencer was she, and so good, that we decided to go for the Grand National with her, although she was only five years old. At the same time, we put her in the Grand International Hurdle

Race at Croydon, to be run on March 1st. When that time arrived, I was again in my usual impecunious state, and I told Joe that we must pull her out for the hurdle race. He was much against it, as it interfered with her National preparation, but " needs must when the devil drives," so out she came. Instead of 10st. 10lb. which she carried before, she now had 11st. 12lb., a big weight for a five-year-old to carry against the best hurdle race-horses in the country. I put all the money I could scrape together on her, backing her to win and also 1—2, as well as for a place, 1—2—3.

Just as I got on my mare, Teddy Hobson, a well-known commission agent who had put my money on, came running out in a very excited state, telling me that I had no chance, and naming another horse as certain to win. But I would not hear of anything beating Bellona.

The going was Croydon at its deepest, which was saying a lot. It was a very fast-run race. Owing to having been schooled over big fences, Bellona, although jumping magnificently, was going right over the top of the hurdles and, half a mile from home, I was in a pretty hopeless position, and the best I hoped for was getting a place and saving my money. But the good old Croydon Hill and the mud came to my rescue, and one by one the horses came back to me. The mare struggled like a tiger and close home I got to the quarters of Silver Sea, who was leading; she could not stand the pressure, swerved badly, and in the last stride Bellona just shoved her grand head in front. What a glorious mare; and what I felt about her I could never express on paper. Curiously enough, at this meeting I again won the steeplechase on Phantom, bringing off the same double as in the autumn.

But all this was not a good preparation for the National. I had been obliged to roust Bellona up like blazes at her hurdles, and it made her a bit wild at her fences, and inclined to take off too soon.

For all that, I went to Liverpool full of confidence,

and backed her to win me £10,000, and if she had not run in this hurdle race I believe she would have done it. As it was, at the second fence, although she never touched it, she overjumped herself and fell. I ran her again in the big steeplechase at Manchester, but this fall had done her no good. She jumped outrageously all through the race, but in spite of that finished a good second.

After this, I sold her to my friend, Mr. T. B. Miller, who already had a half-share in her, and she did many big things for him, but, fine jumper as she was, she never shone at Liverpool. She always wanted to do too much. She gave Charlie Cunningham a bad fall in the National, again over-jumping herself, but Chris Waller who was a wonderful man over fences managed to get her round in the Sefton where she finished third. Croydon was her favourite battle-ground. I remember on one occasion, as we were going down to the post for a steeplechase, a young man, whom I did not know, on a good-looking brown horse, said to me, " I have got £1,000 on mine, and I shall beat you to-day." This was my first acquaintance with Percy Bewicke. Bellona had top weight in this race, 12st. 7lb., but, in spite of this, was a hot favourite, and well did she justify it, for she won by twenty lengths, with Percy Bewicke second.

Later on, Butt Miller sold her to Mr. Abington, but he did not have good luck with her. She had practically won the Paris Steeplechase when a horse fell in front of her at the last fence, and brought her down. Her last appearance was in the National of 1890. Joe Cannon was very anxious for me to ride her and he thought she had sobered down over her fences. Unfortunately, Abington was in some trouble with the Stewards of the Jockey Club at the time, and my brother Durham, who was one of them, did not want me to ride for him. Her jockey fell off her at Becher's Brook; she went on alone, and got very badly staked. After some time they got her home to Newmarket with difficulty, and

Joe Cannon told me that when this grand old mare hobbled back into the stable yard she lifted up her head and neighed with delight at getting home. But it was no good, for in a few days she was dead.

Another good horse that I bought out of Mat Dawson's stable for Captain A. E. Whitaker was Franciscan. He was a lovely little chestnut, full of quality, but as nervous as he could be. He was the property of Lord Cadogan, and, after he had run very badly in some race at Goodwood, his owner sold him to me for £300. In those days, as I have said before, you could buy good-looking horses for these small prices; it cannot be done now. I rode Franciscan about myself, and jumped him over hurdles and small fences. This quickly worked a change in him, and so well did he do that we put him in a small flat race at Derby. We gave him a gallop which he won so easily that it looked too good to be true, so Joe sent me over to Mat Dawson to find out what he thought about the horse. I found the old man not in the best of health, and in rather a crusty mood. In answer to my question he replied, " To tell the truth, it is little that I know about the horse, but I do remember telling my head man I thought he was d—d stingy with his oats." Mat had no use for bad horses.

We sent him to Derby, where he just got home by a neck, but he did not run with much resolution. After that we went on jumping him and he continued to improve. We next ran him in a five furlong race of £500, at Leicester, against some good horses. Joe said that if he did his best there was only one horse that could beat him and that was King of Diamonds. I did not go to the meeting, but shortly before the race I wired to my starting-price bookmakers that I wanted £100 on King of Diamonds, and £100 on Franciscan. The first news I got was a wire from the starting-price office, " King of Diamonds nine to four, Franciscan hundred to fifteen, dead heat, congratulations."

The little horse's next appearance was in a handicap

MR. JOSEPH CANNON

"BELLONA"

ROBERT PECK

Photo: W. A. Rouch

TOM CANNON

Photo: W. A. Rouch

hurdle race at Kempton, where I rode him myself, and won in a canter at a hundred to thirty. Two months later he was in the Sandown Grand Prize, and, in spite of a biggish weight, we thought he would win. The day before I had a fall on some rotten brute in a selling steeplechase and broke my collar-bone, so Roddy Owen rode for us, which was probably a bit of luck, for he rode one of the best races of his life. Never a yard from the rails, and yet riding a waiting race, he won by half a length.

This was a pretty good record—four races in succession for a £300 horse. Small as he was, he was an ideal horse for Auteuil, so we decided to go for the Paris Steeplechase. Rather ambitious, perhaps, for a horse that had never run in a steeplechase, but I had jumped a lot of fences on him. We also had a small school at the Links Farm, in which we turned the horses loose, and he loved going round it. Joe took endless trouble, had a small wall built, and other fences, such as you meet at Auteuil. Everything was going famously, when leg troubles intervened, and the good little horse never ran again.

One Sunday afternoon I remember going to see Joe Cannon and finding this usually delightful and happy-natured man in a very depressed mood. When I enquired the reason he said, " It is really rather heart-breaking when you have brought off two good things to hear that the men you are training for h ve had a bad week." What had happened was that Charles Hartopp and Chris Murrietta, after winning a lot of money on two of Joe Cannon's horses, had yet managed to get into the soup by the end of the week. " Topps," as Charles Hartopp is called by all his friends, was a fine judge of racing, and had a wonderful eye for a horse. In his time he picked up cheaply many good bargains, but excellent as his judgment was he had never any confidence in it himself, and would listen to every " cock and bull " story that was told him by the wrong people, and in the end this cost him a lot of money.

In his younger days, when in the Guards, he was a pretty good rider, and won the Household Brigade Cup at Sandown on Nina for Major Wickham. But his excitable, nervous temperament was not suitable for race riding. One day, at Sandown, Marcus Beresford said to him before he was getting up in some race, " What on earth is the matter with your tongue ? " for " Topps " had got it firmly clenched between his teeth. " Topps " replied that his teeth were chattering so, it was the only way he could keep them quiet. But, like many men of this sort, he was brave enough when once he started, and could ride a good race. He had many useful horses, and always managed them well, but whatever money he might win on his own went west on other people's. Wherever " Topps " went you would find plenty of life and fun, but he was always inclined to burn the candle at both ends. He was, and is, a great friend of mine, but we fell out once for a short time.

Captain Machell had a two-year-old called Madcap, which had been down the course on several occasions. One night at dinner the Captain said this was the worst horse in England. " Perhaps he is," said Topps, " but I'll give you £50 for him." The offer was instantly accepted, and the horse was sent to Joe Cannon. In about a month's time he had him in a selling race at Croydon. " Topps," who could not get away, asked me to go and see him tried, which I did. Ridden by George Barrett, he finished last in the gallop. George told me that he was the worst brute he had ever been on, and could neither go fast nor stay.

In spite of this, " Topps " would have him sent to Croydon. Just before the race he came to me and said, " I don't believe in the trial ; I shall have £200 on him, he looks like a winner." I replied, " You must be mad, what is the use of trying a horse, and, when he finishes last, throwing away £200 on him. If you insist on backing him, I'll lay you the money myself ; I may as well have it as the bookmakers."

As I have said before, " Topps " was easily influenced, so he did not have a shilling on.

When the flag fell, Madcap jumped off in front and won in a canter. " Topps " came bounding off the stand, purple in the face, and said to me, " By God, you ought to be shot," with a few other uncomplimentary remarks. My temper being pretty short, we had a very considerable row. He bought the horse in and lost £200 on the race. So Madcap went back to Newmarket, and shortly afterwards " Topps " went down to try him again. He got Fred Archer to ride, with the same result as before, the horse was beat to blazes. Fred said he could not understand how he had won that race, for he never was and never would be worth a shilling. I was triumphant, and rubbed it into "Topps," who was quite apologetic when he thought of the things he had said to me. However, he entered the horse for a Nursery at Warwick, and although Joe Cannon had another horse in the race, called Jack Frost, which was supposed to be a certainty, and started at even money, Madcap had to run, and again he astonished us, for he ran a real good race and finished second to Jack Frost. But never again did this curious horse show one glimpse of form. No wonder bookmakers grow rich !

The best of companions on or off a race-course, I have had as much fun with " Topps," mixed at times, I must admit, with irritation, as with any man I know.

But all Joe Cannon's owners were not men of straw. One was Jack Hammond, who won the Cambridgeshire and a fortune besides with that grand mare Florence. Hammond's career was remarkable. He began life as a stable-boy in Captain Machell's establishment, when Cannon was trainer, and before middle age he owned St. Gatien, who dead-heated with Harvester for the Derby, Harvester being trained in Captain Machell's stable. Later on he was Joe's richest employer, but the connection, successful as it was, did not last long.

Hammond was a very clever man, and a good judge of racing and horses, but, above all, one of the best gamblers that ever lived. He attributed his great success in that line to the fact that when he fancied a horse, and the price was short, he had a small stake on, but the longer the odds the more heavily he betted. It is easy to see that this is the best policy, but how few of us have the pluck to carry it out.

After three or four years with Joe Cannon, Hammond had a disagreement with him, and his horses left the stable. I will tell the story in his own words, as it brings out Joe's character in a strong light.

It was a year or two after the event that Hammond said to me, " I wish I had my horses with Joe again ; he is the best man in Newmarket, but I insulted him and he won't train for me any more, although he is quite friendly with me." He then proceeded to tell me the story of the rupture, saying, " I had a horse in a race at one of the Newmarket July Meetings. This horse was a bit backward, and I proposed to run him. Joe said I had better not, because, although he was not fit enough to bet on, yet he might win. I said he could not win, and that I should run him, thinking to myself that Joe would give him a bucket of mash the night before to make things safe. But I did not know how d———d particular Joe was, although he warned me again that it was dangerous to run. I was obstinate, the horse ran and won, without my having a shilling on. After the race I lost my temper and abused Cannon. That evening I found a note from him saying that I must take my horses away at once. I wrote back trying to smooth things over, but he replied that if my horses were not out of his yard by the next day he would turn them loose in the street. He also enclosed me a cheque for a thousand pounds, which I had lent him, and you know as well as I do how hard up he was at the time."

Jack Hammond, a good fellow and straight, was a most kind-hearted man and a great friend to the poor in Newmarket.

It is a curious thing that many of the best people in this world seem pursued by ill-luck. Joe Cannon has sustained many reverses of fortune. I have known one thing after another happen to him which would have completely knocked me out, but he has always met these disasters with a joke and the sunniest smile that ever a man was blessed with. The only real good luck that I have known come his way is his extraordinarily happy family life, and his many devoted friends.

I shall always think that if Sir Martin had not fallen in Minoru's Derby he would have won it for Mr. Winans and Cannon. I am sure he was a really good horse, and never completely recovered from the effects of that fall, although he won good races afterwards.

At one time Joe trained for that eccentric and gallant bookmaker, Charles Hibbert. Beyond Mercutio, who won the Lincolnshire Handicap, Hibbert did not have any horses of particular note. He won a lot of money on Mercutio, and I always think it was a wonderful feat of training to win a race of that importance with such a nervous, excitable horse. Hibbert was a dashing layer, and a dashing backer, and in every way a good sportsman.

Another of Joe's patrons was Charles Morbey, who raced under the name of " Mr. Ellis." For him, in addition to many other races, he won the Cesarewitch with Red Eyes, or rather she dead-heated with Cypria, trained by old Tom Jennings, one of the best long-distance trainers that ever lived. Here was an instance of Joe's bad luck ; Red Eyes should have won easily. She was ridden by Tommy Loates, who thought that he could go and beat the little boy on Cypria when he liked, while, if he had set about his business from the Bushes, he would have won by two lengths. On the Monday after there is a lot of difference between dead-heating for a race and winning it.

Charles Morbey, like Hammond, had a remarkable

career, also beginning as an apprentice in Peter Price's stable. He was a fairly good jockey, but it was not long before he was owning horses himself. He was not only exceedingly clever, but also astoundingly lucky, and whatever he touched turned to gold. When Charles Morbey backed a horse his money was good to follow, and the same is the case now.

The history of Red Eyes is worth recording, to show how horses can improve in form. As a two-year-old she belonged to Charles Hartopp. Joe Cannon trained her, and, having tried her very smart, they sent her to run at Liverpool, in a selling race of bad class, and betted on her " till the cows came home." Ridden by George Barrett, she was last. She went back to Newmarket, and was tried again, with the result she won in a canter. She ran again, heavily backed, and was down the course, and so it went on throughout the year. She was a good-looking, well-mannered, sober mare. As a three-year-old there was the same story.

One night in a July week, Topps made a match with Lord Durham, who also had a horse that always ran last, but Red Eyes was beaten by about ten lengths. In disgust, "Topps" gave her to his trainer's son, who sold her to his father for £10. She was sent to Worcester to run in a selling race, with orders that she was to be sold afterwards for what she would fetch, but owing to some mistake, although unplaced, she was brought back to Newmarket. She was then put to jumping, and was as disappointing as ever, until at last she scrambled home in a hurdle race at Derby, carrying bottom weight. She then won another hurdle race in a canter, and before the year was out she had won the Goodwood Stakes, the Lewes Handicap, dead-heated for the Cesarewitch, and had also beaten, at even weights, Lady Rosebery, one of the best mares in training, for the Queen's Plate at Derby.

If she had changed stables previously to these

successes it would have been said how greatly her new trainer had improved her.

When I started training myself, Joe Cannon took as much pains and trouble with me as if I had been his own son, and without his help and advice I should never have got on.

CHAPTER XII

SOME RIDING EXPERIENCES—TOM CANNON OF DANEBURY

DURING these years of which I have been writing, I had been riding a good deal in public and had gained some experience and practice.

I think I got my real start as a jockey in 1885, and Dick Marsh was the man who gave it to me.

At the Liverpool Meeting of that year, I had my first ride in the Grand National on Lioness, a sweet little Irish mare owned by Harry Hungerford,. She had won many races in her own country, but had only run once in England, and then in a hurdle race. She was trained by Alfred Sadler. He was not really a steeplechase trainer, but nevertheless he produced her in the most perfect condition, and she never set a foot wrong in the race. This was the National which Ted Wilson won on Roquefort, with Frigate, who hailed from the celebrated Eyrefield establishment in Ireland, second. Frigate was trained by Mr. H. E. Linde, a man who turned out many great steeplechase winners. A little mare, barely 15.3, all wire and whipcord, without an ounce of superfluous flesh on her, she was not much to look at, but no man could have built a more truly made one, and when that great jockey, Harry Beasley, threw his leg across her, she looked what she was, a mass of vitality and gameness. Arthur Coventry rode Redpath, Charles Kinsky, Zoedone, and Roddy Owen, Kilworth. Then there were many other good horses in the field, such as Gamecock, a subsequent National winner, Downpatrick, Jolly Sir John, Red Hussar, and Dog Fox.

My recollections of the actual race are not too clear, for I never remember things I have taken part in so well as those I have looked on at, and, as this was the first National I had ever ridden in, I was too much occupied with my own affairs to take much notice of what other people were doing. But I remember Zoedone falling heavily with Kinsky, at the preliminary hurdle, which was surprising, as she was the safest fencer in the world. She was a sound second favourite at five to one, and, from what transpired afterwards, I am afraid there were valid reasons for saying the mare was " got at." She ran as dead as a stone, and was pulled up after going about half-way. My mare went round the course without making the slightest mistake, and never once was I interfered with, neither did I interfere with anyone else. The jockeys took a place and kept it, and the horses were jumping their fences as straight as a line. I saw no fall the first time round, and, as my mare was a doubtful stayer, I was not in the front rank, and I had a good view of what was going on.

After jumping the water in front of the stands, I worked up into a good place, about fifth or sixth, when I saw Roquefort going like the devil, Wilson as usual on the inside, and never losing an inch of ground. Frigate was lying handy to him, and Gamecock, also, going very strong ; the latter shortly after took up the running. All went well till coming to Valentine's Brook, three fences from the race-course, where Gamecock turned a somersault, and my mare began to tire. The rest of the journey I was just near enough to see that Roquefort was always too good for Frigate, and I believe that, although he only won a length, he had a considerable amount in hand.

The next morning, much to my astonishment, Dick Marsh came to me at exercise on the course, and asked me if I would like to ride The Captain for the Duke of Hamilton in the Champion Stakes. Dan Thirlwell (who usually rode for him), he said, was not well, and could not ride. Naturally I was delighted, and gladly accepted. The Captain was a champion up to three miles, a beautiful short-legged horse, up to any weight, and a glorious jumper.

There were two other runners, a good horse called Chancery, belonging to Mr. Gubbins, trained by Linde, and ridden by Harry Beasley, and a useful horse in Sidthorpe, with Billy Sensier up. The Captain, who had not been beaten that year, was favourite, but, owing to my riding against these two well-known jockeys, the Ring fielded strongly.

I wonder if Dick Marsh remembers running out on to the course after we had jumped the preliminary hurdle, and saying to me, "They have the cheek to bet evens against the horse. I'm having a dash and we won't carry an ounce extra." With that he took off the heavy woollen bandages that were on The Captain's forelegs. My orders were to stride along, leaving the fences to the horse, and to poach a bit at the fence on the canal turn if I could. In the race The Captain had been bowling along in great style, jumping the fences without the slightest effort, so, when I came to the canal turn, I did take a liberty and jumped the fence on the skew, so as to get round to the next one quickly. This was nearly my undoing, for my horse hit the fence so hard that for a moment I was hanging round his neck, but he shook me back into the saddle. Harry Beasley, who was following me, took the same liberty, with the same result, and he was fishing for a stirrup as he came to the next fence. After that I made the running until the last hurdle but one, where Harry came at me. I dared not look round, but, as we came to the last hurdle, Chancery's head got to my horse's neck and was there when we landed. I was too frightened of Harry Beasley to get my whip up, and this was lucky, as Chancery's bolt was shot and I drew away to win by a length. This race, I think, gave me the greatest pleasure of any I ever rode, and I worshipped Dick Marsh for giving me the chance.

Dan Thirlwell, the Duke of Hamilton, and Dick Marsh, were at that time prominent figures in the steeplechasing world. Dan was one of the neatest and most accomplished riders I have ever seen and when he appeared on one of Dick Marsh's horses in the pretty colours—cerise, French grey sleeves and cap—of the Duke, the combination took the eye of any lover of steeplechasing. Horse, jockey and trainer were always turned out in the very acme of perfection, and, as is not always the case, they lived up to their appearance, for they won a great many races. I cannot from memory recall their many great triumphs, but I can remember, when I was first beginning to ride, that they won races with Thornfield, and Eau de Vie. Before Dan Thirlwell's time, the Duke of Hamilton's favourite jockey was Jimmy Adams. If I had a better memory I could write a book of the quaint and witty sayings of Jimmy.

When I first saw him, he was a little, short-legged man, with the back and shoulders of a prize-fighter, and a good bit more below the belt than was convenient for a jockey. But, even then, to see him ride at the last two fences in a close finish was a revelation of what strength, determination, and skill could achieve. On those occasions I think he could beat any jockey I have ever seen. Before he took to cross-country riding, he had been a first-class flat race jockey, as long as his weight allowed of it. He lived in times when boys of his class got little education, and it was a fact that he could not read, although he never would admit to this. One day he happened to be seen with the newspaper in his hands, upside down. Someone asked him if there was any news. "Not much," was the reply. "I suppose you know you've got the paper upside down," said his friend. "Well, any bl—dy fool can read it the other way," answered Jimmy. Like many people who cannot read, he had a wonderful memory, and always a quick and ready answer to any chaff.

One day going out on some horse for a race at Kempton, Sir John Astley, who was very stout himself, said to him, "Jimmy, hadn't you better leave that corporation of yours behind? I'll take care of it for you while you are riding." " Thank you, Sir John, I think you've enough to do to look after your own," was the reply.

There never was a better and straighter fellow than Jimmy, and, if ever there has been a man who had no enemies, he was the one. He had a supreme contempt for anything outside England. On one occasion at Auteuil, where some good French horse had frightened away all opposition except one of the Duke of Hamilton's, Jimmy, whose language was of the old school, remarked, " I'll tell you what it is, Your Grace, you and I are the only two plucky b———s in this b———y country."

When he gave up riding, he started training at Epsom, which he did with considerable success, two of his owners being Ronnie Moncrieff and Bobby Ward ; the latter must have pleasant recollections of those days.

In the following year (1886), I began to ride a good deal for Tom Cannon. Tom was Joe Cannon's elder brother, a slight, delicate-looking man, good-looking, a bit of a dandy, and a beautiful jockey. I can think of no other word that describes his style so well. In finesse, and the fine art of jockeyship, he had no superior, and in the handling of a two-year-old I should say no equal.

At the time of which I write he lived at Danebury, Stockbridge, where he had a large stable of horses, both on the flat and over fences. He was a good trainer of horses, but I think an even better trainer of jockeys, *vide* his sons Morny Cannon, Kempton, Tom and Charles, Jack Watts and Robinson, who were all under his care as boys, and I cannot leave out Arthur Coventry. He learnt all he knew from Tom Cannon. I remember Archer saying one day that there was no jockey living who could give Mr. Coventry 5lb.

At the Bibury Club and Stockbridge Meetings, Danebury was a great "rendezvous" for all the élite of the Turf world. They would all go there after the day's racing and Tom was a perfect and most hospitable host.

What fun we had in those Bibury Club and Stockbridge days ; fishing, bathing, lawn tennis in the mornings, then racing, and in the evenings most cheery dinners, either at the Bibury Club or at different houses rented for the week. Bridge, which has been the ruin of social life in England, was not then invented.

Matches were frequently made overnight. I remember one between Lord Durham and the late Lord Herbert Vane-Tempest, in which Lord Herbert was beaten, as the horse stuck his toes in the ground at the start and tried to kick him off. Another time there was a private sweepstakes for horses ridden by their owners. Harry Milner, who had married the Duchess of Montrose, had entered a pretty good mare, Shrine. On form, the race looked a good thing for her, but Harry, although he was a plucky man to hounds, did not inspire confidence as a jockey, and Shrine was known to be a fidgety sort of mare. She was very much on her toes, and there was quite a crowd in the Paddock to see him get up.

After half taking off his overcoat, he put it on again, declaring he would not get up on such a beast. At last, he was prevailed upon to do so, but, when Golding gave him a leg-up, he nearly fell off on the other side. Eventually he was despatched down the course vowing he would break his neck.

Everyone went back to the Stand laughing, and saying, " We can't back such a rider even with a stone in hand," and back went Shrine in the betting ; but in the race she jumped off in front and stayed there and Harry Milner sailed home an easy winner, looking quite different from the frightened object we saw going out of the Paddock. It then transpired that he and the Duchess had landed a good stake and that all this funking had been " put on." The Duchess had been annoyed at hearing that people were saying that Harry could not ride, so she said " We will teach them a lesson," and she certainly did, and had the laugh of everyone.

Tom Cannon was king of Stockbridge, and his colours in gentlemen riders' races, with Arthur Coventry up, were good to follow. With all his suave manner and geniality, Tom did not wear his heart upon his sleeve, knew how to take care of himself, and was a good business man.

He made a lot of money selling horses. He sold Humewood to Lord Rodney, as everyone thought very cheaply, before the Cesarewitch. I asked Tom why he had done this, and he said, " Yes, the horse was cheap, but look at the advertisement ; everyone who wants a horse will now come to buy another cheap one from me."

About this time Mr. Coventry gave up riding, and Tom Cannon often put me up on his horses. He taught me what a mistake it is to tie a jockey down with many orders. He would tell you what the horse wanted, and the sort of race that would suit him best, and left the rest to the rider. But it was very rare for him to tell his jockey to go along ; he hated to see a horse of his in front, and this has always been a well-known characteristic of all the Cannons. As I have said, Tom did not wear his heart upon his sleeve, and he was as anxious as many other people to get a good price when he betted.

The first year I rode for him at Stockbridge I was lucky enough to win three races for him. The first horse I rode was Polemic. I used to bet pretty high in those days, and I asked him what sort of a chance the horse had. " Well, just a fair chance, if you are very patient and wait till the last moment," said he. I did so, and the horse came and won the race cleverly.

He was in a race the next day, weights to be declared after the first day's racing. In the evening I saw he had been given 12 st. 12 lb., so I jumped to the conclusion that he would not run, and half engaged myself for some other horse. The next morning Tom said he wanted me for Polemic, and as I went out on the horse he said, " You had better back him again ; what do you want on ? Don't wait with him so long this time, and you will win again," which I did easily. Afterwards I said I wished I had known what a good thing it was the first time, and he replied, with a twinkle in his eye, " Ah ! he worst of it is you young gentlemen will talk so."

A fortnight before that Stockbridge Meeting I am afraid I cost him and my friend, Billy Lurgan, a lot of money. He trained a useful hurdler for Billy called Playful. This horse was in the Paris Hurdle Race, with the nice weight of 10 st. 5 lb., and Tom said that if I could do the weight I should ride, and that the horse was likely to win ; 10 st. 5 lb. was much too light for me to ride, but I determined to do it, and by very hard work got myself down, and still felt fit and well.

The Paris Hurdle Race is run on a Wednesday. The Sunday before I rode a horse called Savoyard in the Steeplechase. A horse ridden by a drunken jockey had come right across me at the wall ; we both fell, and I was knocked out for a time. Incidentally, while I was in that state I was relieved of a valuable pearl pin and some sleeve links. That was not a very good beginning to the week, but I put the lid on it myself. A friend of mine had a real good thing on the Tuesday at Lewes, a horse called Lord Beaconsfield, and I went back and rode it. I won the race by ten lengths, but, when Tom Cannon read in the paper on Wednesday morning that I had been riding at Lewes on the Tuesday, I believe he remarked, " I'm afraid that is good-bye to the Paris Hurdle Race." I arrived back in Paris on Wednesday morning, crossing by the night boat, and when I got there went into the Turkish Baths. After I had been a short time in the hot room I fainted. There was a famous coloured masseur at the bath, who picked me up and said he would put me right. After he had massaged me with alcohol, I felt quite well again. I went to the races and weighed out for my horse in pretty good shape. But just before the starting time a tremendous thunder-storm came on, and the race was put off until it was over. Then for about half an hour we were cooped up in a crowded and stuffy weighing-room, which began to tell on me badly, as I had practically had nothing to eat for twenty-four hours. However when the storm cleared off and I got on Playful, the air being nice and cool, I did not feel so bad. There were only nine runners, Roquefort, ridden by Ted Wilson, being favourite at seven to two, and five to one Playful. Roquefort was giving me two stone, and Tom said he would not do it.

Playful was a lovely horse to ride, and throughout the race was always going like a winner. Three furlongs from home I thought I was certain to win, but three miles and a furlong is a long road for a weak jockey to travel, and Dan Thirlwell, on a horse of the Duke of Hamilton's, with only 9st. 12lb. on his back, kept worrying me, and then Playful, who was not a stout battler, began to hang. There is nothing more difficult than to ride a finish on a horse that hangs, even for the jockey who is fit and strong, and for a weak one it is fatal.

A hundred yards from home I had ridden myself blind, and I was beaten a length and a half. When I pulled up, the course and stands seemed to be going round and round and I could scarcely see.

Neither Billy Lurgan nor Tom Cannon were in Paris, and they never said a word to me afterwards, but they must have thought a lot.

The story of my fainting in the Turkish Bath was never known, for I was so ashamed of myself at the time I never said anything about it. A fortnight later, at the Bibury Club Meeting, as I have said, I won two races for Tom Cannon and one for Billy Lurgan, and it was more than I deserved ever being put up by them again. A jockey, whether amateur or professional, has no right to ride a horse unless he is at his best. The jockey loses a race which he ought to win, and probably is in the saddle again at once riding in many other races. His lapse is soon forgotten, but the unfortunate owner perhaps has no other horses to run. He may have planned " a coup " with his horse, and, having seen it thrown away, has no further interest or excitement.

Writing of Tom Cannon and his love of a " waiting

race" reminds me of a Queen's Plate at Northampton, which I once saw Archer win on a mare of Lord Ellesmere's. Tom used to tell me that he had often won a race by being forced to take a pull at his horse, when if he had had a clear course he would not have dared to have done so.

This race was a case in point. The mare was a great stayer and Archer forced the pace from the start. In the straight for home, two other horses joined him, and a ding-dong struggle took place between three tired horses. A hundred and fifty yards from home, Archer stopped riding and dropped back. Fifty yards from the winning post the other pair literally stood still; Archer's mare came again and won by a neck. We were all thrilled at his wonderful riding; but when I congratulated him he laughed and said, "Well, you know I've been wasting very hard, and I had been riding my mare for a mile; I was beat, and I had to stop; that gave the mare a chance, and she came again. It was really nothing to do with me."

I think myself that the large amount of racing that is done in these days on straight courses is not helpful to jockeys. Riding on a round course teaches the young ones so much more. They are frequently obliged to wait, as they cannot all be in front, and they learn how often a horse will run on again when his rider has been obliged to take a pull.

L

CHAPTER XIII

THE UNLUCKY SAVOYARD—GLENTHORPE AND PARASANG

A VERY unlucky horse was Savoyard, who I mentioned in my last chapter as having been knocked over in the Paris Steeplechase of that year, 1886. The property of Baron Schroeder, and trained at Upton by " Old Jenks," I had many rides on him. On three occasions, with ordinary luck, he might have won the National. He was a lengthy chestnut horse of great quality, with a mouth like silk, and a perfect angel in character, but unfortunately he had one serious defect, a twisted foreleg, which just prevented him from being a smasher.

In his first race for the National he was ridden by a good jockey called Kirby. All through the race he was in a good place, jumping the fences to perfection ; but up the straight for home, when fighting out a desperate finish with Old Joe, he fell at the last hurdle. I was riding Redpath that year, who was as usual going all over like a winner half a mile from home. I remember as I jumped the last hurdle seeing Savoyard and Kirby lying prostrate on the ground, both looking dead to the world. Poor Kirby was not killed, but he was crippled for life, and never properly recovered, but Savoyard was only knocked out, and was none the worse. That year twenty-three horses ran, a grand field of good jumpers, and, until Redpath tired, I had as comfortable a ride as if I had been in a good thirty minutes with hounds.

That fine jockey, Tom Skelton, rode Old Joe, who was a great stayer. I remember seeing him with his whip up a mile from home, but, no matter how hard he was driven at his fences, Old Joe was much too well schooled to fall.

The following year Tom Skelton rode Savoyard when he was second to Gamecock ; the horse who ran so well in the year Roquefort won, and who also had been third to Old Joe.

I think Savoyard ought to have beaten Gamecock, for there was always a doubt in Jenkins's mind whether the former could quite last out the long and tiring journey, and Tom was told to wait till the last moment. Baron Schroeder, the owner, promised him the stake if he won.

In those days we finished up the race-course over two flights of hurdles, and really this made the National a still greater test of stamina than it is over the present course, the last half-mile being against the collar. Savoyard, as usual, slid over the fences with the greatest ease and precision, and Tom Skelton rode a patient, steady race, always being in a nice place. All went well until coming to the turn into the straight half a mile from home. Savoyard then had only the plodding Gamecock to beat, but, alas ! Tom Skelton saw that big stake in his pocket, he was always broke to the world, and, as he said to me, " When I saw that winning post in the distance, with so much money hanging on to it, I had to get there as soon as I could." The result was, he raced to the front, and, after Savoyard had looked a certain winner, old Gamecock, who was well named, for he would never give in, came and worried him out of the race. Although he had fallen, Savoyard was a real Liverpool horse, and a perfect ride over big fences. The following year (1888) I rode him myself. He had a big weight, 12 st. 4 lb., but in spite of that his record was so good that we fancied him very much.

An Irish horse called Usna was favourite. He was a smashing good horse, trained by Linde, and ridden by Harry Beasley. He carried top weight, 12 st. 7 lb. In the field was the Irish mare, Frigate, who had been second to Roquefort in 1885, very much fancied, ridden by another of the Beasley brothers, Willie. In the race, after we had gone a mile, Usna, in spite of his 12 st. 7 lb., went to the front, followed by Frigate, and so great was the pace that, as we passed the stand the first time round, these two had already strung out the field, one of the few who was able to keep anywhere near being myself, on Savoyard. Coming to the fence at the canal turn, they were quite ten lengths in front of me ; on landing over this fence Usna put his shoulder out. He did not fall, but he carried Frigate out almost to the brink of the canal. But for this unfortunate accident I have no doubt that Usna and Frigate would have beaten the rest of the field nearly a quarter of a mile. Up to that moment I had been obliged to keep my horse at full stretch to keep near them, but when they ran out the situation altered. Savoyard went with his head in his chest, jumping like a bird, and the others struggled after me.

This was the first year that the race was run over the present National course, finishing over those two small fences inside the flat race-course ; previously, we had always finished up the flat race-course with two flights of hurdles to end up. That year these two new fences were built, much too straight up and were as strong as a wall. As we came on to the race-course, Ringlet, a mare in Captain Machell's stable, and ridden by Tom Skelton, passed me, but approaching the first of these new fences she was beaten and my nearest pursuer was Playfair, the ultimate winner ; he was quite four lengths behind me and Mawson had his whip up. It went through me then that I was going to win the National if I got safely over the two last fences. Now Savoyard was never so good over small fences as big ones, and I did the most fatal thing a jockey can do at the end of a long steeplechase. Coming to the fence I steadied my horse, he got a little too close to it, just brushed the top and turned over like a rabbit shot through the head, Playfair went on to win easily from

Frigate, who had made up an extraordinary amount of ground, after being carried out (she won the National the following year). When I had picked myself up I first thought of the advice Captain Machell had once given me. He said that at the end of a long steeplechase, even if winning easily, a jockey should never let his horse down but drive him at his last fences.

There were two stories told about me over this fall, which were amusing and both equally untrue. In my fall I lost my whip which I was very fond of, and I kept walking round and round looking for it. Not finding it, I walked back to the fence, thinking I might have dropped it when my horse hit the fence, for he fell some lengths beyond it. Garrett Moore, who was always the first man to go and pick up a fallen jockey, or do any other good-natured action, thought that I had got concussion from the way I was walking round. Instead of that he found that I was not in the least hurt, but only looking for my whip, and on our way home we came across it, thrown an almost incredible distance from where I had fallen. My brother Durham, who was on the stand, declared that I was walking to the canal to throw myself in, and that Garrett Moore had saved me from suicide. The other story was that dear old Jenkins, who trained Savoyard, many times told people that I had lost my head and driven the horse wildly at the fence. I wish I had, all would then have been well.

Ringlet, the mare who had shown such a bold front in the race, belonged to Lord Rodney. He was one of Machell's young men, a good-looking dashing fellow, but headstrong and obstinate.

The next day Ringlet was engaged in the Champion Stakes, and Lord Rodney wanted to run her. The Captain was much against this, as she had had a hard race in the National, but Rodney would have his own way. There were only three runners, the mare, with Tom Skelton up, Johnny Longtail, ridden by Dollery, and Chancellor, with Willie Moore. Rodney, who had been having a bad time, went up and down the rails laying seven to four on his mare. I watched the race with him. I had forgotten my glasses, and, as the three horses came on to the race-course with Ringlet just leading, he gave me his, saying he could not see through them as his hands were shaking so. Ringlet looked an almost certain winner, jumping the last fence, but her effort in the National told its tale, and Johnny Longtail wore her down, beating her a length.

This was practically the end of Lord Rodney on the Turf. Game as a pebble when the race was over, he showed no sign that he was badly hit. His racing career was short, but brilliant. It was only the previous year that he had won the St. Leger with Kilwarlin, and the Cesarewitch with Humewood, and a great deal of money on each occasion, and yet he was a loser on the year.

Tom Skelton, who rode Ringlet, was a jockey I was very fond of. A good-looking, delicate man, with a slight, graceful figure, he had not great strength, but the hands of an angel, and the determination of a devil. He was, perhaps, an even greater artist over hurdles than he was over fences, although, owing to his fearless character, his services were much in request at Liverpool. He once knocked me over the rails in a race at Four Oaks Park when I was riding a horse called Freeny, belonging to Harry Hungerford. He was making running, and coming round the turn he just left room for me to get through, but on seeing this he came back quickly, and over I went. I was knocked out for some time and Tom was most remorseful, but at the same time humorous. "What else could I do?" said he. "If you had got through you would have beaten that horse in our stable, and we were all up to our necks on it." Shortly afterwards, he made amends, for, when again riding Freeny, I was behind Tom on the rails in a race at Warwick. When his horse was beaten, he pulled out, and I slipped through and just scrambled home from some horse belonging to old Alec Taylor.

I HAVE KNOWN

When Tom was quite a boy, he had a fall at some small meeting, breaking his leg rather badly. Having few friends at the time, no money, and being almost unknown, he was left at a small hotel with no one to look after him. Ted Wilson, hearing of this, fetched him away, took him home and cared for him until he was able to resume his profession. Tom walked with a limp for the rest of his life, but he never forgot Wilson's kindness, was devoted to him and would do anything for him. They both rode a good deal for the two Nottingham bookmakers, Bob Howett and Charles Hibbert. These two were about the most dashing bettors in the ring, ready either to back a horse or lay him for any amount of money. Full of fun and chaff, although keen men of business, they both added much to the lighter side of racing. Both were fine judges of form and horses, and Charles Hibbert would put away more champagne than any man of his time, but although it made him bet like blazes he never lost his keen judgment.

In later years Mr. James de Rothschild was an adversary after his own heart, and, when they began tilting against each other, the fun and betting would be fast and furious. Bob Howett, was, I should say, the most popular man in the ring; a real good bluff cheery Englishman. His racing colours were the Union Jack—typical of the man.

But to return for a moment to the unlucky Savoyard. I rode him once more in the National in 1889. Again we fancied him very much. Mr. Jenkins told me to keep on the extreme right of the course until we came to Bechers Brook the first time, for he argued that it was the safest place, horses rarely refusing to the right.

At the second fence, however, a mare called Merry Maiden, ridden by Captain Lee Barber, ran clean up the fence to the right, and I knocked her over and fell myself. The race was won by the gallant little Frigate, ridden by Tommy Beasley; she at last came into her own, beating Why Not, with Charlie Cunningham up, and a wonderful field, including such horses as Roquefort, Gamecock, Voluptuary, Glenthorpe, and Bellona.

If Savoyard had not fallen with me in the National of 1888 I should have brought off a good treble, by winning that race, the National Hunt, and the big steeplechase in Paris. It was unfortunate that the most important of the three did not come off.

That year the National Hunt was run very late in the Spring, at Sandown, on April 14th, in Epsom week. A curious old Lancashire sportsman, Mr. Townley Parker, who always had a useful horse or two, asked me to ride a four-year-old, called Glenthorpe, in this race. I said I would do so if I could ride him a gallop over fences and liked him. So one night I went down to stay with the old gentleman, and the next morning, after an infernally long drive, I arrived on the training ground, only to be told that the horse had done his work and gone home. Naturally I was in a furious rage, caught the first train back to London, and sent a message to Townley Parker saying I would not ride his horse. He wrote back begging me to change my mind, and saying that his trainer had done this on purpose, as he wanted to ride himself, and that he would not run the horse unless I rode him. Two things induced me to reconsider my decision. Townley Parker, though an eccentric, crusty old man, had always been very kind to me and Glenthorpe was got by Glendale, a good horse which had belonged to my father, and had been one of my idols when I was a boy. But there was now no time to have a ride on the horse before the race, and as he had only run once, and then over hurdles, I did not care much about the job.

Being a four-year-old, his weight was 10st. 10lb., which meant hard work for me if I was to ride in a decent saddle. On the morning of the race I went for a walk in Hyde Park to get off some more weight, and while doing this I was seized with an attack of cramp in my side, which completely doubled me up. The late Baron Max de Tuyll, who was with me, put me into a cab, and when I got home a doctor was fetched, who, with fomentations and massage, got me sound again.

When I got to Sandown, I was told that Townley Parker was ill, and had sold his horse to the brothers Oliver and "Wengy" Jones. So I went to Willie Moore, who always rode for them, and said, "You had better ride this horse, I am not fit." Now Willie, at times, was a very cantankerous fellow, and he told me to go to the devil, and that he would not take on my "leavings." After this, I had to make the best of it. Arthur Coventry lent me his saddle, the best light saddle that ever was made. All told, it was under 4lb., and at the same time very comfortable.

I had never seen Glenthorpe, and, when I first set eyes on him in the Paddock, I was delighted. He was a beautiful chestnut horse, full of quality, and with glorious shoulders; but on closer inspection I found, to my disgust, that he had a great long-cheeked double bridle on—my pet aversion for steeplechasing. I wanted to change it, but was told that you could not hold him in anything else. When I got up on the horse he was very excitable and nervous. In those days we always had to jump a preliminary fence before starting. Why on earth this excellent practice has been done away with I cannot imagine. It is far better for the public, the riders, and the horses. But on this occasion my horse refused to go near the fence, and eventually I went down to the Post wishing Townley Parker and Glenthorpe at the bottom of the sea. Even when we got there, for some time he refused to go near his horses, but eventually, with two tremendous fly jumps, we got off. He dashed at the first fence, with his head in the air, completely out of hand, and he hit it so hard that it nearly turned him round, but he was too well balanced to fall. This sobered him; he dropped his head, and from that moment till the end of the race I had the most glorious ride. He stood right away from his fences, and I don't think touched one throughout the four miles. He won in a hack canter by six lengths, from Hidden Mystery (who afterwards proved to be a brilliant horse), ridden by Tommy Beasley, with one of the best fields that ever ran for the National Hunt behind him.

I am blowing my own trumpet, but Garrett Moore, who took the horse back to train after Sandown, paid me this compliment, "I don't know how you ever got that horse round Sandown," he said, " for he does not know even the A B C of jumping." As a matter of fact, the secret was this : he was a bold, impetuous, hard-pulling young horse, and by an accident, I found the comfortable spot in his mouth, and took care never to lose it, letting him look after his fences himself. He was a smashing good horse, and, but for breaking down in the National, he would certainly have won that race the following year.

Just before Sandown, at the Manchester April Meeting, I rode a horse called Parasang. He was a great, raking, bay gelding, who had shown some fairly good form, and was the joint property of Roddy Owen and Ronnie Moncrieff. Curiously enough, he also ran in a big double bridle, being a very hard puller. Although I won the race fairly comfortably, he was not a pleasant ride, for after going two miles he got his mouth set against his bit, and had a dead pull on me, which I hated. That night in London, the joint owners told me that they were going to make a raid on Paris and win the big steeplechase with Parasang.

Later in the month he ran in a hurdle race and did badly. The Paris Steeplechase at that time was a handicap, and when the weights came out Parasang had 10 st. 10 lb. Shortly afterwards, Roddy Owen had a bad fall, and he asked me to ride the horse in Paris. I thought the horse was not speedy enough for the course, and also remarked how badly he had run in the hurdle race. The confederates winked rather mysteriously, said the form was all wrong, and that he would win in Paris, so I agreed to ride.

After my experience on him at Manchester, I was sure that I could never get him round that twisting Auteuil course in a double bridle, so I persuaded Mr. Jenkins, who trained the horse at Upton, to let me ride him in a snaffle, and, although he still pulled very hard, I found him much easier to ride.

That year the race was run in the week between Epsom and Ascot. The partners made my life a burden to me, for if they saw me eating strawberries and cream, drinking a glass of champagne, or smoking a cigarette, they said I was throwing the race away. First thing in the morning Roddy would be in my room and would take me for a walk round the Park, and then make me punch a football.

However, we arrived in Paris the day before the race —all of us stone-broke, my friends full of confidence, and I, though I did not fancy the horse, fitter than I had ever been in my life.

On the morning of the race I still had another pound to get off, so we started for a walk in the Bois about seven o'clock. I remember that even at that early hour it was terribly hot, and there was none of the usual difficulty in getting that last pound off. As the day went on the heat became almost tropical. They said it was the hottest day there had been for twenty years. I remember when driving to the races the sun was so scorching that we had to pull the leather apron over our legs, as it fairly burnt through our trousers. I rode in the two races before the big event. I won the first on a horse of Baron Max de Tuyll's, called Bolero. Max, as a rule, was not a big speculator, but on this occasion, having had a very festive *déjeuner*, he had £1,000 on at two to one. In the next race I was third. When I went to scale for the big race, fit as I was, the sweat was running off me in streams, and I would have given anything for a long drink, but dared not take it on account of my weight. Hot as I was, Roddy and Ronnie were even worse, and, what with excitement and their black coats and tall hats, their collars were already disappearing. They tried to make me back the horse, but, in spite of the mysterious winks over the hurdle race,

I really could not fancy him, and only had £5 on for luck. When we got to the post I noticed one thing, that, while the sweat was pouring off all the other horses, my old skin of a gelding was comparatively cool.

There is not much to tell of the early stages of the race, except that it was one of those rare occasions when everything went exactly as I wished, and, although my horse was pulling very hard, he jumped those little fences as quick as lightning, and was as handy as a polo pony. After two miles, so strong and well was he going that I went to the front, and I could soon hear the other jockeys clicking and driving their horses behind me. Three fences from home the French mare Fierté drew up to me and soon took the lead, but she was going all out, and I still had something in reserve. Half-way between the last two fences, to my delight, I saw her tail go, and her jockey take his whip up. At the last fence she was a length in front of me, but here came the value of the Upton schooling, for, tired as he was, Parasang jumped it to perfection, and I landed at her girths. In another fifty yards both horses were as dead as stones. I hit mine once, but got no response, so put my whip down, whereas my opponent kept on pasting his poor mare for all he was worth. A hundred yards from home I knew I had won the race, for Parasang had got his head in front, and I was sure the mare had not another effort left in her, and so we passed the post. The verdict was a head, but I think it was a good long neck.

When we pulled up I never saw two horses so distressed. After I had weighed in and Parasang was being taken away he collapsed completely and fell down. I think this was the result of the terrific heat. He never got over that race, and never ran again, and I believe it was the same with Fierté. I certainly had to thank Roddy for his strict watch over me, his walks and his punching of the football, for being able to last home myself.

Parasang had pulled so hard at first that two fingers

of my right hand were cut to the bone, and on the following Wednesday I had to ride with my hand bandaged and in a thick glove. I again won the first race of the day on Bolero, then the property of a Frenchman, Max de Tuyll having sold him. I then rode Bellona in the hurdle race. She was a mare that would run longer under the whip than any I have ever ridden, but, owing to my bandaged hand, I dropped mine at the critical moment, and she only finished third. I believe she might have won.

One of the French papers described me as a young millionaire who rode for pleasure. The first part of this statement was certainly far from the truth, but until the myth was exploded I found myself extremely popular with a certain class of ladies in Paris.

Ronnie Moncrieff, who was a brother of the three celebrated beauties, Georgina Lady Dudley, Lady Helen Forbes and Lady Mordaunt, was one of the most attractive and gallant fellows I have ever known. He could do all things well—was a fine cricketer, a good rider, a splendid shot and a cool, bold gambler. Like many men of those days, he lived a reckless life, too fast and too good to last. When he had money he would give it to anyone who needed it, but when he had not he had to get it. On one occasion Charles Kinsky had lost a large sum of money on Saturday night. The year before, having got into serious financial difficulties, his father had paid up for him and Charles had promised, whatever happened, never to go to the Jews again. This time, the money having been lost on Saturday night, there was no time to get into communication with his father in Austria before the following Monday, when the money was due. The aid of that great saviour of gamblers, Mr. Sam Lewis, being thus debarred, there he was on Monday morning at his wits' end to know how to get the money.

Walking down Piccadilly he saw Ronnie Moncrieff driving in a hansom cab. He stopped him and said, " Can you tell of any money-lender who is not a Jew, as I must have £4,000 to-day?" "Yes," said Ronnie, and, pulling out £4,000 in notes, "here you are. I am a Scotchman; pay me back when you like." Ronnie had had a good week, and was just coming back from Tattersalls, where he had collected the money himself.

That year in Paris I first made the acquaintance of one of my best and dearest friends, Monsieur A. du Bos. My readers who have been racing in France any time during the last thirty years will probably know him well, for he has always been the first man to help an Englishman to have a good time in Paris. For very many years he has been one of the leading men in the French racing world, and much of the great success of the Auteuil Steeplechase Course has been due to his energy and clever brains. Du Bos, equally at home in social and Bohemian circles, when you got in touch with him, would show you the best of both. With all his love of gaiety and pleasure, no shrewder man of business ever stepped. Now a very old man, although broken by the tragedies of the war and the death of his gallant son, he is still there to give a ready welcome to his English friends.

The Grand Prix of that year was won by a French horse called Stuart, beating Mr. R. C. Vyner's Crowberry, a rather moderate horse, who had been second to Ayrshire in the Derby.

The three-year-olds of 1888, with the exception of Ayrshire and Sea Breeze, who won the Oaks and St. Leger, were not a very good lot. Ayrshire up to a mile and a quarter was a good horse, but, although he won the Derby easily, he did not really stay, and, good stallion as he was, his stock were more successful in short races than long ones.

Sea Breeze was the property of Lord Calthorpe. I think he bought her from the Duchess of Montrose. Royally bred by Isonomy out of St. Marguerite, she was a beautiful chestnut mare, with lovely quality. Second in the One Thousand to Briar Root, she turned the tables on the latter in the Oaks. Later in the year

I HAVE KNOWN

she trained into a good mare, and, starting second favourite for the St. Leger, she won easily, with the favourite, Ayrshire, unplaced. The following week they met again in a £10,000 race at Manchester, run over seven furlongs. Over a course more suited to him, Ayrshire ran her to three parts of a length, with a big field behind them. In this race the French horse, Le Sancy, who came over with a big reputation, ran well, finishing third. He was a grey horse, well turned and full of quality, with the beautiful head and neck which his grandson, The Tetrarch, has inherited from him, and which he in his turn has transmitted to many of his stock.

Sea Breeze ran once more in the Newmarket Oaks, and that race nearly ended in a tragedy. She was opposed only by a mare called Bellatrix, belonging to my brother Durham. Now Bellatrix was a big brown mare by Ben Battle. When she was a two-year-old, the celebrated horse dentist, Loeffler, had been doing her teeth. He told Alfred Sadler, who was training for my brother, that he considered her a curiously nervous mare, that she was afraid of other horses, and would never run in a big field, but that she was in reality very game.

The mare never having shown any signs of nervousness, and being always very quiet and sober, we thought this was only one of Loeffler's yarns, which he was rather fond of spinning. Up to this time she had not appeared on a race-course, but had been tried to be pretty good. To make a long story short, she ran time after time without making the slightest show in a race, until at last she met the great Sea Breeze, at 14 lb., over the "middle miles" at Newmarket. Odds of twenty to one were laid on Sea Breeze, with Robinson up; Rickaby rode Bellatrix.

A certain French sportsman laid £20,000 to £1,000 on the favourite. The race finished at the Bushes, and, as was the fashion in those days, we, many of us, rode down to see Sea Breeze canter home. Half a mile from home it looked all the twenty to one on, for Rickaby had his whip up, but Bellatrix hung on and kept pulling out a little bit more. Two furlongs from the post, Robinson began to get uneasy, and then there took place one of the most desperate struggles I have ever seen. For the last furlong they ran head and head, the mares racing with unflinching gameness. It ended in a short head victory for Sea Breeze, nearly causing the death of the French sportsman, whose name I cannot remember. Captain Machell told me that it fairly broke Sea Breeze's heart, and she was never any good again.

Bellatrix, on the contrary, came home quite undisturbed, and apparently did not feel the race at all, but three weeks afterwards, when meeting a bad field for the Liverpool St. Leger, she faded out of the race absolutely at the first turn after getting a slight bump.

How can you account for the vagaries of horses, and still less for Loeffler's extraordinary insight into the character of this mare, who up to that time had shown no signs of nervousness?

THE HON. GEORGE LAMBTON IN 1886

Photo: Clarence Hailey

MR. ARTHUR COVENTRY ON HIS HACK, WHEN HE WAS A STARTER

From the painting by Allen C. Sealy

JOHN PORTER

CHAPTER XIV

CHARLIE CUNNINGHAM—JOHN CORLETT—
ABINGTON BAIRD

"It's all d——d rot, I don't talk Scotch," were words that often came out of the mouth of that great North Country sportsman, Charlie Cunningham, who lived near Kelso, on the borders of Northumberland and Scotland, where he trained his own horses. A big, lean fellow, six foot two, as fine a figure of a man as you could want to see, he was hard to beat at any form of sport. He had many warm friends and some enemies, for he had a very fiery, excitable temper, which was continually getting him into hot water. But he was so amusing, so frank and outspoken, that his rows generally ended in a laugh and good humour. He was the easiest of men to "get a rise out of," and his friends were always pulling his leg. When he got excited, he relapsed into broad Scotch; we used to mimic him, and then out would come the words I have quoted.

He was one of the strongest and most resolute horsemen I have ever seen. Perhaps he had not the best of hands, and horses pulled hard with him, but he was at his best when striding along in front over a big country. His weight precluded him from riding much, except in hunters' flat races, but in these he carried all before him, especially in the North. He and Tom Spence, of Beverley, were great rivals. Tom was the opposite to Charlie, being a little dapper man, very particular about his appearance, either on a horse or off one; a splendid jockey, better on the flat and over hurdles than over fences. In one respect he was like Charlie, he had the same fiery, quick temper. I have seen them, on pulling up after a close finish, continue their battle with their whips up against each other. Of course, like every other steeplechase rider, Charlie's ambition was to win the Grand National, but, his ordinary weight being over 12 stone, this was not easy to accomplish. In 1889 he made an heroic attempt to achieve the impossible. His friend, Mr. D. J. Jardine, had Why Not in the National with 11st. 5lb. Charlie had won many races on this horse, and he set about the task of getting down to the weight. How he managed it heaven only knows, but he did so, and, in a field of twenty starters, made nearly all the running, and was only beaten after a gallant struggle by Frigate, with Tommy Beasley up. I believe his defiance of nature laid the seeds of the disease which killed him a few years later.

Twice more did he try to win the National on Why Not. In 1890, with 12st. 4lb. he finished fifth, after falling; this race was a chapter of accidents and many fell. Then again in 1891 did he ride this good horse. The National of that year was an extraordinarily interesting race. In the field there were no less than four previous winners, Roquefort, Ilex, Gamecock, and Voluptuary, added to these Why Not, who had been second to Frigate, and the great raking Cloister, who had already shown that he was a typical Liverpool horse. The favourite was Comeaway, an Irish horse, who had been carrying all before him, and was said by the Irish division to be "walking over." He had the redoubtable Harry Beasley for his jockey. Cloister all his life had suffered from indifferent jockeyship, but now he was to be ridden by Roddy Owen. Trained by Dick Marsh, he had done a splendid preparation, and Newmarket was full of confidence. There was one fly in the ointment, Roddy had hurt his leg, so that he was not able to do the hard work necessary for him to be quite at his best, for, like some horses, he himself wanted a strenuous preparation.

Come Away, Ilex, Why Not, and Cruiser Arc, who was ridden by Tommy Beasley, had not been seen in public that year, and yet they were the four best-backed horses in the race, and six furlongs from home they were all in the fight. Come Away was the property of a young Irishman, Willie Jameson. He and his two brothers were less known in the racing world than in other realms of sport, such as big game shooting, fishing, hunting and yachting. Willie himself was a famous yachtsman, and I believe was as good at that game as his jockey, Harry Beasley, was over fences. He sailed the Prince of Wales's Britannia in many of her famous races. I once had the good luck to be with him on one of these occasions, when he completely "out-jockeyed," or whatever the nautical term may be, his opponents.

Now Come Away was a really magnificent bay horse, and his looks and condition thoroughly justified his favouritism, yet it was no secret that he had a leg which had been causing considerable trouble.

Why Not looked a picture, and filled the eye more than he had ever done before. Ilex, Gamecock, Cruiser Arc, Roquefort, any one of them looked good enough to win, but the latter had not his old pilot, E. P. Wilson. What occurred in the early stages of the race I cannot quite remember, but my impression is that Why Not was always more or less in front. Anyhow, about five furlongs from home, Why Not on the inside, Cloister next to him, and Come Away on the outside, were racing together. So well was Why Not going that it really looked as if Charlie was at last going to bring it off, but coming to the last fence Roddy did not give him too much room, and Why Not came down a fearful crash, he himself being badly hurt. This left Come Away just in the lead, with Cloister creeping up on the inside. Harry Beasley, fearing that his horse's leg would give way, rode very tenderly. A hundred yards from home Roddy drove his horse up to Come Away's girth, but now it was his turn to be squeezed for room, and he could not improve on his position, the favourite getting home cleverly by half a length. After the race Roddy lodged an objection, but it was overruled, and I think rightly.

Charles Greenwood, of the "Daily Telegraph," that best of racing journalists, described the finish of the race most aptly. "Harry had the Captain in the same position as a man with a cork half-way in the neck of a bottle ; one little push and it will go down." I am sure Harry Beasley will forgive me for saying it, but if it had been needful that push would have been given.

After the race, before the objection was gone into, there was the deuce of a row in the weighing room ; the excited Irish Division surrounding Roddy, declaring they would have his blood. I can see him now, with his back to the wall, cool as a cucumber, saying, " All right, but wait till it's settled, then I will fight every one of you, single handed or the whole lot of you together." But hot as the blood was for the moment, there was no ill-feeling left by the next day.

Charlie Cunningham was probably already a doomed man before the race, and he never really got over this fall. George Williamson, afterwards to become the greatest steeplechase jockey of his day, told me that he sat up with him all that night, and more than once thought he was going out, but his pluck and grit pulled him through. Many of my readers must remember him in the few years he lived after this, gallantly struggling, without a word of complaint, against an incurable disease.

I missed him terribly, racing myself. In all the years I knew him we only once fell out, and that was at Ludlow. We were both riding in the last race of the Meeting, and the going was so fearfully heavy the horses could hardly stand up. In the field, coming to the last fence, there was a narrow path, which afforded comparatively sound going, and whoever got first on to it had an enormous advantage. In our race, a long way from home, it became a match between Charlie and myself, and we were both determined to have the path. After a desperate struggle I got it, but in doing this we had both nearly ridden our horses to a standstill. Mine was a great, tall, leggy horse, 17 hands high, belonging to the Duke of Portland.

Owing to everyone in the previous races having gone for this particular place, the fence at this spot was nearly knocked flat, but even then it was too much for my exhausted giraffe. Down he came, and there he lay with me quite unhurt, but unable to get from under him. As I lay there I saw my friend Charlie, on his equally exhausted horse, creeping through a gap the wrong side of the flag. I waited till he was well through and going for home, when I shouted to him to come back and jump the fence. At that moment my horse struggled up, and as I was scrambling on to him, Charlie pulled up and said, " You'll not object to me, I only missed the fence to avoid jumping on you." " That won't do," said I, " there was plenty of room to jump to my left." " D—n—d if there was," said Charlie, " you were in the only gap, and look at my bl—dy horse," and so we crawled past the Post in animated conversation. I ought to mention there was a very long run in from the last fence which could not be well seen from the Stands. When I got into the Weighing Room, I objected to the winner for going the wrong side of the flag, adding that Mr. Cunningham had admitted it. " I admit nothing," shouted the irate Charlie, " but if I hadn't done it I'd have jumped on you, and next time I'll do it and kill you," a speech which was received with roars of laughter, and I got the race.

To his last day Charlie always said I had behaved like a cad over this and I am not sure that he wasn't right !

. . . . .

On looking at the old Racing Calendar of that Liverpool Meeting I find that I rode two winners, both of them on the Flat, and they bring to my mind two well-known characters of that time, John Corlett, Editor of the "Sporting Times," and " Mr. Abington," the assumed name of a young Scotch millionaire, Mr. Baird.

The first of my winners was a horse called William the Silent, owned and trained by Joe Cannon. He had originally belonged to John Corlett. Now John, as became his jovial ruddy complexion, was as cheery an optimist as ever went racing, and while he was his property William the Silent was always tipped in the "Pink 'un" for every race that he ran in. He was always beaten, and I think his continual defeats half broke the theatrical profession, who were devoted adherents of John Corlett and his newspaper. Joe Cannon and I were always on the look-out for some disappointing flat race-horse for jumping, and when at last John Corlett, in disgust, said he would get rid of this hopeless rogue, Joe bought him for £150. After he had had the horse a short time he found that he was not the arch-thief that he was painted, but a poor, weak, shivering creature, who had had his heart broken in trying to live up to a false reputation. With kindness and patience Joe restored courage to this really honest but moderate horse, and after he had run in three or four races and found that he was not going to be flogged when he was beaten he became as true as steel.

The first time he won for us was in a hurdle race on Easter Monday, at Kempton. I rode him myself, and between the last two hurdles we were in the struggle with four or five horses. William, thinking of the whip, began to drop out, but finding that nothing disagreeable was going to happen to him, suddenly took heart of grace, caught hold of his bit and went on to win in a canter. Never again did he do wrong; and this is the history of many a supposed rogue.

Old John Corlett was a notable figure on the Turf at that time. I knew him pretty well. He liked to be well posted with information about horses, but I don't think the betting and financial side of racing concerned him greatly, although he would have his fifty pounds on when the mood took him. He was the best of good company, a wonderful raconteur, with a marvellous memory, and his leading articles on Turf matters were delightful reading. He could sit up all night drinking port and come up smiling next morning. But he had another side to his nature, for I happen to know he was one of the best and kindest men that ever lived, and in his own home at Head Corn, or "Bottom Barley" as it was called, he was loved by man, woman and child.

Now Mr. Abington was quite a different personality. Left with a large fortune early in life, and with no one to look after him, he was an easy prey to the hangers-on of the rich. He was a tall slim young man, built for riding, with a figure something like Fred Archer's. Fond of horses, and with money to burn, he soon was the owner of a big string, and after a time became a very capable jockey. He was a good judge of horses, but a d———d bad one of men, and was surrounded by the worst crowd in Europe. Once that lot gets hold of a man they never let go. Poor Baird, I often felt sorry for him; he was not a bad fellow at heart, and good-natured to a fault. He made one or two attempts to break loose from his surroundings, and on one occasion I thought he was going to succeed.

In his keenness to ride winners he bought horses all over the country, and although he had installed Charles Morton at Bedford Lodge as his private trainer he had many horses in other stables.

Charles Morton, as usual, made a success of the job he undertook, but after a time, finding the life and entourage at Bedford Lodge too much for him, he resigned.

Baird was very keen on prize-fighting. Now there are two classes of people who go in for this game, one a good sporting lot of Englishmen, the other a crowd of the greatest ruffians in the world. Amongst the former, Joe Cannon was an enthusiastic devotee, and he there became acquainted with Baird. When Morton gave up, Baird asked him to take his place, which he agreed to do. So Joe was installed at Bedford Lodge with a real good stable of horses, and for a time all went well. Baird had not only a great respect for his trainer, but a wholesome fear of him besides, for Joe was a man who would stand no nonsense, but spoke his mind freely. The first year was very successful. They won a great many races, including the Dewhurst Plate, with Meddler, the best two-year-old of his year, with the exception of Isinglass. Baird was taking great interest in his horses, and I remember him telling Arthur Coventry and myself that he was never going back to the gang which had so nearly ruined him. But when the racing was over, having nothing to do, he got amongst his old associates again in London. It came to Joe Cannon's ears that he intended going to America with a party of these people, a very rough and undesirable lot. Joe told me that he was sure if he did this he would never return, and he instantly went up to London to try and prevent it. On arriving at his house he found Baird in a deplorable condition from the life he was leading. He was, however, overjoyed to see Joe, and begged him to rescue him from these surroundings, promising to return with him to Newmarket. Joe left the house for a short time to make some arrangements, and that was the last he ever saw of Baird, for when he returned it was too late. He could not get into the house for the gang did not mean to let their prey escape. Baird went to America, and, as Joe had so truly prophesied, he never returned, and died there that winter.

CHAPTER XV

LORD RANDOLPH CHURCHILL—JOHN PORTER—
THE DUKE OF WESTMINSTER

As I look back upon the past there are certain people I have known who, on account of their strong characters and great qualities stand out very clearly in my memory. There is an old saying, " On the Turf and under it all men are equal." This cannot perhaps be argued convincingly, but there is no question that the glamour of the Turf is far reaching and is felt by all sorts and conditions of men. Nowhere, I think, do they show more truly or more quickly what their real character is, according to the way they meet success or failure.

Princes and politicians, soldiers and sailors, the working man and the millionaire, all go to swell the ranks of the racing community, all have a common interest in the winner of the Derby.

Before my mind, at the moment, is the memory of a particularly vivid and brilliant personality, that of the late Lord Randolph Churchill. When Lord Randolph announced that he was sick of politics and was going to turn his attention to racing, it caused some sensation in Turf circles.

In 1887, he began buying yearlings, which he placed under the care of Bob Sherwood, who was not only a good trainer but an extra good judge of a yearling. He launched out very freely and one day his friend Sir Frederick Johnstone told him that he was not rich enough to race on such a large scale, and that he would be broke. Randolph laughed, and replied, " Nearly all you people who go racing are fools, and no really clever man has ever taken it up seriously, but now that

I have done so I shall succeed." His words nearly came true.

In his early life, Lord Randolph had been too much occupied with politics to take much interest in racing, but he had always been very fond of hunting. I first met him in Leicestershire, hunting with the Cottesmore. He was very keen on hounds, saying, " I go out hunting not to jump fences, but to see hounds work," and although, when hounds checked, Randolph, who had a wonderfully good eye for country, always mysteriously turned up, we came to look upon him as a man who was afraid to jump. But one day, when, towards the end of a good gallop in Fernie's country, we saw him sailing over a great big black fence with an ox-rail on the far side, we changed our opinion. Someone said to him, " Hallo ! Randolph, what on earth were you doing ? " " Well," he replied, " there was no gate, so what else could I do but jump the d——d fence if I wanted to see hounds run into their fox."

That was typical of the man, for, when once he had made up his mind what he wanted to do, no obstacle would turn him from it.

To return to his racing, as he had jokingly prophesied, he quickly made his mark, collected a nice stud of horses, and won many races, including the Oaks, the Hunt Cup, the Manchester Cup, and the Portland Plate, with a very good mare called " L'Abbesse de Jouarre."

He took tremendous interest in his horses and really loved them ; when he went round stables his pockets were bulging with apples and sugar, and his favourite was the Abbesse. I remember going with him to see her when she had gone out of training and was at Mr. Lacy's stud at Borough Green near Newmarket. When we arrived we went first to look at some mares and foals, and Randolph began talking. Suddenly we heard the most tremendous hullabaloo going on in a box a little farther down the yard, something kicking, squealing and neighing like the devil. " Good God," said Lacy, " that is your mare ; there must be something wrong with her." Out he dashed followed by Randolph and myself, opened the door of the box, expecting to find some tragedy, but instead of that the old Abbesse came rushing at Randolph like a dog, trying to put her nose into his pocket for sugar and apples; he had not forgotten them, and, being a most emotional man, tears rolled down his cheeks. What memories horses have. Randolph had not seen the mare for nearly twelve months, and yet the sound of his voice in the yard was enough.

On another occasion I travelled down from London to Newmarket with him. He told me that he had running in the first race a very promising two-year-old, of which Sherwood had a very high opinion. We arrived just in time to see the horses going out of the paddock, and met Sherwood, who told him that the horse was still backward, but that he expected him to beat all except the favourite. Rickaby was riding, and was told not to be hard on the horse if he could not win.

We watched the race together. The favourite was always going like a winner, but coming out of the dip Rickaby made his effort, and for a few strides his horse looked to have a winning chance, and, though beaten, put up a very promising performance.

Randolph was delighted; rushed off to the paddock, and went up to Rickaby as he was riding in, saying, "Well, how did he run?" Rickaby had a good look at the questioner and replied, "What the hell is that to do with you?" Randolph was furious, and told Sherwood, "Don't you ever put up that jockey again." Sherwood assured him that Rickaby did not know who he was, and Sir Frederick Johnstone, who overheard the conversation, chipped in with, "Of course, with that old hat and coat of yours he took you for a tout." But it was not till half-way through a good dinner that night that he became mollified, and then enjoyed the joke more than anyone.

Sherwood was a very clever trainer, and devoted to his master. I am sure that their success would have continued, though I rather doubt whether Randolph's racing had been financially as satisfactory as he anticipated. When bad health, which for long he struggled against bravely, at last forced him to give up racing, he was a great loss to the Turf, and certainly to me personally, because, although I was a good deal younger, I found him the most delightful of racing companions ; his wonderful charm, his quickness, his love of horses, even his changeable moods, had made me deeply attached to him.

Bob Sherwood was a fine fellow, a most kind-hearted and generous man, with a very quick and fiery temper. He used to be very severe on his jockeys when they did not win on some horse that he fancied.

I remember once, at Lewes, Tom Cannon, who frequently rode for him, throwing his saddle into the corner of the weighing room and exclaiming, " You ride your horses yourself : I won't." But the storm blew over quickly, and he was riding for him again the next day. His son, the present Robert Sherwood, has these same characteristics, and is well known to be the most hospitable and generous man in Newmarket.

. . . . . .

At the time of Lord Falmouth's retirement from racing the Duke of Westminster was already challenging him for supremacy on the Turf, and in the year following the yellow and black cap of the Duke, with Archer in the saddle, or the " Boy in Yellow," as the public termed him, took the place of the magpie colours of Lord Falmouth.

The Duke was a tall, distinguished-looking man, with rather an ascetic cast of countenance, reserved and self-contained, but, when he chose, with a wonderful charm of manner. A beautiful horseman himself, I question if there was ever a man with greater knowledge of breeding, racing, the training and riding of horses.

With him there was no chopping and changing of trainers and jockeys with every wind that blew. He went for the best, and he got it, and when a horse of his, trained by John Porter and ridden by Archer or Morny Cannon, came out for a big race, they carried the confidence and money of the public. On these occasions, the Duke appeared to be the most unconcerned man on the course, but that his appearance belied his real feelings I think the following story will show.

In 1899 Flying Fox, with Morny Cannon up, started a hot favourite for the Two Thousand. The horses were at the Post and as soon as the starting flag went up (this was before the days of the starting gate) Flying Fox began to give trouble. Time after time did he bolt out into the country to the left. In those days I have frequently seen a start delayed for thirty minutes or more.

I had a good deal more money than I could afford on Flying Fox, and so hopeless did the prospect of his getting off appear that I had sat down on a seat a little way below the Jockey Club Stand, gloomily thinking of the next Monday. The Duke walked off the Stand and came and sat down beside me, saying, "This is one of the most painful moments of my life." I thought to myself, the way of the rich is easy.

At that moment, the starter and Morny Cannon somehow or other managed to get Flying Fox off, and, as he passed the Post an easy winner, the Duke let out a piercing " View holloa," which re-echoed through the Stands. The shocked amazement of his friends was comical to see. No member of the Jockey Club had ever committed such an atrocity, and I think, after the race, there was as much talk of the Duke's " View holloa " as of the Duke's Flying Fox.

Flying Fox, of course, was a good horse, but I shall always believe him to have been the luckiest horse in the world to have won the Derby. The favourite for the French Derby had been a grey horse called Holocaust, the property of Monsieur de Bremond. Although in this race he was beaten by Perth, good judges in France said he was a great horse ; moreover, he was to be ridden by Tod Sloan, who, although a new-comer, had established a wholesome fear among the English jockeys.

Holocaust, on his arrival at Epsom, did not create a favourable impression, as he was pronounced to be coarse and common, and Flying Fox started a very hot favourite. In the race, when safely round Tattenham Corner, it was evident that it was a match between the two. A quarter of a mile from home Cannon was distinctly uneasy on his horse, while Sloan had never moved ; but in another stride Holocaust fell and broke his leg, leaving the race at the mercy of the Duke of Westminster's horse.

Sloan told me directly after the race that he had got Flying Fox beaten when the accident occurred. Although this coincided with my own view of the race, I had so often heard it said by jockeys that I did not attach too much weight to it.

Now Arthur Coventry, who was then the Jockey Club Starter, was a great admirer of Morny Cannon, and not too partial to Sloan, or to the new style of riding which he had introduced, but when I told him what Sloan had said he remarked, " By God, it's true," adding that he had galloped his hack across the downs and was on the rails just a few yards from the place where Holocaust fell, and in his opinion Sloan had won the race. Arthur Coventry knew Morny Cannon's riding so well that his opinion was most valuable.

I think it is probable that Flying Fox was not a true stayer, and there is no doubt that John Porter was not anxious to train him for the Ascot Cup the following year. If he had been, I believe the horse would not have been sold.

Porter trained more winners of the Derby than any other man. Besides the Duke of Westminster, he at one time trained for King Edward, then Prince of Wales, Lord Alington, Sir Frederick Johnstone, Baron Hirsch, Mr. Gretton and others. Year after year great winners came from Kingsclere. He was the most unassuming of men, practically never betted, a great believer in hard work for men and horses, and, when a horse trained by him came to the front in a race a quarter of a mile from home, it was a rare thing for him to be beaten.

He gave up training, greatly to the regret of all racing people, but he did not give up work, for he put his keenness and energy into the construction and management of Newbury Race-course, the success of which is notable. The great old man died, as he would have wished, in harness, at the age of 83, in January 1923.

To return to his chief patron, the Duke of Westminster, he bred and raced Bend Or, Ormonde, Flying Fox and Shotover, all winners of the Derby, Orme, and innumerable other good horses, and his success continued up to the day of his death. At the sale of his horses, in 1900, that brilliant mare, Sceptre, was sold as a yearling for ten thousand guineas. Great as her performances were, I think if she had remained under the skilful management of John Porter she would probably never have been beaten.

As I have shown, the Duke owned four winners of the Derby, and it was generally supposed that he should have owned a fifth in Orme, who was said to have been poisoned a fortnight before the race. I have often seen this stated as a fact, but I have great doubts myself as to the truth of the story, in spite of all I have read and heard on the subject.

La Flêche, the property of Baron Hirsch, was also trained by John Porter, and she had not been beaten as a two-year-old. Many people thought she would beat Orme, as she, too, was to run for the Derby. When two good horses in different ownership, trained in the same stable, are in a big race, it oftens leads to trouble and jealousy, and on this occasion there was very keen partisanship in the different camps.

When Orme, a fortnight before the race, went badly amiss and was scratched, there was talk of foul play. As usual there were plenty of people who believed the story, and when La Flêche, owing to the bad riding of George Barrett, was beaten for the Derby, there was undisguised satisfaction in certain quarters. As a matter of fact, I believe that Orme suffered from wrong treatment by a veterinary surgeon, who blistered his throat when he was suffering from a poisonous tooth and a disease called horse-pox, which in those days was not well understood, at least that was the opinion of the horse dentist, Mr. Loeffler, who was called in to see him.

Orme recovered sufficiently from the ailment, whatever it was, to win the Eclipse Stakes in July. He and La Flêche were both engaged in the St. Leger, and naturally there was keen rivalry between the supporters of these two three-year-olds.

Orme was ridden by George Barrett and started favourite, but La Flêche, with that good jockey Watts in the saddle, beat him easily.

Orme, like his son Flying Fox, was not a true stayer, but a brilliant horse up to a mile and a quarter. La Flêche was a really good mare and put up a great performance when she won the Cambridgeshire of that year with 8st. 10lb. She won the Ascot Cup two years later, but she was then trained by Dick Marsh, at Newmarket, for, at the end of the season 1893, the Prince of Wales's horses and those of Baron Hirsch left Kingsclere for Newmarket.

Here was the beginning of another of those fine combinations which lead to success. A great owner in the Prince of Wales, a great trainer in Richard Marsh, two fine jockeys in Watts and Jones, with the valuable assistance of Lord Marcus Beresford as manager. The partnership continued to the day of King Edward's death. King George carried it on, and it only terminated on the death of Lord Marcus in 1922.

Common, who won the Two Thousand, the Derby, and the St. Leger for those two patricians of sport, Lord Alington and Sir Frederick Johnstone, was also trained at Kingsclere by John Porter. As my readers will remember, the two partners had won the Derby

CAPTAIN THE HON. CHARLES LAMBTON, D.S.O., AFTERWARDS BRIGADIER GENERAL.

CAPTAIN THE HON. HEDWORTH LAMBTON, AFTERWARDS ADMIRAL OF THE FLEET SIR HEDWORTH MEUX.

LADAS WINNER OF THE DERBY, 1894, WITH THE EARL OF ROSEBERY, MAT DAWSON AND JACK WATTS

Photo: Clarence Hailey

seven years previously with St. Blaise. Common was only once beaten as a three-year-old, and that was by Surefoot, in the Eclipse Stakes, who, when he won this race, was trained by my friend, Garrett Moore.

Got by Wisdom out of Miss Foote, by Galopin, Surefoot was a grand specimen of the thoroughbred. A big massive bay horse, full of the fire and dash characteristic of Galopin. His owner, Archie Merry, was a rich young Scotchman in the Royal Horse Guards, very popular in his regiment and in London society, although, true to the habits of his native country, he did not wear his heart upon his sleeve. Slight and thin in build, he was a great contrast to his trainer, the burly, jovial, Jousiffe, not only in physique but in character, for Jousiffe was the most sanguine of men, and shouted his good things all over the course.

Surefoot came out as a two-year-old in the Woodcote Stakes at Epsom, where he beat a "hotpot" in Lord Calthorpe's Heresy, trained in Machell's stable. His next appearance was on the Tuesday, at Ascot, when he was beaten by the flying little Semolina. The following Thursday he came out again and won the New Stakes. He only ran once again that year, when he beat a moderate field at Goodwood.

His Ascot conqueror, Semolina, was a wonderful little bay filly, by St. Simon out of the speedy Mowerina, the property of the Duke of Portland, then in the heyday of his success. She won thirteen races as a two-year-old, and the following year the One Thousand Guineas, with her stable companion, Memoir, second.

To return to Surefoot, as a three-year-old he made his first appearance in the Two Thousand. Jousiffe told all his friends that the horse was sure to win, having done all that he had asked him. But when he appeared in the Paddock he created by no means a favourable impression, for he looked as big as a bull, and, in appearance and manners, was more like a covering stallion than a race-horse. In spite of this, the opposition being moderate, he started favourite, and confounded his critics by winning with ease. When he came back to the unsaddling enclosure accompanied by his trainer, I don't know which of the two was sweating and blowing the more; both horse and man being highly excited; Jousiffe shouting at people to keep away, and the horse lashing out in all directions. He was then trained for the Derby, and, when the day arrived, was supposed to have come on a lot. But the ordeal of Epsom was too much for him, and he was so upset by the noise and the crowd that he never settled down to racing. With nine to four betted on him, he only finished fourth to Sainfoin, Le Nord and Orwell. In spite of his great bulk, he must have been a very sound, hardy horse, for he ran three times at Ascot, winning one of the Biennials, and being beaten in the Prince of Wales and Hardwicke Stakes; and then, a fortnight later, he won the £10,000 race at Leicester, beating Memoir and a good field. Hard work and racing were getting the beef off him, and he was getting fighting fit, but unfortunately, at the same time, his temper was getting worse. He ran twice more that season, running badly in the St. Leger and the Free Handicap at Newmarket.

I shall always think that the anxiety and excitement of training Surefoot killed poor Jousiffe, who suffered from a weak heart, for he died some time the following spring, and the horse was sent to Garrett Moore to train. His first appearance after this was in the Eclipse Stakes at Sandown, and when he came into the paddock before the race there was a remarkable change, for, instead of the excitable, sweating horse we were accustomed to see, he was walking about quietly and soberly.

When Marcus Beresford saw him he said to Garrett, "How did you do it?" and Garrett replied, "Well, one of us had to be master, and it was not going to be Surefoot."

The Eclipse Stakes at Sandown has been famous for great horses, and interesting races, and on this occasion there was a real good field. Among the runners were the lengthy Common, the French horse Gouverneur, a splendid massive chestnut, who had won the French Two Thousand for Monsieur Blanc, and had also been second to Common for the Derby, the Duke of Portland's Memoir, winner of the previous year's St. Leger, making her first appearance of the season, but said to be in her old form, and several other very smart horses.

There was then, and I think there is still, a considerable feeling of rivalry between the followers of cross-country sport and flat racing, and the steeplechasing lot looked upon Garrett Moore as their champion against all these flat racing " swells." Common was thought by many to be looking lighter than when he had won the Derby, but in spite of that he was a hot favourite, and started at two to one on, with Surefoot at the nice price of a hundred to eight. Half-way up the straight Gouverneur and Common were fighting it out when the great Surefoot stormed past them and won handsomely by a length, and then I am afraid Garrett's friends, myself among them, joined with the Irish Brigade, and made rather an unseemly noise. This was certainly by far the best form Surefoot had ever shown. It was a great feat on the part of Garrett to produce the horse in such grand condition, as he not only had a temper but a suspicious leg as well, and I doubt if any other man could have tamed that fiery spirit without breaking it.

Common did not run again till the St. Leger; he was a strong favourite all the summer, but when he arrived at Doncaster he looked so light, especially over his loins, that no one liked him, and, in spite of his having a very moderate field to beat I felt very nervous about a big bet which I had made. So much so that the evening before the race I asked John Porter if he would advise me to get out or stand it. He made some wise remarks on the folly of betting more than you could afford to lose, but ended up by saying, " Don't worry about Common looking light : he is fit to run for his life and has killed half the horses at Kingsclere." So, although I thought the horse looked half-dead himself I stood the bet. The race gave me some shocks, for Common was never going like a winner, and, when I saw George Barrett get his whip up at the Red House, I gave up all hope, but the horse kept gamely struggling on, wore down one opponent after another, and in the end won by a length. I believe Common to have been a good horse when he won the Two Thousand and the Derby, but I think he had greatly deteriorated when he ran for this race.

CHAPTER XVI

HOLLINGTON AND THE GRAND MILITARY—LORD ROSEBERY
AND LADAS

When the late Lord Londonderry was Lord Lieutenant of Ireland, he used to give a Cup, to be run for at Fairy House, which was called "The Viceroy's Staff Cup." As might be supposed, he had on his staff a real good lot of riding men, and among them was my brother, Captain Charles Lambton.

Charlie was a very good horseman and a first-rate man to hounds, but no one ever looked on him as a race-rider. He always had the knack of picking up a useful sort of horse, and in 1887 he had a little Irish mare called Diana, of whom he had a great opinion. To everyone's surprise, he entered her for the Conyngham Cup at Punchestown, trained her in the Phœnix Park and ran her. Although she got round safely, she naturally did not make any show.

Shortly after this was the race for the Viceroy's Staff Cup, and I remember Lord Londonderry telling me that it was looked upon as a joke, and rather a ridiculous one, to run a hunter against a lot of thoroughbred horses. But Charles had method in his madness, and his school in the Conyngham Cup had done both him and the mare a lot of good. When the Staff Cup was run, he quickly recognized that, though the weights were higher, the pace was far greater than it had been in the other race, so he let the field go, and when he passed the stands the first time round a very long way behind, he came in for a considerable amount of chaff from the spectators. But, continuing his steady gallop, two fences from home he caught a lot of thoroughly beaten horses, and finally won the race by ten lengths. The next year on the same mare, carrying 7 lb. extra, and pursuing the same tactics, he won again, and in 1889 he won on a sister to Diana, called Maid of the Mist, but this time only getting up in a close finish to win by a neck.

I believe that these three successive victories drove the Viceroy's sporting staff nearly mad. They could not understand it, but came to the conclusion that the two mares must have been extraordinarily good to win under such conditions. So much so that, when shortly after Maid of the Mist ran with another jockey up, she started a hot favourite, but finished nowhere. Lord Londonderry was much amused about all this, and said to me, " They may say what they like about your brother, but I believe he is a d——d good jockey."

Captain Whitaker, whom I have mentioned before as the owner of Franciscan, was a brother officer of Charlie's in the Northumberland Fusiliers. He had at that time a five-year-old called Hollington, in training with Joe Cannon. The horse was in the Grand Military, and he decided that Charlie should ride him. Hollington had only won two small races as a four-year-old, but he was much improved, and was going like a good horse at home. Charlie came down to Newmarket to ride him once or twice before the race, and his performances did not inspire confidence, but he himself was satisfied and liked the horse, which was the main thing. There was a real good field for the race, which was run at Sandown, and some first-class men riding—Roddy Owen, Captain Fisher, Eustace Crawley, Mr. Lathom— all good jockeys. Banstead, with Eustace Crawley, was a six-to-four chance, and a brilliant horse, Midshipmite, Roddy Owen up, three to one. But Hollington was so good-looking and had such a reputation at home. that he started at seven to one. Joe Cannon was confident about his horse, but, naturally, not so much so about his jockey.

In the race, when they passed the stands the first time,

having gone about a mile and a half, Hollington was a very long way last, and the story of the Viceroy's Cup passed through my mind. But when they came to the pay-gates, on the far side, and he was still last, with his jockey taking apparently no interest in the race, or riding as if it was five miles instead of three, I gave up all hope. As they turned for home he began to close up, but in very leisurely fashion, and I turned my glasses on to what I thought were the horses likely to be concerned in the finish ; but, as they came to the last fence, Hollington suddenly appeared on the scene, and you could see it was ten to one on him. He swept past and won by five lengths. It was the most extraordinary performance, and I'm hanged if I can understand it any more now than I could then. The general opinion was that Hollington must be a smasher to have won under such disadvantages. But we were wrong, for only once again did this horse ever run such a good race, and then he had the same man on him, when he was third for the Grand Military in 1892, carrying 13 st. 7 lb.

Perhaps I am prejudiced, for he finished my riding days ; but a more unenterprising, sulky brute on a race-course I never rode. Arthur Nightingall and George Williamson tried their hands on him, and, although he won small races, he always failed when asked to do anything more. George Williamson told me only the other day that his first mount in the National was Hollington. When riding him at home Hollington had carried him like a real good horse, and he fancied his chance tremendously, and in a very big field he started at ten to one, but ran very badly. George said Hollington felt like a bit of damp string under him, a different horse altogether from what he was at home. I hate the memory of the horse, for, as I have said, he finished my riding and nearly finished me.

This was in February, 1892, at Sandown, in a three-mile steeplechase, for which he started favourite. After going half-way he was jumping and galloping in such slovenly fashion that I caught hold of him and tried to make him do things a bit quicker, with the result that he entirely disregarded the fence at the pay-gates, taking it by the roots. I fell clear of the horse, but the first thing that hit the ground was my back. For three or four minutes I was in agony, but this went off, and I was able to walk to the stands. For six weeks after this I went about as usual, and even rode a few races, but I was no good, and felt very bad. Eventually inflammation of the spine set in, and I was on my back for months. It is not a pleasant thing to be told you can never ride again or take part in any active form of sport, but that is what happened to me. Fortunately, it turned out to be untrue, although for several years I was more or less of a cripple.

Captain Whitaker won the Grand Military the second time the following March, with the four-year-old, Ormerod. Curiously enough, he also was a rattling good horse, but as soft as butter. It was well known that year that Why Not, with Roddy Owen up, was to go for the race. This took a good deal of interest from it, for what chance had the ordinary soldier to find a horse to beat such a pair in a weight-for-age race?

Shortly before the time for the entries, Captain Whitaker told me that if I could find a horse to beat Why Not he would buy him and give £2,000 for him. There was not much time to do it in, and the only possible chance was a maiden four-year-old, if it could be found. But even that would be no good without a first-class jockey, and, as the weight would be 10 st. 7 lb., it was not an easy matter.

But I asked Percy Bewicke if he would ride if I found the horse. This being arranged satisfactorily, I went down to Danebury to see Tom Cannon, who always had a lot of young horses, and told him what I wanted. He told me that he had the horse if I had the jockey, and showed me a four-year-old chestnut gelding by Ocean Wave, which had never run. He was a grand-looking horse, except for his small prick ears, and Tom said, "Here is the horse to beat Why Not at the weights, but I want £2,000 for him." There was no time to try the horse or examine him, and, Tom being a man of his word, I bought him there and then. It came off all right, and he won the race. Why Not fell, but I do not think that made any difference, for Percy Bewicke said his horse was winning easily at the time. Ormerod was a good horse that day, and had a great pull in the weights; but those prick ears told a true tale, and his after career was by no means glorious.

It was about this time that I was taken ill, and, after a long time on my back, I was at last able to get about in a sort of plaster jacket, which I wore for several years. It was then that I first made the acquaintance of William Allison, who at that time was editor of the *St. Stephen's Review*. Knowing that I was at a loose end he asked me if I would care to write the Sporting article for his paper. Having nothing to do and no money I gladly accepted his offer. Allison in later years became famous throughout the sporting world as the "Special Commissioner" of the *Sportsman*. He is one of the most remarkable men I have met on the Turf. His love for horses and his enthusiasm for racing is as unbounded as is his store of knowledge on all matters concerning Turf history. I shall always think he is by far the best writer on racing matters in my time. His articles in the *Sportsman* on the horses entered in classic races for the last twenty years have been wonderful, and his judgment of first-class horses is unrivalled. Selling platers and moderate horses he has never troubled about, neither does betting or the financial side of racing concern him. Enthusiasm for certain strains of blood and occasionally for some particular horse at times carries him too far, but I know no man who has a greater love for a good horse.

I wrote for some time for the *St. Stephen's Review*, and then Reggie Brett, now Lord Esher, who at that time was very fond of racing, and always had a horse or two, suggested to me that I should start training myself, for which I shall be ever grateful to him. Moreover, he had two yearling fillies, which he said he would send me. There were three objections to this : I knew very little about the inside management of a stable, I was in very bad health, and I had no money. But, with the help of good friends, two of these difficulties were overcome. My brother, Durham, guaranteed an overdraft at the bank, and Joe Cannon gave me one of his best men to be my head lad. So I started at Newmarket with a small yard in St. Mary's Square and about a dozen horses.

Really my first patron was Lord Molyneux, as, before Reggie Brett's yearlings came into training, he sent me several jumpers—Sheridan, Fugleman, Mosquito, Emin and Orangepeel by name.

" Little Mull," as he was called, was a dear little fellow and always ready to help a lame dog over a stile. Tremendously keen on cross-country sport, he was a good rider in a quiet, unpretentious way. No horse ever pulled with him, and he had that great quality or art of leaving them alone, with the result that they seldom fell ; but he had not the strength to get much out of a horse that required riding. He was a wonderful man to train for, delighted when he won, and pleased with his horses when they ran well, even if they did not win. Altogether that year, 1892-93, I had six horses of his, and they won twenty-eight races. Usually he rode them himself. The races were of small value, but he was content.

There was only one thing that spoilt it. His father, Lord Sefton, strongly objected to his riding over a country and did all he could to prevent him. Both father and son were obstinate men, and neither would give way an inch. In consequence, things did not go too smoothly between them. I knew Lord Sefton pretty well, and at the root of the matter was the fear that his son would get hurt, for he was really very fond of him. He told me that, if I could persuade him to give up steeplechasing, he would give him as much money as he liked to buy horses to run on the flat. I did my best, but the little man was too keen on the game to give it up, also he did not care about flat racing, although, to please me, he did occasionally run horses under Jockey Club Rules. On one of these occasions we had a really great success.

I had seen a horse called Pampero win a race at Brighton, and then get disqualified. He looked a likely sort of horse, and I bought him for " Mull." He also had a mare called Ejector, who was a failure for jumping, and I proposed that we should enter these two at Epsom, which we did. It so happened that Ejector was in the race before the Derby, and Pampero in the race after it. Both horses had done extraordinarily well, and, although we did not know much about flat-racing form, we went there thinking they would not disgrace us.

Ejector won her race after a desperate finish, ridden by George Barrett, and then after the Derby, which was won by the great Isinglass, we went down to the paddock before the next race.

I remember Rickaby, who was to ride Pampero, began talking about the Derby, which had been a most exciting race, for Tommy Loates had to ride Isinglass like the devil before he got rid of Ravensbury, with a steeplechase jockey, Harry Barker, in the saddle. " Mull " said, " Never mind about the Derby, that's over ; what you've got to do is to win this race for me." " So I shall," said Rickaby, and he did, after a tremendous struggle with Morny Cannon on a very hot favourite. " Mull " was highly delighted, and declared that he would never have a better day in his life. It was wonderful, he said, for two steeplechasing men to come to Epsom and win two races on Derby Day. So fond was " Mull " of riding that he never could bring himself to refuse a mount, however bad it was, and one day, at Liverpool, although I implored him not to do so, he insisted on riding some wretched horse that ought never to have been allowed to run over such a course.

He got a fall and had concussion of the brain. He never entirely recovered from this, and it was really the cause of his death, after a long and painful illness.

When writing of the Derby of 1893, I cannot help thinking that if you were to put Papyrus and Pharos, the Derby horses of 1923, alongside Isinglass and Ravensbury, even allowing for the glamour of the past, the comparison would not be to the advantage of the younger generation. The two latter were magnificent horses. Surely Ravensbury must have been one of the most unlucky horses in the world, second for the Two Thousand Guineas, Derby and St. Leger, each time to a champion like Isinglass, and also beaten a short head for the Grand Prix. It must have been heartbreaking for his trainer, William Jarvis, but fortunately he had a character which enabled him always to come up smiling after any reverse. Morny Cannon rode him in Paris in the place of Harry Barker, who was on his back in the Two Thousand Guineas and Derby. I did not see the race, but Morny told me that he was absolutely certain he had won, and he was not a man to make that sort of statement without good reason.

Harry Barker was also very unlucky, for, besides being second for the Two Thousand Guineas and Derby, he had been second for the National that year, a really remarkable performance for any jockey. Getting beaten in these two classics did him a lot of harm, for in each race there was a moment when Ravensbury looked as if he had got Isinglass beaten, but the latter was very lazy and Tommy Loates, good jockey as he was, never could really ride this great, long-striding horse. His legs were too short, and, until he had picked up his whip and hit him five or six times, Isinglass would be doing nothing. But, of course, the fact of Harry Barker being a steeplechase jockey made many people think that Tommy outrode him at the finish. I believe the case was exactly the reverse, and, if you had changed the jockeys, Isinglass would have won without giving his backers the fright he did on both occasions, for Harry

Barker was not only a very strong jockey but a beautiful rider.

The Derby of the following year (1894) was won by Lord Rosebery's Ladas. For various reasons, after 1882 and 1883, Lord Rosebery did not take an active part in racing for some years, but about 1890 he started again. At that time I think Matthew Dawson had practically made up his mind to retire, when Lord Rosebery asked him to train his horses. Lord Rosebery was then at the zenith of his great career, and Mat could not refuse. He told me that no other man could have made him go into harness again. I think it must have been in the first year of his training for Lord Rosebery that Ladas came out as a two-year-old.

Some time before the Epsom Summer Meeting, I was coming down to Newmarket by the early morning train, and I travelled down with Lord Rosebery, who told me that he was going to try Ladas for the Woodcote, and that Mat Dawson had told him he was a good horse. I was considerably in awe of the great man, but he was so pleasant and amusing that by the end of the journey I wondered how I could ever have been afraid of him. I remember that he had a bad cold, and I noticed that he had on very thin low shoes. I remarked that I hoped he had a change, as the grass on the Limekilns was very long and wet. He replied that he never worried about trifles of that sort, but Mat Dawson, however, did, and I believe he would not let him go off the road beside the Limekilns when his horses were tried.

I did not see the gallop, but I imagine that it was not quite satisfactory, and in a small field for the Woodcote, at Epsom, Ladas started at ten to one, but, ridden by Tiny White, he won in a canter, upsetting a three-to-one on chance in Glare, owned by Sir Daniel Cooper, and trained by George Blackwell. The beautiful Ladas was a brown colt by Hampton out of Illuminata. I should say just about 16 hands, and near perfection in make and shape ; what a gentleman he was in manners and appearance, well worthy of carrying the colours of not only a great sportsman, but the Prime Minister of England !

After winning all the four races he ran for as a two-year-old, ending up with the Middle Park Plate, he went into winter quarters favourite for the Derby, and carried the hopes and good wishes of not only the racing community, but the people of England, although the Nonconformist conscience pretended to be shocked at the Prime Minister owning the favourite for the Derby.

Now Mat Dawson was famous for the tremendous preparations that he gave his classic horses. When it was seen that Ladas, on the contrary, was having rather an easy time of it, people began to think that there might be a screw loose. So much so that a friend of Lord Rosebery's, General " Bully " Oliphant, who had a lot of money on the horse, invited himself to stay with me, so that he might see what was going on. Mat Dawson had told me that he was well satisfied, but that, owing to Ladas' breeding and constitution, he did not require a strong preparation. I forget the name of the horse that led him in his work ; he was a bad one, but at his own pace could get any distance. Mat told me that, although Ladas could give him four stone, he was always carrying level weights in his work. There was the great trainer who understood his horse !

In the afternoon, General Oliphant went to see Mat Dawson and Ladas. He came back full of confidence, and full of whisky, for, like Mat, he was a Scotchman ; he stood his money and he won it.

Ladas first came out as a three-year-old in the Two Thousand Guineas ; he was a picture walking round the paddock ; won easily, and followed it up at the next Newmarket Meeting with the Newmarket Stakes.

As he had beaten all the best three-year-old form, the Derby looked a foregone conclusion. Sure enough, ridden by Jack Watts, he won in a canter from his constant opponent, Matchbox, and the enthusiasm was almost as great as it was two years later over Persimmon's victory. Then came the sad part of the story of Ladas. In the earlier days of Mat Dawson's great successes, the Two Thousand Guineas, the Derby, possibly a race at Ascot and the St. Leger were the objectives of the good horses. Now there is the Newmarket Stakes sandwiched in between the Two Thousand Guineas and the Derby, and after Ascot the Princess of Wales Stakes and the Eclipse Stakes. Mat, who aimed at perfection when he trained a horse for a classic race, did not believe it possible for any man to keep a horse keyed up to his best for so long. He told me that he wished these races at the bottom of the sea, and he would in his heart have liked to have missed these rich prizes, but he could not really advise Lord Rosebery to do so as the races were worth about £10,000, and Ladas had a great chance of winning them both.

I have no doubt whatever that Mat was right in his opinion as to the continuous strain being too much for a three-year-old, and I believe that the deterioration of really first-class horses that can stay a reasonable distance comes from this abuse of them when young. The fact is, that now there are too many valuable races for three-year-olds and not nearly enough for four-year-olds and upwards. You cannot expect owners to resist the temptation. I don't blame them; it is the system which is wrong.

To return to Ladas, there is no more difficult job for a trainer than to let a horse down when he has been thoroughly fit, and then to produce him again at the top of his form, unless he has plenty of time in which to do it. Now Ladas had an " easy " after the Derby, missed Ascot, and then was brought out again on July 5th for the Princess of Wales Stakes at Newmarket, where, with the odds of three to one laid on him, he was third, beaten three lengths from Isinglass, who just beat Bullingdon a head. A fortnight later he again had to tackle Isinglass in the Eclipse Stakes at

Sandown, at the same weights. Although he was again beaten, he put up a much better show, and he was running against one of the best horses ever seen, who at the moment was at the top of his form.

Ladas was then put by for the St. Leger, but when he got into strong work again he showed unmistakable signs that his rather high-strung and delicate temperament had suffered from his strenuous season. He had now taken to pulling very hard, and was inclined to be irritable, but, in spite of all this, as the time approached for the big race he bore the hall-mark of Mat Dawson's skilful training, and it looked a good thing for him.

In all his races as a three-year-old he had been ridden by Jack Watts, who was exactly the jockey he required, but in the St. Leger Watts was claimed by Baron Hirsch for Matchbox, and Ladas was to be ridden by Tommy Loates. Tommy was a very good jockey, but he had neither the length nor the strength to ride Ladas. I believe that, after he had ridden him a gallop, he was not at all keen on having the mount, as he was afraid that he would not be able to hold him. His fears were justified, for in the race, after fighting hard for his head for a mile, Ladas took charge of his jockey, dashed to the front, and ran himself to a standstill. Morny Cannon, on Throstle, realizing that the pace was too fast to last, had been a long way behind at the Red House, but, gradually making up his ground, and coming with one of his irresistible runs, he caught Ladas a hundred yards from home, and beat him three parts of a length. The finish of the race reminded me much of Dutch Oven's St. Leger.

There is no doubt that if Watts had ridden Ladas he would have won. In writing this I don't want in any way to depreciate Tommy Loates' jockeyship, but physically he was not the man for the horse. He was a light-weight riding 7 st. 4 lb.

Ladas only ran once again, as a four-year-old, in the Jockey Club Stakes, where he was fourth to Laveno, giving him 26 lb. I don't think he was seriously fancied. Once you get to the bottom of a highly strung generous horse he is never so good again.

The career of Ladas reminds me of a talk I had with Mat Dawson one day. He had been saying to me that I ought to make money racing. I reminded him of how he had once told me that betting was no good, and that ninety out of a hundred people lost money. " Yes," he replied, " that is so, but you should make money by breeding and selling horses, if you study their make, shape and constitution, but remember this, horses are getting more delicate and nervous every year." I asked him how he accounted for this, and he said, " Horses for years have had too great a strain put on them in their two and three-year-old days, consequently every succeeding generation becomes less robust, and you will find that as time goes on horses will less and less be able to stand the work that their more hardy ancestors did." He added that, if he was a young man, he would aim at breeding from the best staying blood available. I say that these prophetic words have been proved to be right, for year after year do we see the high-class two-year-olds degenerate into non-stayers in their three-year-old careers, and you have only to look through the entries for the Cups and long distance Handicaps of these present years to realize their truth.

Lord Rosebery had made many attempts to win the Derby before doing so with Ladas, but, when he had once broken the ice, another success quickly followed. In 1895, the year after Ladas triumphed, he won again with Sir Visto, a bay colt by Barcaldine.

Sir Visto was rather a plain but lengthy horse with sickle hocks. He only ran twice as a two-year-old, winning the Imperial Produce Stakes at Kempton on his second appearance in public. I don't think many people marked him down as a likely Derby winner, but he had the good fortune to be born in a year of moderate horses. In a small field for the Two Thousand he was third to Kirconnel and Laveno, and in the

Newmarket Stakes he was third again, but this time he beat the non-staying Kirconnel, who started a six-to-four favourite. In this race he stayed on so well that for the first time Mat Dawson began to have visions of another Derby. I never liked Sir Visto, which was rather ungrateful of me, for on Mat's advice I had quite a nice bet about him. Starting at nine to one, he won Lord Rosebery his second Derby. He was ridden by Sam Loates, a good jockey, and a wonderful judge of pace, who gave nothing away in a race. Sir Visto then won the St. Leger with the same jockey up, beating a bad field.

Lord Rosebery's next Derby winner was a horse of totally different character, the beautiful little Cicero, but that was ten years later.

On looking back on the history of the famous horses he has bred and owned, one cannot help being struck by the fact that his good horses, with the exception of Sir Visto, were all of exceptional beauty and quality. There is no doubt that Ladas, Neil Gow, Cicero, Velasquez, Chelandry and Bonny Jean were types of the bloodlike quality horse, and to this day his horses seem to retain much of that character.

Of his own wonderful personality, and his great charm, I had often heard, but for a long time I had no opportunity of experiencing it, for he was considerably older than I was, and also moved in circles which I did not frequent. I have told how I travelled down to Newmarket with him, and how quickly he dispelled my feeling of awe. On another occasion I had the good fortune to dine alone with him at the Jockey Club Rooms at Newmarket. After that I completely understood the extraordinary fascination there was in the man.

In that anxious and almost painful time, when horses are at the post for a big race, it has always interested me to watch the faces of the owners of fancied horses. In their different ways they generally show the intensity of their feelings, but Lord Rosebery, with his sphinx-like face, gave nothing away. For all that I believe him to have been always a most sensitive man, and I am sure that the victory or defeat of his favourites went to his heart more nearly than is the case with most people. He had always taken, and takes to this day, the keenest interest in the breeding and racing of his horses.

CHAPTER XVII

MY START AS A TRAINER—LORD DERBY AND HIS
EARLY RACING

THE two fillies that Reggie Brett so kindly sent me to train came up in September, 1892. They were not very promising, and Reggie was under no illusions about them, for he said, " I am afraid they will not do you much good, but, anyhow, they will be something for you to practise on." One was a well-bred chestnut by Peter out of Venus's Looking Glass called Hettie Sorrel, a plain, angular filly, very much back at the knees, but with a game, lean head. The other was a pretty little thing, but I cannot remember either the name or the breeding, and she never came to any good.

When Hettie Sorrel got into good work there was something to like about her, although she was slow in getting on to her legs. After running once she was put in a selling race at the First July Meeting at Newmarket. After being hopelessly outpaced, she struggled on to second place, and the winner fetched £600, which was a big price for a plater in those days. Rickaby rode her, and when he got off her he said, " Don't let anyone claim her, for she will make a useful mare over a distance of ground," so I quickly got the owner of the third to put in a friendly claim. Rickaby was right, for, keeping her till the nursery season began, she won five races straight off the reel. She gave me my first confidence in training, for although her races were either seven furlongs or a mile, being sure of her staying powers, I never worked her more than five furlongs, and tried to improve her speed.

After her third victory, Reggie sold her to Lord

Stanley, who was just starting racing. Hettie Sorrel was a wonderful game filly, and would race with a donkey. She would win her races by a neck or half a length, and, when the handicappers put her up five or six pounds, she always pulled out just enough to win again, and kept on repeating the job, much to the astonishment of handicapper, owner and trainer.

My first jockey when I began training was Fred Rickaby. I don't say he was as brilliant as Danny Maher or Frank Wootton, who succeeded him, but he was the soundest and most hard-working jockey I ever had. There was nothing flashy about him, but it was very rarely that he threw a race away. But he did so on one occasion when riding Santa Brigida in the Park Hill Stakes at Doncaster. She whipped round at the start and lost many lengths, but she got to the leaders a quarter of a mile from home. Instead of taking a pull here he went to the front, and then her bolt was shot. She was caught by something ridden by Morny Cannon and beaten. "Rick" was very unhappy, and declared he ought to burn his boots and breeches and never ride again. That is what I like, a man who knows when he has made a mistake and owns it. When he was quite a boy he was riding in a match for Lord Durham, the other horse being ridden by Tom Cannon, who was a great match rider. My brother said to him, "Are you afraid of Tom Cannon?" and he replied, "No, my lord, but he always beats me a head."

One morning, on the Heath, Mr. Coventry was talking to him when a batch of horses came thundering along. "I suppose that's what they call a half-speed," said Mr. Coventry. "Yes," said Rick, "but it would take them a long time to find the other half." He had a quaint way of saying rather clever things.

Rickaby was a most determined jockey, especially good on a round course. He would take any risks, and was always as fit as a prize-fighter. I saw him ride a tremendous finish on Mr. Douglas Baird's Mazagam for the Lowther Stakes, one and three-quarter miles, at Newmarket, against Tommy Loates on Skopos, the latter a seven-to-four chance. Mazagam, who was at seven to one, was the idlest horse in the world, and would do nothing save under compulsion. At the Bushes it looked any odds on Loates, as Rickaby had been riding his horse very hard for a long time : but again and again he squeezed a bit more out of him, At last Loates and Skopos began to get uncomfortable, and, when Rickaby and his horse put in one more tremendous effort, they both fell to pieces, and Mazagam won by a short head. When Rickaby came in he was speechless and white with exhaustion, although, as I have said, he was as fit and hard as a prizefighter. Sloan, who had been watching the race, remarked to me afterwards, " I guess that Rick is a real demon when it comes to a long bout."

I think there is a considerable difference between jockeys of old times and those of to-day with regard to fitness. There are several reasons for this. For one thing, motor-cars make things much easier, and we all take less hard exercise than our predecessors did, also the jockeys of the present day are, as a rule, smaller men than they used to be, and they have not to take the strenuous measures that used to be necessary to keep their weight down. I can remember the day when you would see parties of jockeys starting off to walk from Newmarket to Cambridge and back loaded with sweaters. Life is made too easy now, and the worst thing of all is the habit of smoking cigarettes. There is nothing so bad for the wind and nerve. When I say " nerve," I do not mean that a man is going to be a coward because he smokes, but it makes him jumpy and excitable. I remember years ago going to see a horse of mine run, trained by Tom Green : his race was last on the card, and my jockey had no mount before this race. I saw him in the paddock smoking a cigar, so also did Tom Green, who walked up behind him, took the cigar out of his mouth and threw it away. I remarked to Tom that I could not see any harm in it. He replied, " If it comes to a tight finish that cigar might just make the difference of a head : you can't afford to throw any chance away when you are betting." To quote another case, E. P. Wilson was a non-smoker. He said that, if it came to a long struggle, his lungs and strength would last longer than those of the man who had been smoking. Donoghue seldom smokes, neither did Fred Archer : here are two examples which might be followed by young jockeys who are ambitious. A few years ago, Lord Durham, when he was a Steward, told the Clerks of Courses that smoking should not be allowed in the jockeys' room and weighing room. I am afraid that this excellent rule has been allowed to lapse, and, in some weighing rooms I have been into, you could hardly see from one end to the other for smoke. When I was riding steeplechases, although I did not follow the spartan methods of Ted Wilson, I never smoked until the day's work was over : and when Danny Maher, who was a heavy smoker, was my jockey, I persuaded him to practically give it up. He told me afterwards that it was the best piece of advice, and almost the only one, that he had ever taken.

. . . . . .

Early in the summer of 1893, I had a great surprise, and a very pleasant one. I was staying at Ascot with Mr. Leopold de Rothschild, and Lord Stanley (the present Lord Derby), who had just come back from Canada, was also there. He told me that his father intended to start racing the following year, and hoped to revive the old prestige of the Derby stable. Greatly to my surprise, he asked me if I would train for him. On thinking it over, I did not feel that with my little experience I was equal to taking on a job of this sort, and I suggested that he should let Joe Cannon train the horses, and that I should manage them : but this he would not have, and stuck to his original proposition. So then began my association with the Stanley family, and for thirty years I have trained for father and son.

At that time I did not know the late Lord Derby. If I had I do not think I should have been so diffident in accepting the offer of training his horses. I have had many good friends in my life, and known many delightful men, but the most perfect gentleman of all was Lord Derby.

In some ways he was rather a shy man, but he had, which is unusual when combined with that trait, such a delightful charm of manner that everyone—no matter what his station of life—at once felt at ease with him. A more modest man never lived, yet his opinion, when he could be induced to give it, was always worth having on any sort of question, and his store of information on all subjects was wonderful. He took a great interest in his horses, and the breeding of them, and there was nothing he enjoyed more than coming to Newmarket when there was no racing, and when he could see his horses peacefully without any fuss or bother. On these occasions, when he stayed with me, he was never in a hurry to go to bed, and, as long as there was anyone who would sit up with him, he would talk and smoke cigarettes till any hour of the night. But, no matter what time we went out next morning, he always put me to shame by being down before anyone else, and walking about in the garden with the inevitable cigarette in his mouth.

I thought at first that he did not know much about racing, but I soon found out that little escaped his notice. As a young man he had been very fond of it, and had seen a great deal of John Scott, of Whitewall, who trained for his father. What he had learnt there he had not forgotten.

It is impossible to give any idea of his extraordinary kindness to me, for on more than one occasion my health was so bad that I had to give up and go abroad for two or three months, also I was not a good business man, and things certainly did get into rather a muddle at times, but he always made allowances for my shortcomings. I really loved him, and would have done anything in the world for him, and I do not think any young trainer ever started with a better chance.

Before the Liverpool Summer Meeting of that year, Lord Stanley asked me to find him a horse to win some little race there. I bought him old Greywell, a horse belonging to Charles Kinsky, for there happened to be a race with conditions which I thought would suit him well. Greywell, by Marden out of Seakale, was a dear old horse and had done us in his time some good turns, although he had on occasions let us down badly. But this time, when carrying the Derby colours, which had not been seen on a race-course for many years, he did his part nobly. In a great finish, for the first and last time, he ran as game as a fighting cock and won, setting an example which has been followed by many another bearer of the Black and White cap. It is really quite extraordinary how many horses I have had who have loved that peculiar tricky course and shown far better form at Liverpool than anywhere else.

I am proud to say that I have never had the reputation among racing people of being "clever," but I think that many people have thought that I almost deserve the title over many of my Liverpool successes. It is remarkable when horses have once shown a liking for the Aintree course what big things they can accomplish there.

Old Greywell led off well, and then Hettie Sorrel emphasized the "beginner's luck." As I have said, Lord Stanley bought her from Mr. Brett, and she won for him at Kempton and Newmarket.

The first yearlings I bought for Lord Derby were Dingle Bay, a bay colt by Minting; Oleander, a bay colt by Isonomy; and Propeller, by Ayrshire. I bought them privately from Sir Daniel Cooper, and very useful horses they were, although neither of the two former won as two-year-olds. Propeller ran second at Ascot, and then won the Mersey Stakes at Liverpool, beating Mr. Fairie Cox's Solaro, who afterwards won the Champagne Stakes.

Oleander was a big, fine horse, but split a pastern in a race at Sandown as a two-year-old. Nevertheless, he afterwards won the Dee Stakes, and was second for the Goodwood Stakes, then he broke down and was sold.

Dingle Bay was a very big, heavy horse, and about as bad as he could be as a two-year-old. He was always beaten off in any sort of gallop, and yet he had good action. As a three-year-old, in the early part of the year, he was no better, and appeared to have no course.

By that time, although I still had to wear my plaster jacket, my back was better. I was able to ride again, and sometimes rode a gallop. Dingle Bay, being as quiet as a sheep, up to any weight and no good, I used to amuse myself on him. I thought I would like to have another ride, so I entered him in the Bibury Stakes at Stockbridge. His weight was 10 st. 3 lb., and it shows what illness had done for me that I could do the weight easily, when formerly I used to ride 11 st.

On the morning of the race, Tommy Lushington, who was the crack amateur of the day, came to me and said, " I have not got a ride, do let me ride yours." I said I would if the horse had any chance, but that I thought he was no good. At that moment my jockey, Rickaby, came up, and I asked him if he thought there was any hope whatever, as Mr. Lushington wanted to ride. " He would not win if you started him overnight," said Rick, so I decided to stick to the mount myself.

In the race, Dingle Bay jumped off first, sailed along in front with his head in his chest, and won by four lengths, starting at a hundred to seven. This was a great surprise. I rode him again later in the week, with a lot more weight, and was second. After this he improved at the rate of about 5 lb. a week, won again at Liverpool, and the next year won some good races, including the Ebor Handicap and a two-mile race at Ascot.

He also won the whip at Newmarket, and this race

was a great affair. The other runner was a horse called Bevil, belonging to Mr. Leopold de Rothschild, and was ridden by Morny Cannon.

The race finished at the old Cambridgeshire Stand. Dingle Bay being a great stayer, Rickaby forced the pace from the start, and came a rattling good gallop. After they had passed the Cesarewitch Stands, Morny Cannon drew up and lay just in his heels, so that Rickaby could not see what he was doing. Coming to the old Red Post, Rick, who was up to all the tricks of the trade, just left room for Cannon to come up on the inside, hoping to tempt him to make his effort sooner than he should do. But Morny resisted the temptation, so Rickaby went back again. Still Morny did not come to him, so Rick tempted him with an opening again, this time with success, but the opening was so narrow, and Dingle Bay just happened to roll slightly back again, that Morny changed his mind and delivered his challenge on the other side. Again Rick's horse just rolled the other way, threw Bevil slightly out of his stride, with the result that he was beaten a head.

Leo, good loser as he was, naturally was rather cross and said he ought to object, but he did not, and Morny Cannon declared that he had been trying every sort of trick on Rickaby, and that the latter was quite right to look after himself. But it was as fine an exhibition of the craft of riding as I have ever seen. Gameness in a horse was a quality that Lord Derby greatly appreciated. He was very fond of old Dingle Bay, and no money could have bought him.

At that time Morny Cannon was at the zenith of his fame, and he was a delightful jockey to watch—naturally, as he was a Cannon, his great art lay in riding a waiting race. It really was extraordinary, after apparently being out of a race, how he would sweep down on three or four struggling horses and beat them. It was the more remarkable for in those days races were not run from pillar to post as they are now. Taking him all round, I have seen no better jockey than Morny. He had a beautiful seat on a horse, was very strong, and had the best of hands. He always turned up fit and well for the job before him; and, with a character beyond suspicion, it is no wonder that for years he was the favourite jockey of the public. There were perhaps times when he carried this practice of waiting too far. He may occasionally have lost a race by it, but against that must be put the many that he won.

There is no doubt that most of the jockeys were frightened to death of Morny, with his tremendous rush at the finish, but there was one who was not, and that was Jack Watts. How many beautiful races I have seen these two ride against each other! Although their style was different, I do not think there was a pin to choose between them. Jack Watts apparently did so little; there was nothing theatrical about his riding. In a race he was always stealing quietly along in a good place, and very seldom getting shut in, winning his race at the right moment. I remember once at Manchester he rode a good game mare of ours, called Birch Rod, in the Prince Edward Handicap, in which she carried top weight. I was not there, but I had a wire saying that she had finished third, but had run a great race, and was second best.

When Harry Sharpe, who was my head man at the time, came back he told me that, although the mare had a long struggle with the winner, Watts had never hit her, and given her an easy race. That same morning I met Watts himself, who said she had run a great race. "But I am afraid," he added, "I gave her a very hard race, for she kept pulling 'out' a bit more every time I asked her." I was surprised, and told him that I had heard just the opposite, and that he had never picked his whip up. "No, that's true," he replied, "but I nearly squeezed the life out of her, and she gave every inch she had in her." And so it was, for it took her a very long time to get over the race. That was Watts—he got the last ounce out of a horse apparently doing nothing, whereas Morny Cannon could be seen balancing his horse and preparing him for his run, then sitting down and riding a most vigorous but artistic finish. Both jockeys, in their way, were as good as they could be. There was one characteristic they had in common —after winning a big race, they would come into the unsaddling enclosure looking as solemn as a judge who has just passed a death sentence.

Birch Rod was somewhat of a freak as a race-horse— I bought her very cheaply out of the Blankney stud, which was owned by Mr. Henry Chaplin. By Hazelhatch out of Fright, she was a washy chestnut with four white legs, nearly up to her knees and hocks, and with soft blood on both sides of her family. When we started to break her, she appeared hopeless, and we could do nothing with her, neither in the stable nor out of it. It was six weeks before we could get a saddle on her, but eventually she became as kind as a Christian, and as game as she could be. She won us many good races.

It was not till 1894 that Lord Derby really started to lay the foundations of the Knowsley Stud. At the sale of the Duchess of Montrose's yearlings he bought Canterbury Pilgrim for 1,800 guineas, and the broodmare Broad Corrie for 600 guineas. The descendants of these mares have won many great races. At the same sale he was also the underbidder for Roquebrune, who won the New Stakes at Ascot, and was the dam of Rock Sand. He did not buy extensively that year, but Lord Stanley and Sir Horace Farquhar, the latter having joined the stable, bought several horses. They were very lucky, for between them they bought some good ones, such as Melange for 600 guineas ; The Quack 400 guineas ; Golden Rule, 600 guineas ; Chiselhampton, 500 guineas ; Nouveau Riche, 170 guineas ; East Sheen, 600 guineas ; all of whom were horses far above the average. I wish I could buy horses of that class now for such prices.

At that time Count Lehndorff, manager of the Imperial Stud in Germany, was a great deal in England.

He was supposed to be the finest judge of bloodstock in the world. He was a typical Prussian, a fine-looking, tall man, with rather an overbearing manner. I got to know him well, and learnt a great deal from him. He said to me one day, " There are three great things to bear in mind for the foundation of a stud. The first is soundness, the second is soundness, and the third is soundness." And that is the principle I have tried to follow all my life.

CHAPTER XVIII

KING EDWARD—PERSIMMON'S DERBY—MR. LEOPOLD DE ROTHSCHILD

IN the season 1895, Persimmon and St. Frusquin stood out as the star performers among the two-year-olds. They had met only once in the Middle Park Plate, when St. Frusquin won and Persimmon ran badly. But there was a valid excuse for the latter, who had not long recovered from coughing, and I believe that his trainer, Dick Marsh, was against running him. Anyhow, his form in the Middle Park Plate was too bad to be true.

As in Ormonde's year, we had again two great horses in Persimmon and St. Frusquin, owned by great sportsmen in the Prince of Wales and Mr. Leopold de Rothschild, trained by masters of the art in Dick Marsh and Alfred Hayhoe, and ridden by Jack Watts and Tommy Loates.

The latter was a good and strong rider, and a great public favourite, not such a fine jockey as Watts, but well suited to St. Frusquin, who was a hardy, game customer, able to stand any amount of riding ; while Watts, who had been brought up by Tom Cannon, and had his beautiful, delicate style, was as fine a horseman as ever lived, and just the jockey for a high-strung, delicate horse like Persimmon.

Equally happy were these horses in their trainers. Alfred Hayhoe was one of the old school. A splendid trainer, but a very hard man on his horses, who needed iron constitutions to stand what he gave them. When they did so, the result was the very perfection of fitness. Whereas Marsh was the most patient of men, and could nurse a delicate horse into the same state of perfection.

As to the owners, it is not for me to write about King Edward. His character and life are too well known to everyone, but as a sportsman he was by far the most popular man in England, and in this respect Mr. Rothschild was second only to him. It is when you get the rivalry of such men and horses as I have just described that racing deserves the title of " The Sport of Kings."

In the spring of 1896, both horses were reported to have wintered well, and in the Craven week at Newmarket everyone was keen to see them at work. St. Frusquin came out in the Column Produce Stakes, which he won easily, pleasing everybody. He was well forward in condition, while Persimmon was backward in his coat, and did not altogether satisfy the critics.

Report for once was correct, for Persimmon was struck out of the Two Thousand Guineas, the Prince taking the sound advice of Lord Marcus Beresford and Marsh, that if he wanted to win the Derby he had better forgo the Guineas. St. Frusquin won the race in great style, beating a good horse in Love Wisely (afterwards winner of the Ascot Cup and the Jockey Club Stakes) and settled down into a good favourite for the Derby.

Meanwhile, Persimmon was doing well, and Thais, the property of the Prince of Wales, won the One Thousand Guineas, which raised the hopes of his supporters.

As I have already said, Persimmon did not please everyone in his work, and he certainly was not a taking mover in his slow paces, but one gallop I saw him do convinced me that he was a great horse. The last fortnight before the Derby the going was very hard, and both Hayhoe and Marsh were very anxious, as neither horse really liked such conditions. I think perhaps St. Frusquin was the chief sufferer. But good horses and good trainers can overcome most things, and they arrived at Epsom both fit to run for their lives.

F. RICKABY (Senior)  FREDDY RICKABY (Junior)

JACK WATTS  HARRY BARKER

MORNINGTON CANNON  TOD SLOAN

All photos by Clarence Hailey except Harry Barker, which is by Robinson

THE HON. GEORGE LAMBTON
AT BEDFORD LODGE

Photo: Clarence Hailey

From the drawing by Lynwood Palmer

CHAUCER

I was staying with Lord Rosebery at the Durdans, and went out in the morning to see the work. It was very hot when I got on the Downs. One of the first horses I met was Persimmon, rather irritable, the sweat running off him, and not looking in the least like a Derby winner, with Dick Marsh, quite as hot and nearly as irritable, his hopes having sunk almost to zero. Then I met St. Frusquin and Hayhoe, the horse looking beautiful, but moving a little short, and Hayhoe in a very bad temper, declaring that the course was beastly. Mr. Rothschild was there, beaming as usual, but also hot and nervous. Such are the pleasures of owning and training Derby favourites!

In the paddock and parade there were only two horses that people wanted to see, but Persimmon was saddled at Sherwood's stable, not far from the start, and he took no part in the Parade (there was no rule then that horses had to go past the Stands before a race), and St. Frusquin was saddled in the grounds of the Durdans, adjoining the paddock.

He was a brown horse of lovely quality, on short legs, with a wonderful back and loins, and a real good game head. If you could pick a fault you might have said that he was a trifle short. Now, Persimmon, also a horse of great quality, was an exactly opposite type. A great lengthy bay, slightly on the leg, with the most perfect shoulders, bloodlike head and neck, great quarters, and very straight hocks. The public like a horse that has been out, and in consequence of that, added to the report of Persimmon's nervous state in the morning, St. Frusquin started at eleven to eight on, Persimmon at five to one against. Like Ormonde and The Bard, it was a two-horse race, St. Frusquin taking up the running when fairly in the straight, followed by Persimmon. Then ensued the most exciting struggle, and a beautiful one to watch. Tommy Loates on the rails riding for all he was worth, St. Frusquin gamely answering every call, and Watts patiently holding his horse together for one run. When he did call on him he gradually but

P

surely drew up to St. Frusquin, then he appeared for one moment to falter, and Watts had to balance him once more perilously near home, but in the last hundred yards he shot up and won by a neck.

I shall always think that Watts's quietness and nerve in such a critical moment was one of the greatest feats of jockeyship I ever saw. When you think what it means to a jockey to win or lose the Derby, add to that the responsibility of riding for the Prince of Wales, one can imagine Watts's feelings when he found it necessary to take that pull so close home, for if it had not come off it would have looked as if he had ridden a tame finish, and he would have come in for much criticism.

The scene after the race will remain in the memory of all who were fortunate enough to be present. The Prince walked down from the stand amid a wild tumult of excitement and enthusiasm, and went with his equerry and Marsh on to the course to lead his horse in.

The crowd broke through the cordon of police, and it was with difficulty that the Prince could get near his horse. I think in later years, when Minoru won for him as King of England, that the enthusiasm was even greater. The police were then quite unable to cope with the crowd, who patted the King on the back and shook him by the hand with cries of "Good old Teddie." Some distinguished foreigner who witnessed it said that nothing like this could happen outside England, which recalls to one's mind what Bismarck said to Disraeli, "You will never have a revolution in England as long as you keep up your racing."

Dick Marsh told me that when the King was leading Minoru back through the cheering crowd some music-hall singer struck up with "God Save the King," which, as we can all remember, was taken up and sung right down the course.

Ardent supporter as I was of Persimmon, I thought at the time that the brilliant riding of Watts had just turned the scale, and subsequent form in the Prince of Wales Stakes at Newmarket showed how evenly matched the two horses were, for on that occasion St. Frusquin, in receipt of 3 lb. from Persimmon, won a splendid race by half a length.

St. Frusquin after this carried off the Eclipse Stakes in fine style, and showed himself to be getting better and better. Everyone looked forward to a great struggle for the St. Leger, but unfortunately St. Frusquin broke down in his preparation, and he never ran again.

It was a thousand pities, and I know that no man more genuinely sympathized with Mr. Rothschild than the Royal owner of Persimmon, who, good sportsman as he was, looked forward to the great battle for supremacy. With his great rival out of the way, Persimmon won the St. Leger in a canter from Labrador, the property of the Duke of Westminster. The North Country crowd, loyal to the backbone, and dearly loving a good horse, went wild and eventually the police had to escort the Prince back to the stands. As he walked back, surrounded by a cordon of police, some wag shouted out, " Never mind, Teddie, it will be all right: we'll come and bail you out."

Persimmon ran once more that year, winning the Jockey Club Stakes and beating Lord Rosebery's Sir Visto, winner of the Derby the year before. Then the enormous responsibilities of Dick Marsh and Lord Marcus Beresford were over for the moment, and the horse retired into winter quarters with his next objective, the Ascot Cup.

Good as he was as a three-year-old, he improved like good wine with age. Some time before Ascot of the following year, Lord Marcus wrote to Marsh, saying, " If you will tell me that Persimmon will win the Cup, Queen Victoria will come to see him run." This was asking a good deal of any trainer, so Marsh set Persimmon a very hard task in his trial. To his surprise and delight the horse came home alone, and he was able to answer that the Queen might come with safety.

Persimmon won the Cup, beating Winkfield's Pride in a canter by eight lengths. Robinson, who trained the latter, was very confident that he would win. He told Marsh the evening before the race that his was a great horse, that he was going to jump off and come as hard as he could all the way, and that no horse could live with him. Dick replied, " The faster your horse makes the pace the further will mine win." When Persimmon was stripped for the Ascot Cup he stands out in my memory as the most perfectly trained horse I ever saw, and on that day it would have given my two heroes, St. Simon and Ormonde, as much as they could do to beat him.

For seventeen years did Dick Marsh train and Lord Marcus manage for King Edward, and, great as their successes were, they had their periods of dire disaster and misfortune, but in these bad times no word of complaint ever came from their master, who took success and failure in the same fine spirit.

There was no place where the King was happier than at Newmarket, riding out in the morning to see his horses work, going to tea at Egerton House after the races to see them in the stable : he, for the moment, was free from the cares of State, for, greatly as he appreciated the lighter side of life, his capacity for hard work was even greater, and no man in any station of life fulfilled his duties with greater ability or more conscientiously than did King Edward.

Both Lord Marcus Beresford and Marsh had been fine cross-country riders in their younger days. Marsh rode many times in the Grand National, was third on two occasions, and nearly always got round. Moreover, he trained seven or eight horses for the race, and not one of these horses fell.

Marsh rode and won a hurdle race for Lord Marcus on Blue Bonnet in 1874. That is something to look back upon and be proud of—forty-eight years, and they were still working together when Lord Marcus died last year.

The sayings and doings of Lord Marcus would fill a book, and a devilish amusing book it would be. He was the wittiest man in the world, the best of friends, and a pretty good enemy : and Dick Marsh is one of the most entertaining of men. I do not often give advice, but, if anyone who is fond of racing has the chance of spending a day at Egerton House, do not let him miss it. There is Turf history written on the walls of the house, and he will also meet Mrs. Marsh, that most charming daughter of another great trainer, the late Sam Darling.

Writing of Turf history on walls makes me think of Palace House, the Newmarket home of the Rothschilds, and the wonderful collection of pictures there. I have heard some people say they do not like pictures of horses. Perhaps, from an artistic point of view, they may be unsatisfactory, but to those who are fond of racing what pleasant memories they bring back.

There is no more honoured name on the Turf than that of Rothschild, and I should say it stands alone in this respect, that their colours have been carried on the race-course without a break for a longer period than those of any other family. I have known many good and kind men, but one of the best friends I ever had was the late Mr. Leopold de Rothschild.

Many people do kind things when it comes their way, but Leo was for ever looking for an opportunity to help those who might be in difficulties. The following words always reminded me of him : " I pass through this world but once : if, therefore, there be any kindness I can show, or any good thing I can do, let me do it now : let me not defer it or neglect it, for I shall not pass this way again."

These words were the favourite quotation of a very gallant gentleman, Major Charles Beatty, who was so impressed with them that he had them written over the mantelpiece in his home at Newmarket, saying he liked to be reminded of them every day.

I believe that in his long career on the Turf, Mr Rothschild had but two trainers, first Alfred Hayhoe and then John Watson, and his son Anthony carries on in the same way. The latter has already won the Grand Prix with a good horse in Galloper Light, and is certain to revive the glories and successes of the Blue and Yellow cap.

Leo was a busy man, but no one ever loved the game of racing better. He managed his horses himself and arranged the trials and, carrying on an old custom of the family, made his jockeys wear colours, boots and breeches in all trials.

He was very fond of betting, but his satisfaction over a good win was greatly spoilt if his friends were not " on " too. He was very proud of his horses, and sometimes inclined to overrate them, but we most of us can plead guilty to that fault, if fault it is.

Excitable and emotional, with a quick temper, I have known him flare up and attack people sometimes without reason, but so generous and open-hearted was he in making amends that one liked him better after one of these breezes. He had many great horses, and the Rothschild family have won all the big races.

Unquestionably St. Frusquin was the best horse he ever owned, although St. Amant won the Two Thousand and the Derby. St. Amant's Derby was run in a most terrific thunderstorm, deluges of rain and thunder and lightning. He was a brilliant horse, with tremendous speed, queer-tempered and easily upset.

Kempton Cannon, who rode him in all his races, told me the following story. When he got up on the horse in the paddock at Epsom, and was being led round the ring, St. Amant kept on putting his ears back and turning his head round, as if he were trying to catch his jockey by the leg. When Kempton asked the boy what on earth was the matter with the horse, he replied, " That's all right : I've been pinching him all the morning. He'll be fairly on his toes now."

Whether it was the effect of the pinching or the thunder and lightning I do not know, but St. Amant jumped off in front and nothing ever got near him. I never saw a happier or a wetter man than Mr. Rothschild when he led in his horse.

While Mr. Rothschild was always a staunch supporter of any jockey who rode for him, he perhaps liked George Fordham best, and among the many stories he told me of him here is one I particularly remember.

Mr. Rothschild was going to have a big bet on a two-year-old on its first appearance on a race-course, and told Fordham that he must be sure and win. " Oh dear, oh dear," said Fordham, " you ought never to bet on a two-year-old first time out." " Why not," said Mr. Leo. " I have tried it very well." " Well, you know," answered Fordham, " when I get down to the post on these two-year-olds, and I feel their little hearts beating under my legs, I think, why not let them have an easy race, win if they can, but don't frighten them first time out."

I once told Mr. Rothschild that I thought he tried his two-year-olds too high, saying that if I had a promising horse I believed in giving him an easy trial to give him confidence. He answered, " Yes, that is what I like, too, but if I do it my horse gets a false reputation. When he runs, half the City of London is on him : he may be beat to the devil—and then where am I ? "

Fordham, great jockey and good fellow as he was, did not always quite like to own up when he made a mistake. One October meeting at Newmarket, I was with Lord Alington, when Mr. Rothschild told us he had a certainty in a selling race, and having had a bad day I went to get out of it. Later on, when riding down to see the race, which finished at the T.Y.C. Post, with Mr. Rothschild, Lord Alington came cantering up and Mr. Rothschild asked him what he had got on. He answered, " Twenty-five pounds." " Why, you ought to have had more than that," said Mr. Leo, and turning round put the same question to me. £500 was my stake, and I told him so. " Good God," said Lord Alington, " I wish I had your pluck." " All right," I said, " you can have my pluck if you will give me your money."

Nimble, the supposed certainty, was beaten a head.

Fordham was riding one of his "kidding" races, and for once was caught. Mr. Rothschild declared his intention of buying the winner. Fordham begged him not to, but having seen nothing apparently wrong in the race he did so. The horse turned out to be no good. Archer happened to be on his hack close to me while the race was being run. When I saw Fordham's whip go up 200 yards from home, I thought he was beaten, but Archer, who had studied his methods so closely, assured me that he was only "kidding." He lost the race by a head, and I turned to Archer, saying, "Well, you made a mistake then." "No," he replied, "I made no mistake, but the old man did and threw his race away." It took an expert like Archer to know whether Fordham was all out or had a stone up his sleeve.

Besides being a great racing man, Mr. Rothschild was very fond of hunting, and hunted from his house Ascott, near Leighton Buzzard, with the Whaddon Chase and also with Lord Rothschild's Stag Hounds.

Stag-hunting is generally, to my mind, a somewhat tame performance, but the Rothschild hounds were splendid, and showed great sport, running with the dash of fox-hounds. Some of the best hunts I have ever had have been with them and many of the happiest days of my life were spent hunting from Ascott.

CHAPTER XIX

THE FOUNDATION OF LORD DERBY'S STUD—CANTERBURY PILGRIM—LORD WILLIAM BERESFORD AND TOD SLOAN

In 1894 Caroline Duchess of Montrose died, and Lord Derby engaged her stud groom, John Griffiths, for the Knowsley Stud. He could not have chosen a better man, for the Griffiths family is well known among breeders of bloodstock to-day. John Griffiths is still in charge at Knowsley, and his sons hold good positions in other large studs, one of them, Walter, being Lord Derby's stud groom at the Woodlands Stud, Newmarket.

It was largely on John Griffiths's advice that Lord Stanley bought Canterbury Pilgrim for his father, at the sale of the Duchess's yearlings, after her death. Beautifully bred by Tristan out of Pilgrimage, she was, as a yearling, rather on the small side, with a good back and loins, but with a short neck and very low withers. But Griffiths's judgment was good, for undoubtedly this little filly has been the foundation stone of Lord Derby's Stud. She grew very little during the winter, and did not show any particular promise. She was excitable in her work, and had a very bad mouth. I tried her twice, and all she did was to show speed for about $3\frac{1}{2}$ furlongs. She ran five times as a two-year-old and was unplaced on every occasion except one. That was in the Knowsley Nursery, at Liverpool, when, thanks to a flying start, she was only just caught close home, and finished a good third, but with only 7st. 6lb. on her back.

I have previously told how the late Robert Peck,

after seeing her run very fast in the Champagne Stakes, for which she finished last, had encouraged me by saying that she would probably win the Oaks the next year, adding that she reminded him of that great mare, Marie Stuart, whom he had trained, and who had also been a very short runner as a two-year-old, and then developed into a great stayer.

In the winter and early spring of 1896, Canterbury Pilgrim improved immensely in appearance, but, when she began to do fast work, she became so irritable and pulled so hard that it was difficult to do anything with her. She was as spiteful as a cat, and kicked at anything that came near her. We had a big bay gelding called Flare Up in the stable, who had won many races for us. He was as quiet and sedate as an old sheep, and I sent him about with her away from the other horses. At first she would kick at him whenever he came near her, but suddenly she took a great fancy to him, and so long as he was beside her she would behave decently. So old Flare Up constituted himself her schoolmaster, and he really seemed to take the most intelligent interest in his job. They had adjoining boxes in the stable, and we made the partition very low, so that they could always see each other. It was no pleasant job to do her in the stable for she would kick and bite like the devil, but when she was making an extra fuss the old horse would put his head over the side of the box, and if ever a horse talked to another he did. We even sometimes took him into her box and let him stand beside her while she was being dressed over. So long as she was in training he never left her and accompanied her to every race meeting she went to.

She pulled so hard that she did most of her gallops by herself, with old Flare Up ready to look after her when she pulled up and to take her home.

I had made up my mind early in the year to train her for the Oaks, and miss all other races, and she did a tremendous lot of long work. It was at the Second Spring Meeting at Newmarket that she had her first and only trial. She had done so much work alone that I was not at all sanguine as to the result, and told Rickaby to ease her if she tired. She fairly astonished us by winning in a canter by many lengths, and when she pulled up would not have blown a candle out. It was not what she beat in the gallop, but the way she did it which impressed us. I never tried her again, and she still did most of her work by herself.

It was a dry season, and the ground was very hard. In those days, in dry weather, the whole of the Lime-kilns were open, and you could go where you liked. Rickaby and I found one track which had escaped being used, and was much better than anywhere else, so every other day she would come a good gallop up this particular bit of ground. The harder she worked the more she ate and the bigger she got, and that is a characteristic of many of her descendants. They are often most difficult and disappointing in their early work, but, if once you get them going the right way, the more you give them the better they like it.

The day before the Oaks it was frightfully hot, and, when Canterbury Pilgrim stepped out of her box on arriving at Epsom, the sweat was running off her in streams, and even Flare Up could not put her in a good temper. That day she ate nothing, so we gave her some stout with eggs beaten up in it, a beverage that Flare Up knew well in his younger days, and was very fond of. By the next morning she was herself again.

The One Thousand of that year had been won by the Prince of Wales's Thais. She was a strong favourite for the Oaks, and, Persimmon having won the Derby, a great double was anticipated for the Royal colours. But the men of observation at Newmarket had not forgotten Canterbury Pilgrim's gallop, and, in spite of her bad record as a two-year-old, she had a good many supporters. Lord Cadogan had been round my stable the week before Epsom, and as he was leaving he said to me, " You have shown me the winner of the Oaks," and he told everyone she was sure to win. As she walked in the Paddock beside the great Flare Up many people mistook the old gelding for the filly, and said what a great fine, slashing mare she was.

I was so sure of her stamina, and she had done such a preparation, that I wanted Rickaby to jump off and go all the way, but he would not hear of it, and said, " I must get her in behind, or she will run herself to a standstill." So I let him do as he liked, only saying, " For God's sake, don't get on those rails, but give her a clear run whatever you do." Rickaby told me the other day that I always gave him those orders when I thought I had a good thing, but that he never obeyed them. He had a passion for being on the rails, yet he always managed to get through at the right moment. So in the race he waited with her till they came to Tattenham Corner, and then somehow, in the straight, there he was on the heels of Thais. About half-way up he dashed his mare at the favourite and settled her in a few strides. It was the fashion in those days for a jockey, when he challenged in a race of that sort, to come as close to the other horse as possible, with the idea, I suppose, of demoralizing his opponent. So much so that Tom Cannon said no man was a jockey who could not, at the crucial moment, pick his whip up just in front of the challenging horse's head. Certainly on this occasion Rickaby was very close to Thais, and afterwards, when the Prince of Wales congratulated me, he said " Tell your jockey from me that he came too close to my mare," and I think he was right for the least swerve on either side might have led to trouble.

I was desperately hard up at this time, and my only bet was a thousand to eighty, but as I was getting in the train that night, going home to Newmarket, a letter was put into my hand from Lord Derby, containing a cheque for £1,000 and I went home a very happy man, thinking what a lucky day it was for my creditors.

Canterbury Pilgrim's next race was in the Coronatio..

Stakes, at Ascot, and here I made a complete fool of myself. I was very much afraid that the mile, which is the distance of this race, would be too short for her, and I told Rickaby that he must jump off and come along with her from the start. He was dead against it, declaring that was the way to get her beaten, but I was obstinate, and I suppose had got a swelled head after winning the Oaks. I insisted on it, with the result that after tearing away for six furlongs she went out like a snuffed candle. Her next appearance was in the Liverpool Summer Cup, which she won in a canter, beating a very hot favourite of Bill Beresford's, a good horse called Paris III.

By that time my back had got very bad again, and I was not able to go to Liverpool, and shortly afterwards I had to give up training and go abroad. I did not come back till the First October Meeting. The horses were left in the charge of Harry Sharpe (my head man) and Charles Morbey. They had a very successful time, and won a lot of races.

Canterbury Pilgrim did not run in the St. Leger, as Persimmon blocked the way, but she won the Park Hill Stakes from a good field in a canter. She was then trained for the Cambridgeshire, which I thought was a great mistake, as it was not the sort of race for her. She would have been much more at home in the Cesarewitch. In the Cambridgeshire she ran moderately, but two days later came out again for the Jockey Club Cup, where she had to meet a good horse of Mr. Rothschild's called Gulistan. He had won the Free Handicap for three-year-olds that week with 9st. on his back. I remember Rickaby who, as a rule always tried to stop me betting, saying, " Now this is an occasion when you can really let yourself go," and I did. He was right, for she galloped Gulistan to a standstill, and won by fifteen lengths.

At the end of the racing season 1896, Lord Derby asked me if I wanted to keep her in training for the following year, and what I thought of her chance of winning the Ascot Cup. I knew that Persimmon was to be kept for this race, and good mare as ours was she would never beat this great horse. Also, she was such a highly strung mare that she took a lot out of herself in training, so I advised him to send her to the stud.

This question of racing mares after three years old has been much discussed. I know that the general opinion is that they are more likely to breed good horses if retired early, but I am not at all sure that this theory is correct, neither do I believe that it is founded on fact. I have often heard it said that great race mares do not make good brood mares. When people make this statement they forget that every year there are some hundreds of fillies born, and that out of this number there are perhaps two that become really good racehorses. Of course, every now and again one of these good mares proves a failure at the stud, but if you were to take a percentage of the brood mares you would find that the produce of the great race mares is easily first in the field.

Mat Dawson, who trained for Lord Falmouth, was of this opinion, and used to cite the instance of Alice Hawthorn, dam of Thormanby, who ran, I believe, till she was aged. Then there were Lily Agnes, dam of Ormonde, Donnetta, who was at her best on a race-course when she was seven years old, was the dam of Diadumenos, Diadem, Diophon, and has this year the best-looking foal she has ever produced.

I could give many more instances, but these few are sufficient to show that racing mares after three years old does not necessarily harm them from a breeding point of view. Of course, as in everything else, judgment and common sense must be used. The moment a filly shows signs that she is getting tired of racing, out of training she should go. However, to take a case for the other side, Canterbury Pilgrim was a great success at the stud. Her second foal, Chaucer, by St. Simon, was a good horse, and Swynford, by John o' Gaunt, was by far and away the best I have ever trained. Her sons are good stallions, and her daughters good brood mares, and anything of her blood commands a high price. As I have said, Canterbury Pilgrim herself was, an excitable, irritable mare, but game and hard as steel. She, no doubt, got these characteristics from her sire, Tristan, who must have been made of cast iron, but was certainly a bad-tempered horse. Her descendants have nearly all got a touch of the old mare's disposition, for although they are as a rule generous, good-tempered animals they want careful treatment. Many of them look like horses that would come out early, but it is very rarely that they do so, and if you try to force them it means ruin, for their temper is sure to go.

In the year 1896, Lord Derby had a good two-year-old running called Crestfallen—I think one of the best-named horses I have ever known. The present Lady Derby (then Lady Alice Stanley) was responsible for the name : he was by Ocean Wave out of Dolores. I bought him from Alfred Sadler for £300. He won six races that year, beginning by winning at the Liverpool Spring Meeting, and ending with a victory in the Knowsley Nursery at the Liverpool Autumn Meeting.

That winter, 1896-1897, I had again to go abroad for my health, and did not come back till the day before the Derby. I did not go to Epsom, but came straight to Newmarket. I then lived at Bedford Lodge.

The stable had been having a very bad time, and Crestfallen had run the first day at Epsom, starting at three to one on, and had been down the course. When he arrived back at Newmarket, he had a temperature of 104, which accounted for his defeat. When I told Lord Derby, instead of being upset he smiled, and said, " I am delighted to hear it, because some of my friends have been trying to persuade me that Rickaby was not trying on the horse, and here is a much better answer than any I could give them." But I was not so pleased, for this was the beginning of a disastrous epidemic in my stable, which did not miss a single horse. It was a nice thing to come home to after six months abroad. Our first winner was Melange, at the Liverpool Summer Meeting, and he was the only horse we were able to run.

. . . . . .

In 1896 the colours of Lord William Beresford appeared on the English Turf. He was the eldest of those three remarkable Beresford brothers, the other two being Lord Charles and Lord Marcus. Bill Beresford had been for some years Military Secretary to the Viceroy of India, and in that country he had carried all before him, both socially and on the Turf. These Beresfords were a wonderful trio, a devil-may-care lot, who took and gave all the joy that was to be got out of life, but in addition to this they made their mark in whatever line of life they adopted. Bill was a distinguished soldier and a V.C. : Charlie was one of the most able and gallant of our naval heroes : and Marcus was for years the manager of the Royal Stud.

The three brothers were extraordinarily devoted to each other, and in particular Marcus adored Bill, who, in spite of his distinguished record, had always something of the reckless boy about him. Bill Beresford had not been in England long before he married Lily, Duchess of Marlborough, an American by birth, and he became the owner of a large stud of race-horses, which were trained in company with Mr. Lorillard's by the American trainer, J. Huggins.

This was the beginning of what we at that time called the " American invasion." American owners, trainers and jockeys played a large part in the racing world, and perhaps the most remarkable figure among them all was that wonderful little jockey, Tod Sloan. The first occasion that I can remember seeing him ride was when he was beaten a head on St. Cloud for the Cambridgeshire, in 1897. Kempton Cannon, on Comfrey, won the race.

From the painting by John Beer
CHAUCER WINNING THE LIVERPOOL CUP, 1905

From the painting by Isaac Cullen
STEDFAST WINNING THE CORONATION CUP, 1912, FROM PRINCE PALATINE

STANLEY HOUSE STABLES

GOING OUT FOR MORNING EXERCISE

I HAVE KNOWN

At the time we most of us thought that Sloan on St. Cloud ought to have won. Little did I imagine that this same Sloan in a short time would revolutionize the whole system of race-riding.

Sims, another American jockey, had come over a little while before with a great reputation, but he never made good, and I, in common with many others, despised and ridiculed the monkey seat of these jockeys. At the same time I could not be blind to the fact that Sloan, during the short time that he was in England, in 1897 won twenty races, and often on horses that did not appear to have particularly good chances.

Huggins told me some interesting facts concerning the origin of the present style of riding. In the old days there used to be a lot of what they called "Up Country" race meetings in America. These were very primitive affairs with partially untrained horses and inexperienced riders competing for the races. But often a useful horse was to be picked up at these meetings, and Huggins used to make a practice of sending some good old plater round the country. If anything beat him he would buy it, bring it home, where he usually found that good training and riding would work immense improvement. Then there came a time when the country people began putting up nigger boys on these horses. Huggins, having bought two or three horses that had won, and had been ridden by black boys, took them home, but, instead of finding they were improved by his training, they turned out not to be so good as when he bought them. This puzzled him considerably, and he could not make it out. Then one day, having bought a horse, the black boy who rode him begged to be bought too, as he wanted to go with his horse. Huggins, liking the look of his face, agreed to take the boy. When he got home, he tried his new purchase, and he was beaten easily by the very horse he had defeated up country. The black boy went to Huggins and said, " You let me ride, you see what will happen " ; so the experiment was tried, and the Darkie rolled home. To make a long story short, whatever Huggins put the boy up on was sure to win. It may not be generally known that the American jockeys in those days, who I believe were most beautiful horsemen, rode with even longer stirrups and sat more upright than the English. The black boys got their peculiar seat in this way. No one took the trouble to teach them to ride, they were thrown up on some old broncho with only a rug instead of a saddle, and they used to catch hold of the mane and hang on the best way they could until they had found their balance. You have only to picture the scene in your eye and you will see the origin of the present seat. Huggins soon tumbled to this, and to the advantage it gave the horses. There you will find the beginning of the present style of riding. You cannot oppose it, but you cannot like it. It has spoilt much of the beauty of race riding, but it has come to stay, and we must make the best of it.

In 1898, shortly after the Doncaster September Meeting, Sloan returned to England, and became first jockey to Lord William Beresford. He began at once to ride winners, but I was still stupid enough to oppose him. At the Newmarket First October Meeting he carried all before him, and, owing to my obstinacy, by the end of the week I was very nearly " broke." My jockey, Fred Rickaby, was a man of few words, and never gave an opinion without good reasons behind it. I asked him what he thought of Sloan. He answered, "If I were an owner I should not run a horse unless Sloan rode it."

I was so impressed by this that from that moment I determined to put up Sloan whenever I could get him and when my horses were in at weights that Rickaby could not ride.

At the time Rickaby gave me his opinion of him I trained a three-year-old filly belonging to the late Lord Derby, called Altmark. She was a beautiful little chestnut mare by Marcian out of Altiora, but all through the year she had greatly disappointed us in her races. I had won the Liverpool Spring Cup that year with a five-year-old, Golden Rule, the joint property of Lord Stanley and Sir Horace Farquhar. Before the Craven week I tried Altmark, and another three-year-old, Schomberg, at even weights with him. Altmark won easily, with Schomberg a neck behind the old horse. She ran in a small welter handicap in the Craven week, where she was receiving lumps of weight from moderate horses. I had by then given up high betting, but on this occasion, and for the last time in my life, I had £500 on, and I almost thought I was robbing the bookmakers. Ridden by the best light-weight of the day, Nat Robinson, she was a bad third.

The very next race was the Craven Stakes, and, to rub it in, Schomberg, in a good field, was second, only beaten half a length by Jeddah, who subsequently won the Derby. The following week Altmark was a good third for the One Thousand, not two lengths behind the winner. After that, although you could not make her do wrong at home, she ran worse and worse. Having now become a believer in Sloan, I resolved to try to win the Liverpool Cup with this jady mare if he would ride her. Bill Beresford gave his consent, and, as she was well handicapped, we all backed her once more, trusting in Sloan to work the miracle.

Tod hated riding gallops, especially early in the morning, and I never could get him on her back previous to the race. But, as he had won two or three races for me on shifty horses, I somehow felt confident that he and Altmark would hit it off. When it was known that he was to be her jockey she became a hot favourite. I remember on the morning of the race feeling very frightened that she would let me down again and make a fool of me. When Sloan came into the Paddock I could see he was not on good terms with himself, and he said to me, " They all tell me this is the meanest mare on earth, and that I have no chance." Now, unless he was confident, half his greatness was gone, so I did not feel happy. He then said " Where is the mare ? I have never seen her." She was walking just outside the Paddock, and she certainly looked beautiful. He gave one look at her. In a moment he was a changed man, exclaiming, " Oh ! I shall win." Now it was well known that Altmark was an impetuous, nervous mare, and naturally the English jockeys were not particularly keen on Sloan winning, which perhaps accounts for the fact that they were 40 minutes at the post. In the many false starts the mare three or four times went nearly a furlong before Sloan could pull her up. But, to my great surprise, instead of returning thoroughly upset, she was as cool as a cucumber. Her jockey seemed to have hypnotized her. When they did go she was off like a rocket. Nothing ever got near her again, and she won.

The start for the Liverpool Cup is close to the Stands. After the first break-away, when Sloan had pulled Altmark up, she looked as if she was going to " play up." I saw him lean right over on her neck. He appeared to be whispering in her ear ; anyhow whatever he did she calmed down and behaved perfectly from that moment.

Sloan won on another curious old horse for me at the same meeting, Sir Horace Farquhar's Nouveau Riche. He was well named by Carlton out of Novice, and was a great favourite of his owner. Horace had bought him himself, for when the horse went into the sale ring he was standing next George Barrett, who happened to tell him that the sire and dam were two of the gamest horses he had ever ridden. He turned out a very useful horse, and had in his time won many good races, but he had become very cunning and sulky. He was in the habit of beginning so slowly that he would be quite out of the race from the start. With Sloan up, he jumped off like a two-year-old and won, running away, by eight lengths. I think the old horse thought he had a devil on his back. It certainly is a fact that Sloan produced a marvellous effect on all sorts and kinds of horses. Nouveau Riche was in another handicap on the Saturday of the same Liverpool week, and we proposed to run him again, but, as Sloan was sailing for America that morning, we had to find another jockey.

Rickaby could not ride the weight, and I could not find a single one who would take the job on. At last I persuaded Sam Loates to do so. " I shall pull up my stirrups," he said, " and do Tod Sloan on the old brute." So out went Sam with his knees under his chin, looking very uncomfortable, and away went Nouveau Riche from the fall of the flag as though he had the same devil on his back. Coming to the canal turn he was leading the field by ten lengths, but about then he began to discover that his rider was a jockey and not a devil, and he pulled up into a canter. After two or three horses had passed him Sam Loates scrambled back into his old seat. He picked up his whip and shouting out " Here's two for old England," he hit the horse two terrific clouts which set him going again, with the result that, dashing through his field, he won by ten lengths. Nouveau Riche never won a race again.

That week was a good one for Knowsley and my stable. We won eight races, and were three times second, but, as so often happens, the " good thing " of the week came unstuck. This was a two-year-old belonging to Sir Horace Farquhar. It was entered in a mile selling race. With Sloan up it was something to bet on without fear. Sloan had won the race in a common canter, but, pulling his horse up, he was shot on the post and beaten a head. Sir Horace not only lost his money, but he also lost his horse, for the latter was promptly claimed. Bill Beresford had backed it to win him £2,000, which he declared before the race he intended to invest on Altmark for the Liverpool Cup.

The best year Lord William Beresford ever had was in 1899, when he won 60 races, value £42,000. They included the One Thousand, the Jubilee, the Champagne Stakes, the Middle Park Plate, and the Dewhurst Plate. If he had stuck to his own horses he would have won a fortune, but he would bet on every race, which drove his trainer, Huggins, almost to despair. It is most disappointing for a trainer, after he has brought off one or two good things for his owner, to hear that, after all, the latter has had a bad week.

There is no doubt that the " American invasion " taught us in England a lot, especially in regard to the plating of horses. Their racing plates were far better made and lighter than ours. I remember Huggins telling me once in July that, in his opinion, having American plates on instead of English made the difference of at least four lengths in a mile race. He added that he would rather run his horse without shoes at all than in English ones. This so impressed me that I asked Sloan to cable to America ordering a box of these plates to be sent over. Meanwhile I ran several of my horses without shoes, with considerable success, but to do this you must have a horse with particularly good feet, and the going must be perfect. I did not get my American plates until the First October Meeting at Newmarket. I was running a sharp little two-year-old called Handspike, belonging to my brother Colonel Charles Lambton; Sloan was riding her.

When I told him that I thought she might just win he said, " I wish she had our plates on." " So she has," I replied, " for they arrived last night." The little man fairly jumped, and, saying " Please excuse me, I have forgotten something in the weighing room," he ran off, presumably to get his money on. Having found what he wanted, he came back declaring that he was sure to win, and so he did, beating a field of eighteen by two lengths.

The Americans also taught us that open doors and cool stables were far better than the hot-house atmosphere usually to be found in English stables at that time.

It was Sloan's misfortune to be always surrounded by a crowd of the worst class of people that go racing. Once a man gets into that set, I have hardly ever known him get out of it, even if he wants to. This was the ruin of Sloan, and eventually brought about his downfall.

I HAVE KNOWN

He was a genius on a horse; off one, erratic and foolish. He threw away a career that was full of the greatest promise. As a jockey, in many ways he reminded me of Fred Archer. He had the same wonderful hands, and was as quick as lightning to take advantage of any opportunity that occurred in a race. Like Archer, once he had been on the back of any horse, he had an almost uncanny intuition into its peculiarities and nature.

A race I remember well was when he rode Knight of the Thistle in the Jubilee. The Knight was a great big good-looking horse, but a loose-made sort of customer, and easily unbalanced, in addition to which he was not too generous. He was owned by Lord William Beresford, who had backed him very heavily for the race, and he started favourite.

In the parade, Sloan seemed like a pea on a drum on this big horse, and, knowing that other good jockeys had found him more than a handful, I would not back him. The horse was as obstinate as a mule at the post. During the long delay it looked very much as if he would be left. In the end he got off fairly well, but all Sloan's usual quiet persuasive efforts to induce him to race properly were unavailing. He had to fall back on the whip, and in the end slammed him home by a length. When he rode back to the unsaddling enclosure, Sloan looked quite exhausted.

I had engaged him to ride a two-year-old filly of Horace Farquhar's in the next race. Bill Beresford came to me and said, " Sloan has asked me to tell you he can't ride for you, as he is so tired." I tried to get another jockey, but as there was a big field I found every one was engaged. So I went to Sloan and told him he must ride. With his funny American twang he replied, " That was the meanest horse I've ever ridden. I'm tired to death, and I can't ride any more." But I insisted and weighed him out. When he came into the paddock he lay on his back in the grass, repeating. " It's no use: I can't ride."

Bobette, who was a beautiful little filly, was walking about close by. Sloan, still lying on his back, asked, "Is that my horse?" When I said, "Yes," he was on his feet in a moment, and all his depression and lassitude disappeared. He won the race easily. Sloan was like that: when he was full of life and confidence he could do anything, but when he was down he could do nothing, and would get beaten on the best thing in the world.

Chiselhampton was another good horse I trained about this time. He never ran as a two-year-old, for he was continually going wrong in his back. Twice I had a sheep killed and the skin put on his loins, an old-fashioned remedy. This eventually cured him completely, but left him very sour in his temper. As a four-year-old he was a regular savage, but a real good horse. I don't think I should ever have got a race out of him if it had not been for my jockey, Rickaby, and Bill Newman, my present travelling lad. The latter did him in the stable and rode him at exercise. I know before the York Summer Meeting I had nearly given him up, for we could not get him to start for any gallop. But one morning, when he had been playing up at the bottom of the Limekilns, Rickaby, who was on him, said, "Leave him to me: if I stop here till dark I'll get him to go." I can't say from memory how long he was there, but it was for some hours, and the horse three times got rid of his jockey, but "Rick" never let go, and at last he got him thoroughly beaten, and did what he liked with him.

After that Chiselhampton went to York for a handicap where he was top weight. Owing to my train being very late, I got to the course thirty-five minutes after the time set for the race the second on the card. As I went in I asked the man at the gate what had won. "They're not off yet," he said, "and Chiselhampton has been behaving like a mad horse." At that moment the bell rang and they were off, and my horse won in a canter. I wonder what the public would say now if the starter waited forty minutes for a bad-tempered horse. It was frequently done in those days.

Chiselhampton then won three good handicaps running, ending up with the Liverpool Cup, beating a raging hot favourite of Percy Bewicke's in General Peace, and giving him 17 lb. He was ridden by Sam Loates, who rode a splendid but severe race, and his temper was worse than ever afterwards.

CHAPTER XX

SOME AMERICAN OWNERS AND TRAINERS—DOPING—SAVAGE HORSES

THE first American owner I knew was the late Mr. Ten Broeck. I was only a boy at the time, but he struck me as typical of the shrewd, dry humorous American that one reads of in the novels of Mark Twain. I know that he was very much liked over here, and his colours were popular on the English Turf.

Mr. Lorillard and Mr. Whitney were the type of sportsman that any country would be proud of, and their trainers, first Huggins and later Andrew Joyner, were two good fellows. Both of them, especially Joyner, were very popular with the racing world. Their horses were always run out in the most straightforward manner. I can say that at the time when Joyner made up his mind to leave England and return to America there was no more popular man in Newmarket, and I shall always look back with pleasure on the dinner we gave him before he left. The more Americans of this sort that come over the better.

At the time I write of, Mr. P. Lorillard had a large string of horses in England trained by J. Huggins. He was as great a gentleman and as good a sportsman as ever went racing. He was not a new-comer on the English Turf, for in 1881 he had won the Derby and St. Leger with Iroquois, and in 1879 he had a wonderful old gelding called Parole. This horse created a sensation by beating Isonomy for the Newmarket Handicap in April. He was ridden by Charles Morbey, and started at a hundred to fifteen. His victory was not unexpected by his connections, and he followed it up by winning the City and Suburban and the Great Metropolitan, in both of which races Archer was his jockey. Mr. Lorillard's horses were then trained by a curious character, Jacob Pincus, who remained in this country when Mr. Lorillard for a period gave up racing in England and returned to America. Pincus had practically given up training, but occasionally had a horse or two of his own. I remember one year when, as a very old man, he owned two shocking bad horses, and, much as everyone would have liked to see the old man win a race, they were so bad that they were the despair of the handicapper. Yet on the same day at Lingfield both these horses managed to get their heads in front, and the public was as delighted as the owner.

I believe it was the interference of the Government with racing in America that brought Mr. Lorillard and his horses back to England. He had an enormous stud in America: his yearlings were broken and tried at home, and he brought the best to England, where he had considerable success for some years. Mr. Harry Cuthbert, well known to race-goers of to-day, then quite a young man, came over with him as his secretary, made his entries, and had much to do with the breeding of his horses. Mr. Lorillard was a great believer in English blood, and frequently replenished his stud with it. Eventually, Lord William Beresford entered into partnership with him, and, with Sloan as their jockey, they had a royal time.

The late Mr. Whitney and his son were both of the same class of owner. When they gave up and retired to their own country, they were a great loss to English Racing. Mr. Whitney got his racing colours in rather a curious way. One August Meeting, at York, I was in a vein of bad luck, my horses being continually second. Mr. Gerald Paget came to me after one of these reverses and said, "Are you fond of your colours?" They were light blue with a brown cap. "No," I replied, "I hate the sight of them." He then asked me if I would take £100 for them. "Give me the money,"

I answered, " and they are yours." The deal was completed at once, and then I learnt that it was Mr Whitney who wanted my colours, and as long as he lived his horses carried them. At his death I got them back again. Partly on account of my old colours I was always fond of backing his horses, and I had a good race on Volodyovski when he won the Derby.

Another American trainer, Wishard, was a very shrewd man, who won a great deal of money. He went in for a different class of race, and trained for a different class of owner, but I personally liked him very much. He was a remarkably clever man with horses. There is no doubt that he supplemented his great skill as a trainer by making use of the dope. In those days there was no law against this pernicious practice.

Wishard brought over with him as jockeys the two brothers Lester and Johnny Reiff. Lester was a very tall man, and had great difficulty in keeping his weight down. He was a fine jockey, and a wonderful judge of pace, while Johnny as a boy was the best light-weight I ever saw, excepting Frank Wootton.

I always thought it was a great pity that Wishard ever took to doping, for he was somewhat of a genius with horses, and would, I am sure, have made a great name for himself without it. His horses generally looked beautiful, and I am sure whatever dope he used could not have been a very powerful one : they looked too well for that, and kept their form too long. I had many a talk with him, and found him a most agreeable man, but we never got on to this subject.

Perhaps his greatest success was with Royal Flush. He was a very handsome chestnut horse by Favo, and had passed through more than one man's hands, but at the time Wishard bought him he belonged to Mr. F. W. Lee, who is well known to the present-day racing public as the Handicapper at most of our big meetings. I am sure that Royal Flush must have taught his genial and kindly owner what an uncertain thing a race-horse may be, for he, while well known to be a good horse, seldom produced his home form in public, and he continually disappointed Fred Lee. But when he had been for some time in the hands of Wishard he began to show what he could do. After running a good third for the Jubilee at Kempton, he won amongst other races the Hunt Cup at Ascot and the Stewards' Cup at Goodwood

I remember Wishard telling me to back him for the Hunt Cup, but, knowing how often he had disappointed his former owners, I would not do so. And what a fool I felt when I saw him run a game, honest horse and win a head. From that time on " he got better and better," and ended the season by running a match for £500 at Hurst Park against Eager, the best sprinter in England at the time, at even weights. The excitement over this match was intense, and the betting close. I was firmly convinced that Eager would win, which he did with ease, but the career of Royal Flush bears out my theory that Wishard was a great trainer as well as a good doper. Whether Royal Flush was helped by a dope of course I do not know, but if he was it cannot have been a very injurious one, or he would not have kept his form throughout the season as he did, and come out always with the appearance of a perfectly trained horse.

There is no doubt that the Americans started the practice of doping, though it must not be supposed that they all doped their horses. Both Huggins and Joyner detested it. They had seen too much of the mischief it caused in their own country, but, when they came over, there was no law against doping and those people who, like Wishard, made a study of it were perfectly within their rights.

It was Huggins who told me how it originated. In America they used to race eight or nine days in one particular place, and would then move on to some other district, where the same thing would take place. The consequence was that towards the end of these meetings most of the horses had run several times and would be played out. In fact, it became a survival of the fittest, and every dodge and device was used to keep the poor devils up to the mark, and some man hit on the marvellous properties of cocaine for the jaded horse.

After the Americans brought the dope over here, many Englishmen took it up, but they were not very successful, as they did not really understand enough about it. My own experiences were rather interesting.

I remember at the Newmarket First October Meeting of 1896 running a horse belonging to Sir Horace Farquhar, called East Sheen, in the Trial Selling Stakes. He was a useful plater, and anything that beat him was worth buying. In this race he was beaten a neck by a chestnut mare, Damsel II. When she was put up to auction I bought her for £450. She was pouring with sweat, looked very bad, and I thought that I could probably improve her. That evening, when I went to my stables my head man remarked that the mare I had bought was a wild brute, and had been running round her box like a mad thing ever since she came home. I went to look at her, and she certainly was a miserable object, with eyes starting out of her head and flanks heaving. This was the first doped horse I ever saw, although at the time I was quite unaware of what was the matter. I gave the mare a long rest, and got her quiet and looking well, but she was no good. Eventually Charlie Cunningham bought her for jumping, but he could do no good with her. He afterwards put her to the stud, where she produced a dead foal, and beyond that I know no more of her. But in 1896 doping was in its infancy, and it was not till about 1900 that it really began to be a serious menace to horse-racing. Even then, although there were mysterious hints of its wonderful effects, few people knew much about it, or really believed in it. After 1900, this horrible practice increased rapidly, and by 1903 it had become a scandal. I myself was still sceptical about any dope making a bad horse into a good one. But very strange things occurred, and one constantly saw horses who were notorious rogues running and winning as if they were possessed of the devil, with eyes starting out of their heads and the sweat pouring off them. These horses being mostly platers, and running in low-class races, did not attract a very great deal of attention, but three veterinary surgeons told me that the practice was increasing very much, that it would be the ruin of horse-breeding, and ought to be stopped. Then there occurred a case when a horse, after winning a race, dashed madly into a stone wall and killed itself. I then thought it was about time that something was done, so I told one of the Stewards of the Jockey Club what my three friends, the veterinary surgeons, had said. He was as sceptical as I had been, and declared he did not believe there was anything in it. At that time I had in my stable some of the biggest rogues in training, and I told the Stewards that I intended to dope these horses. They could then see for themselves what the result was.

The first horse I doped was a chestnut gelding called Folkestone. This horse had refused to do anything in a trial or a race. He was always last and would come in neighing. I first of all doped him in a trial. He fairly astonished me, for he jumped off in front and won in a canter. I sent him to Pontefract, where he beat a field of fourteen very easily, and nearly went round the course a second time before his jockey could pull him up. He won a race again the next day, was sold and never won again. I had told my brother, Lord Durham, who was not a Steward of the Jockey Club at that time, what I was doing. So much did he dislike this doping that he was inclined to object to my having anything to do with it. But when I explained that my object was to open the eyes of the Stewards, he withdrew his objection, but begged me not to have a shilling on any horse with a dope in him. To this I agreed.

I obtained six dopes from a well-known veterinary surgeon. They were not injected with a needle, but just given out of a bottle. Their effect on a horse was astonishing. I used five of them, and had four winners and a second. Not one of these horses had shown any form throughout the year. One of them, Ruy Lopez, who had previously entirely defeated the efforts of the best jockeys in England, ran away with the Lincoln Autumn Handicap with a stable boy up, racing like the most honest horse in the world. At the end of that Liverpool Autumn Meeting I had one dope left. I had made no secret of what I had been doing, and Lord Charles Montague asked me to give him one of these dopes. He wanted it for a horse called " Cheers," winner of the Eclipse Stakes, belonging to the Duke of Devonshire : so I gave him my last one. " Cheers " had run badly all the year. The following week he beat a big field for the Markeaton Plate with the dope in him, including a horse of my own, Andrea Ferrara, which I very much fancied.

By the following year, doping was made a criminal offence, the penalty being " warning off." Some people think there is a great deal going on now. I don't believe it : the penalty is too severe, although it is possible there are trainers who will take the risk.

A dope undoubtedly has a wonderful effect on a bad horse, but I am told it acts in just the contrary way on a good, honest one. In the bad horse it supplies the pluck and energy that are wanting, in the good one it overdoes it, and he will run himself out quickly.

Rather a curious case occurred with a horse that I trained. He came to me from another stable, and his trainer told me that he was sure he had been doped previously, for after he had got him the horse was in a most peculiar state, and that all his coat had come off. Acting on this information, I gave the horse a good chance to recover, and after a long rest got him in splendid condition, and tried him well. But directly he got on a race-course there was nothing doing. After several races I advised the owner to get out of him, as by this time doping was illegal, and I was convinced that he would not win a race without it. So he was entered in a selling race, and advertised to be sold after the race. I said to the owner, " You

THE EARL OF DERBY, K.G.

THE LATE EARL OF DERBY, LEADING IN KEYSTONE II,
AFTER WINNING THE OAKS, 1906

FINISH OF THE ST. LEGER, 1910, SWYNFORD WINNING FROM BRONZINO

Photo: Sport and General

will see this horse will be bought by the man who did so well with him before." In the race the horse was nearer last than first, and when he was put up for sale I saw the agent of the man I suspected bidding for him, and he fetched quite double what he was worth on the form he had been showing. Ten days later I went to a race meeting, and just got there in time to see the first race. Something ridden by Danny Maher came out looking all over a winner, when I saw the horse I had sold ten days before come up like a whirlwind, with his tail going round, and snatch the race from Danny in the last hundred yards. Now there is no doubt that a change of stables and a change of trainers sometimes works wonders with horses, but that is not done in ten days! This race attracted considerable notice, and the activities of this particular trainer ceased not long after this event. Not that he was warned off, but I believe that he was closely watched from that moment, and being a clever man he knew that the game was up.

As I have said previously, the Americans certainly taught us much that was simple and intelligent in the treatment of the horse.

When I began racing horses were not given enough fresh air in the stables, which were often badly ventilated, and without sufficient light. Open doors and windows were unknown at that period, and horses were heavily rugged up when at exercise. I think the change in this respect partly explains why horses of these days are so much better tempered than they used to be, and also so much sounder in the wind. Roaring in horses used to be exceedingly common, and it was not unusual to hear a string of horses coming up the cantering ground making as much noise as a band. Nearly every stable would contain one or two really savage horses, and when, as occasionally happened, one of these got loose, there would be a regular stampede to get off the Heath. Time after time I have seen a loose horse galloping about for half an hour or more before he could be caught, trumpeting like a wild beast. Now, when you see one, he generally trots up to his stable companions and stands quietly eating grass until he is caught. I remember on one occasion when I was the only person left on the Limekilns, and it happened in this way: it was at the time that I was suffering from my back and could not ride. I was on foot waiting for my horses to come up the gallop when I heard a most extraordinary noise proceeding from the plantation that runs along the side of the Bury road. Then a loose horse dashed out from the trees, and stood there roaring and trumpeting in a way that I have never heard before or since. I at once recognized that it was a noted savage called Prince Simon, owned by the French sportsman, Monsieur Lebaudy, and trained by Golding. My assistant, Harry Sharpe, was with me, and I hurried him off to turn my string on to the Waterhall ground out of the way of this mad brute, who would savage anything he came near. Away went Sharpe, and everyone else made themselves scarce. I could see and hear Prince Simon charging about the plantation in a mad state of fury kicking and biting at the trees. He then went for Golding, who rode a white pony. Golding discreetly left his hack: it was said that he climbed up a tree. The pony galloped off towards Moulton, pursued by Prince Simon, and I thought all was well. But somehow the pony eluded his pursuer, and the Prince again appeared on the Limekilns. Standing there, lord of all he surveyed, he was a fine sight, although rather too close to be pleasant. Still, I did not think he would bother about me on foot, but, finding nothing else worth his attention, he suddenly came charging down at me. It was not a pleasant position, as I was more or less of a cripple. I had my shooting stick with me, and when he came at me I gave him a crack over the head which made him stand on his hind legs and roar with rage. At this moment, by the greatest piece of luck, Golding's white hack emerged from the trees on his way home. Prince Simon, catching sight of him, went after him like a dog after a rabbit, and chased him home to his stables, where they managed to let the pony into a box and shut the door on his pursuer. They were not able to catch the savage till late in the afternoon, when, I suppose, being hungry, he went into his box of his own accord. Prince Simon was well bred and a good performer. After this episode, he was sold to the French Government as a stallion, but when they got him over to France he was so unmanageable that they shot him and rightly refused to pay for him.

On another occasion, two horses, the property of Mr. Abington Baird, got loose, also on the Limekilns. One was King of Diamonds, a good sprinter, the other a big chestnut called Snaplock, who was a good stayer. Mr. Baird's horses were then trained at Bedford Lodge, Newmarket, either by Charles Morton or Joe Cannon, I forget which. When they got loose, these two horses went for each other, but King of Diamonds soon had enough of it, and away he went as hard as he could down the Bury road for home, pursued by Snaplock. It must have been much like a hare and a greyhound, for, when they came to the entrance to the stables, Snaplock was so close on King of Diamonds' heels that he could not turn, so they went straight through the town down to the Rowley Mile Stands. Jack Watts followed them on a hack. They went into the enclosure for hacks, by the Birdcage, and came to a barrier by the steps in the Jockey Club Stand. There they had another scrap, and then King of Diamonds jumped the barrier and Snaplock knocked it down. Then they both jumped a similar barrier out again, and on they went across the Heath, for, whenever King of Diamonds stopped, Snaplock attacked him. Eventually they both came to a standstill just beyond the Cesarewitch starting post. Jack Watts found them there, both so thoroughly exhausted that there was no fight left in them, and they were taken home without any difficulty. Neither horse was ever worth a shilling again.

All this has taken me some way from the Americans, and their doings. I must say that at first the " American invasion" was not much appreciated over here, and I frankly confess that I hated it for it upset so many of my old theories and ideas. Also, the crowd that came over was a pretty tough one. I remember saying to Huggins one day that I supposed there were a good many rogues and thieves racing in America, and he replied, "There is not one, they have all come over here." But there is not the slightest doubt that the coming of the Americans did us a lot of good and roused us from that feeling of superiority and complacency which is fatal to all progress. When I came to know them I found there was so much to be learnt from them and they were so ready to be friendly that I changed my opinion. "Skeets" Martin was one of the first American jockeys really to make his home in England. He was first jockey to the Whitneys and J. Huggins. No man was ever blessed with better hands than Martin. He was a wonder at getting away from the gate, and I never met a starter who was not loud in his praise. He never gave them trouble, and they could always trust him. There was no more popular jockey in England, both with owners and his brother professionals. He was a fine rider, especially on two-year-olds and free-going horses, but, good jockey as he was, he would have been a great one if he had only had more confidence in himself. If he was riding a horse that was greatly fancied he would worry himself to death before the race and be over-anxious, and if he was beaten, whether it was his fault or not, he would be terribly down in his luck. He won the Derby on Ard Patrick for Mr. Gubbins and Sam Darling.

Two other American owners whose colours were always popular in England were Mr. Keene and Mr. Belmont. Mr. Keene was the owner of that good horse, Foxhall, who won the Grand Prix, beating Tristan, and the following year won the Ascot Gold Cup.

Foxhall was trained by old William Day, of Wood-yeats. William had trained at one time for my father, and, when I was about seven or eight years old, I was staying with my mother at some place about eight miles from his training establishment. I got hold of a donkey, and somehow found my way to his stables, and when I turned up and told him who I was he was tickled to death.

He never forgot it, and when, as a young man, I was racing and betting, he would sometimes tell me things which he would hardly let his own right hand know. William was of the old school, and went in for big coups and handicaps.

There is no doubt that things were done then that would raise a storm in these days. I remember three horses running in a race at Winchester, an open course, with no rails round it. One of these was trained by my old friend. He was one of those mystery horses which appeal to the public, had been entered in the Cesarewitch, and was supposed to be a " rod in pickle " for some good handicap.

I had been losing a lot of money, and I asked the old man if his was good enough to bet on. He hesitated a moment, and then replied, " If you know which of the other two will win, back it." I had no idea which was the best, so I backed them both for as much as I could get on, ending up by laying four to one on the pair. I went up to the Stand to watch the race, which was a mile and a half. Coming to the turn into the straight, to my horror I saw William's horse ten lengths in front. There was a beautiful field of standing corn on the left-hand side of the run-in. Whether the horse was hungry or not, I do not know, but instead of coming round the turn he dashed into the cornfield, and there was an end of him as far as the race was concerned. The funny part of the story was that the horse, whose name, I think, was General Scott, was really not worth a shilling, and was a good-looking impostor. William Day knew this when he advised me to back one of the others, but when, after the race, there were nods and winks about General Scott's extraordinary dash into the cornfield, and talk of the Cesarewitch, he held his tongue and looked mysterious. He knew that when the weights came out for the Autumn Handicaps the horse would be thought by many people to be his best, and would afford a screen for getting his money on the real goods. The handicappers were so afraid of William that it was not easy for him to get his horses well handicapped.

There was a tremendous plunger in those days called Sir Beaumont Dixie. At some race meeting, where he was entertaining a large party, very early in the day Sir Beaumont asked William if one of his horses would win a certain race. William told him he fancied it, but said, "You must keep it quiet, or I shall get no price." The horse started a hot favourite, and was beat to the d—v—l. After the race Sir Beaumont came up reproachfully to William, who said, "Never mind, you will get your money back on him another day." "Oh," said Sir B, "I'm not worrying about my losses, but all my party have lost their money." "Ah," said the old man, "that's just what I expected," and went off rubbing his hands.

Writing of Foxhall, who no doubt was the best horse William Day ever trained, reminds me of Tristan, a very queer-tempered horse, but game. Tristan was a dark chestnut by Hermit, just under sixteen hands, most beautifully made, with legs and constitution of iron. All courses came alike to him, and shortly after winning three long-distance races at Ascot, the Vase, the Hardwicke Stakes and a Biennial, he won the July Cup, six furlongs, at Newmarket.

The following year, as a five-year-old, he won the Ascot Cup and again the Hardwicke Stakes.

He was the property of Mr. Lefevre, a French owner, and was trained by "Young Tom" Jennings, the son of old Tom. Like his father, young Tom believed in a very strong preparation, and I remember Tom Corns, the commission agent, saying of their horses that they were so hard "you couldn't drive a nail into the beggars." Tristan remained in training till he was six years old.

That year St. Simon was entered in the Ascot Cup.

A curious match was made between these two horses at Newmarket over, I think, a mile and a half, each with his own pace-maker. Good as Tristan was, he met more than his match here ; St. Simon won in a canter. Shortly after they again met in the Cup, which was won easily by the younger horse. But Tristan won the Hardwicke Stakes again for the third time.

Tristan was not a great success at the Stud, but he was the sire of Canterbury Pilgrim, the wonderful little mare who, as I have said, laid the foundation of Lord Derby's great successes on the Turf, and whose descendants I have trained for the last twenty years.

CHAPTER XXI

CHAUCER—DANNY MAHER AND ROCK SAND

CANTERBURY Pilgrim's first foal was a brown filly by St. Serf, called St. Victorine. She met with an accident as a yearling, and could never be trained, but she was the dam of Entebbe, a useful mare, who has bred White Ant, and the two-year-old Equator, now in training.

Her second foal, Chaucer, by St. Simon, was a little pony when he came into training, but small as he was he soon showed that he could go, and on his first appearance ran second for the British Dominion Stakes at Sandown. But, like all the breed, he did not mature early, and he only ran once again before winning the Gimcrack Stakes at York.

I had tried him very well for this race, and he started a hot favourite at six to four, and won easily. At that time he was just under 15 hands. Like his dam, as a two-year-old, he was very low in the withers, and when Danny Maher got on him at York he appeared to be sitting on his neck.

After York he won the Boscawen Stakes at Newmarket, and finished the season by running second for the Clearwell Stakes. He improved greatly during the winter, and by the following May he was a beautiful little horse. Not being well engaged, we kept him for the Hunt Cup. When the weights came out it looked so good a thing that Danny Maher, who was then riding for us, advised me to run him at Hurst Park, as the penalty would bring his weight up and we would be able to put up a good jockey. He went to Hurst Park, started a hot favourite, and ran badly. The horse looked well and there was no excuse. We could not understand it, so he went to Ascot, where he again ran moderately.

I took five or six useful horses to Ascot that year and expected to have a good time. They all ran disgracefully, except one, Gay Gordon, which I fancied the least of all, and he ran second to Sceptre for the Hardwicke Stakes. The horses looked well and were feeding all right, but they were so distressed after their races that I began to think I must be the worst trainer in the world.

When I got home I could find nothing the matter— no temperature or other bad symptoms, but they showed no life on the training grounds, and the following week the whole stable went down with an illness called " Pink Eye," which was practically unknown among race-horses. With one or two exceptions they none of them recovered their form, and I think the first race I won was with a horse called Outsider, at the Houghton Meeting at the end of October.

Little Chaucer had a very bad attack, and did not run again that year; and the following year, as a four-year-old, although he won three races, he was very delicate and nervous, and could not get over six furlongs. He could not stand any hard work. As a five-year-old he began to gain confidence and strength. He won the Liverpool Summer Cup, but it was not till he was six years old that he really came to himself.

That year—1906—he again won the Liverpool Cup, beating one of the best horses on the Turf at the time, Velocity. This was one of the finest races I have ever seen, and Danny Maher, who was then Lord Derby's jockey, fairly excelled himself.

Velocity was a beautiful big bay horse, over 16 hands, with wonderful quality. He was a great horse and won races over all distances, but a mile and a quarter was just about his best course. In the race for the Liverpool Cup he was giving Chaucer 11lb. When they got into the straight the pair came away from the rest of the field ; the big horse had the best of it, but the little one hung on to him. Twice Chaucer made a great effort, only to be shaken off, and it looked all over, but Danny pulled him together, and had another go. This was too much for Velocity ; he threw his head up in the last few strides and was beaten a neck, with the third six lengths away. I have never seen a jockey more pleased with his horse than Danny was, and he said the little fellow had the heart of a lion. These two game fighters met again in the Chesterfield Cup at Goodwood, this time Velocity giving 9lb. After a tremendous struggle he finished a head in front of Chaucer, but the pair were just beaten by the beautiful mare Gold Riach, carrying a light weight.

I had great hopes of winning a third Liverpool Cup with the little horse that autumn, and I think he was better than ever, although he had a suspicious tendon. But the morning before the race he half ran away with Danny, and his leg went. Like his dam, he was always a very hard puller.

Danny Maher, his jockey, first came over to England in 1900, quite late in the season. He brought with him a great reputation from America, and quickly showed that it was not a false one. From the first I liked his manners and his riding. The following year he again came to this country, and was first jockey to Blackwell's stable, Sir James Miller being the chief patron. The first classic winner he rode was Sir James's Aida in the One Thousand Guineas. She was rather a flighty sort of filly, and her jockey showed that combination of delicate handling and strength which put him at the top of his profession as long as he was able to ride. Rickaby, than whom there was no better judge of riding, said he was better than Tod Sloan on his best day.

Sir James Miller, a young man in the Army, was most extraordinarily lucky on the Turf, and at this moment he was just entering the years of his greatest successes— without doubt they were largely due to his trainer,

George Blackwell, and his jockey. Never did two men work better together, and they had the greatest confidence in each other. When Danny took a fancy to a horse he wanted to be on his back every day if possible, and, when a jockey does this, it is wonderful how much he can improve a horse. I know that Danny, when he rode for me, made one or two quite ordinary horses into good ones, and I am sure that Blackwell could tell the same story.

Of course, Sir James Miller's best horse was Rock Sand, a very bloodlike brown horse by Sainfoin out of Roquebrune. From his early days in training Rock Sand was the worst trotter I ever saw, and did not move much better in his steady canters. Anyone who saw him hobbling along before he got warmed up would have put him down as a hopeless screw. But when fully extended in a good gallop he was a lovely mover. He was only beaten once as a two-year-old, and that was in the Middle Park Plate. Blackwell at that time also trained for Sir Daniel Cooper, and he had the very useful colt, Flotsam, in the race. I believe the two owners tossed up for Maher's services, and Sir Daniel won. Rock Sand was a moderate third, although ridden by a very good jockey, Lane, and Danny squeezed Flotsam home by a head. Probably Rock Sand missed his old pilot, for this was not his true form, and he came out again for the Dewhurst Plate, to win in a canter with Maher up.

There is no doubt in my mind that Rock Sand was a better horse than Flotsam, but Dan Cooper would never admit this. They met again as three-year-olds in the Two Thousand; Danny was again up on Flotsam, and Skeets Martin rode Rock Sand, who won cleverly by half a length from Flotsam, on whom Danny rode a wonderful race.

There were some good three-year-olds running that year, and none of them better than the beautiful Quintessence, who belonged to the late Lord Falmouth. I wish we could see those famous old colours back on the Turf again. I have said that Rock Sand was always lame, or appeared to be so, in his slow paces, but he was a park hack when compared to Quintessence. It is a curious thing that the two best three-year-olds that year of either sex should have been afflicted in the same way. Quintessence was the dam of that good horse, Paragon, who, I am sure, was a great loss to this country. He was sold to go abroad.

But, good as these two were, the three-year-olds of the year before had been of an even superior vintage. I remember going to Sandown for the Eclipse Stakes of 1903 with the intention of having a dash on Rock Sand against Ard Patrick and Sceptre. But when I saw these three champions walking round the ring, much as I loved Rock Sand, and often as I had won money on him, I had to give him third place. A beautifully made horse and not by any means a small one, yet the other two were a pair of giants, both in performances and stature, and the old saying that a good big one will beat a good little one was borne irresistibly into my mind.

Martin rode Rock Sand, as Maher was ill, and I think, perhaps, the horse ran just a little below his best form, but whenever he met Sceptre she beat him. About the best thing in racing is when two good horses single themselves out from the rest of the field and have a long-drawn-out struggle. So it was in this Eclipse Stakes, for, when well in the straight, it was apparent that the two four-year-olds had Rock Sand beaten. Half-way up Sceptre looked the winner, as she had drawn slightly ahead, but Madden was a jockey who knew exactly where the winning post was, and he nursed Ard Patrick beautifully for that last hundred yards, with the result that the horse just outran the mare and won by a neck. Hardy, who rode Sceptre, was quite a capable jockey, and rode a good race, but Madden rode the best race of his life, which is saying much, for he was a fine jockey, especially over a long course. In spite of the result of this race I believe

Sceptre was the better of the two, for she was more distressed afterwards than Ard Patrick, and blew more than Alec Taylor's horses usually do, however long and severe the race. The mare had not been long in his care, and if he had known as much about her as he did later on she would probably have been the winner.

Rock Sand met Sceptre twice afterwards, in the Jockey Club Stakes at Newmarket and the Coronation Cup at Epsom, and each time with the same result, though in the Coronation Cup they were both beaten by another of the grand big horses of that period— Zinfandel.

As a two-year-old Zinfandel had been too big to arrive at his proper form, and I don't know how good he might have been if his lines had been cast in luckier places. Owing to the death of his owner, Colonel McCalmont, all his engagements were void, so Major Charles Beatty, who trained him for Lord Howard de Walden, had to look for other fields than weight-for-age races in which to make his name.

Zinfandel was a magnificent great chestnut horse and it required some pluck and confidence to produce him for the first time as a three-year-old in the Manchester Summer Cup with a 6st. 12lb. boy on him. The Major, who was a very highly strung man himself, was doubtful as to the wisdom of the policy, as Zinfandel was a bit of a handful, and I remember meeting him and his horse one morning, both in a state of violent temper, which did not look too promising.

But the venture came off all right, greatly to the delight of Newmarket, for the whole town was on him. Major Beatty was a great favourite with everyone, although he would at times let fly all round in great style. I remember the Special Commissioner of the "Sportsman," Mr. Allison, writing something very descriptive of Charlie Beatty when the latter fairly got going. Allison was describing how he watched some work at Newmarket on a morning when there was a biting north-east wind which blew right through him. He declared he never got warm till he accidentally got mixed up with Major Beatty and his string. No better or finer fellow ever stepped than Charlie Beatty. Whatever he did, he did well, and he left his horses to go out with the Yeomanry in the South African War. He greatly distinguished himself there, and became A.D.C. to General Alderson, who was in command of the Light Cavalry. I think he liked the life of a soldier better than that of a trainer. There are too many petty worries in the latter profession to suit a man of his temperament.

When he came back from South Africa he started to train again, but only because his great friend, Harry McCalmont, said he would give up racing unless he did so. Unfortunately for Charlie, Harry McCalmont died the following year, and I don't think his heart was ever in the game again, although he always did his work conscientiously and well.

Again, in the Great War, did Charlie Beatty, although he was forty-nine, go out to fight for his country. His old general, who commanded that gallant Canadian Division which did such wonderful work in France, asked for him again as his A.D.C.

Later on he was very badly wounded, losing an arm, and came home a wreck. He never really recovered, and died in 1917. He was a great friend of mine, and I think one of the straightest, most conscientious men I have ever met.

To return to Zinfandel, the one defeat of his three-year-old career was in the Cesarewitch, and that was perhaps his finest performance. Ridden by Morny Cannon, with 8st. 4lb. on his back, in very heavy ground, he was just beaten by the aged horse, Grey Tick, carrying 6st. 9lb. But for Colonel McCalmont's death Zinfandel, and not Rock Sand, would probably have been the hero of 1903. In the Coronation Cup as a four-year-old, he beat both Sceptre and Rock Sand.

He was second the same year to Throwaway for the Ascot Cup; he should have won easily, Morny Cannon for once riding a very bad race. The following year he won it and showed that he could stay as well as go fast. For some reason or other he was a great failure at the stud, whereas Rock Sand was a great success.

In thinking of these great horses, I have strayed a long way from my own stable and Danny Maher, but at that time, owing to the epidemic of Pink Eye, my horses were useless, and their doings of little interest.

When Rickaby retired I got Maher to ride for me whenever possible, and eventually he became Lord Derby's first jockey.

Certainly in his day, as a jockey and a horseman, he stands supreme in my opinion, and I think in that of every other man who then went racing.

I was talking to Frank Wootton the other day, who became his great rival, and he thinks he was a marvel, especially on courses like Newmarket, York and Ascot. When he first came to England he rode in pronounced American fashion, but he told me that he soon found out that this did not suit our race-courses. He said that it was all very well on American tracks, which were as level as a billiard table, but that on our courses, with their ups and downs, and inequalities of ground, it was impossible to get horses balanced again if once they changed their legs and rolled about. His seat was the perfect mixture of the old and the new style. His patience was wonderful, and nothing would induce him to ride a horse hard unless he had him going as he wanted.

Sometimes this caused him to lie a long way out of his ground, and occasionally it lost him a race, but this can be said of nearly all great jockeys. He was always a delicate man in a way, for even when I first knew him he was inclined to be consumptive, but this never prevented him from putting an extraordinary amount of devil and strength into his finishes, although I have often seen him speechless from want of breath after one of these efforts. Naturally, he was the popular idol of the public, and everyone conspired to turn his head, but he always remained the same pleasant, well-mannered man whom I first knew.

But there was one thing no one could make him do, and that was to take the care he ought to have done of his health. He had many good friends, and some very bad ones. I think his greatest and best friend was Skeets Martin, but neither he nor anyone else could keep Danny from burning the candle at both ends, with the usual result, the end came too soon.

LORD DERBY LEADING IN SWYNFORD AFTER WINNING THE ST. LEGER, 1910—FRANK WOOTTON UP

Photo: Sport and General

From the painting by Lynwood Palmer

SWYNFORD

From the painting by Lynwood Palmer

STEDFAST

CHAPTER XXII

THE FIRE AT STANLEY HOUSE—KEYSTONE II—
PRETTY POLLY AND THE ASCOT CUP

For three years in succession, 1901, 1902 and 1903, we had an epidemic of what was called " Newmarket Fever " at the Bedford Lodge Stables, and Lord Derby decided to buy the Sefton Stud Farm from the Duke of Montrose and build the Stanley House Stables. They were finished in 1903, but our ill-luck pursued us there, for the first year that the horses were in them we had that horrible illness, Pink Eye, of which I wrote in my last chapter.

Owing to the clever treatment of Professor McQueen, of the Royal Veterinary College, and Mr. Livock, the Newmarket Veterinary Surgeon, we only lost one horse, but I remember when I told the late Sam Darling this he remarked that it would have been better for me if they had all died, as they would probably never be any good for racing, and his words proved more or less correct. Chaucer was one of the few that ever recovered their form.

But by 1908, the stable was looking up again, and after three very lean years I was hoping for a good one. On May 16th I had been to Kempton to see the race for the Jubilee, and I came home by the 7.30 train, which used in those days to arrive at Newmarket about 10 o'clock. I was met at the station with the news that my stables were on fire, but the horses were said to be safe. On arriving at the stables I found them in a blaze, and a desperate fight was going on in the endeavour to save one portion of them. When I asked what had happened to the horses, I was told that there had only been time to get them out and turn them loose, and that some were still loose and could not be found, but the majority were safe in the boxes at the Stud Farm, about half a mile away. The fire had begun at 8 o'clock in the evening. There had been some entertainment on in the town, and after evening stables everyone had gone to it except two old men, who were left in charge. Owing to a high wind the fire had spread with such rapidity that all they could do was to get the horses out of the stables as quickly as possible. Fortunately a neighbour, Mr. Charles Waugh, had seen the fire, and, running across, had given most valuable assistance. Most of the horses when free galloped round and round a circular track which I have at the back of the stables, until they were thoroughly tired out when they were caught and put into any vacant stabling that could be found, but a few disappeared completely, and two were not found until the next morning.

Fortunately, my boys had been well schooled in fire drill, and they, with the assistance of the Town Fire Brigade, prevented the fire from spreading to the house and the boys' rooms, but the hero of the night was Mr. Cecil Marriott, manager to the Jockey Club, who did the work of ten men and kept everyone going. There were some humorous incidents : one concerned a clergyman, Mr. Young, a great friend of Marriott's, who was anxious to be of use, but who kept getting in everyone's way, until Marriott at last turned the fire hose on to him and drenched him to the skin. There was a very savage horse in the stable at that time, Vedas, who had won the Two Thousand Guineas and other good races. Mr. Livock, when he heard that the horses were all loose, said to one of the boys, " I wonder what has become of Vedas." " I hope the b—— is burnt," replied the boy. As a matter of fact, Vedas was in a box at the Stud Farm when the fire broke out.

The next morning I expected to find half the horses broken down, but to my great surprise there seemed to be nothing more than a few cuts and bruises, and they all appeared perfectly well. Someone said that if this was the case I must have got a d——d bad lot of horses, for if they had been any good they would have broken their necks or done something of the sort, but this pessimist, whoever he was, turned out to be wrong, for these horses won £37,000 in stakes that year, and placed me at the head of the winning trainers.

It was a hard task to work the stable after the fire, for the horses had to be lodged out all over the place, but I have always had a wonderfully good lot of men to work for me, and without them it would have been impossible.

Amongst the horses that were turned loose that night was one of the best mares I have ever trained, Keystone II, a bay filly by Persimmon out of Lock and Key. I saw her the day after she was foaled, and I thought, " There is an Oaks winner, if ever I saw one."

She was a typical daughter of Persimmon, a big, lengthy filly, with glorious shoulders, and that beautiful straight hind-leg which was such a marked characteristic of the horse and the best of his stock. Her dam, Lock and Key, had been a useful little filly that Lord Derby had bought from Charles Morbey. By Janissary out of Seclusion, she was full of the best blood from the Duchess of Montrose's Stud.

Persimmon himself had been a difficult subject to train, and I have written before that, without the skill and patience of Dick Marsh, we might never have heard of him as a great race-horse after his two-year-old career. When Keystone came into training as a yearling, it was evident that she also would require time and patience. I have always had one great advantage over most of my profession, in that the late Lord Derby and his son have allowed me to train their horses as I wanted, and have never been in a hurry to have their good horses produced too soon, and Keystone's first appearance was in the Champagne Stakes at Doncaster. Skeets Martin had ridden her in a rough gallop about a fortnight before. She had showed great speed, and Martin, when he got off her, told me he thought she would be a real good filly Skeets Martin was a wonderful jockey on a two-year-old ; he had the most beautiful hands, and we all used to be anxious to get him to ride our two-year-olds at home. There was no more obliging fellow in the world, and he was always ready to ride a gallop for you, even if he had no prospect of riding the horse in a race.

In the Champagne Stakes at Doncaster, Lord Derby had two fillies engaged, Victorious and Keystone II. Victorious was a great fine mare, own sister to Volodyovski, winner of the Derby. She looked a pretty good thing for the race and ridden by Danny Maher she started favourite. But we also ran Keystone II, with Wheatley up, declaring to win with Victorious. After looking a certain winner, the latter fell all to pieces in the last few strides and was just beaten. After the race, Wheatley, who rode Keystone II, told me that she had run extraordinarily well, and he thought she might have even won the race had he not pulled her up, thinking Victorious had won easily.

From that moment I had my eye on the Oaks, and Keystone did not run again as a two-year-old. She did very well in the winter, but in the spring she was very troublesome, and her winter coat stuck on long after all my other horses had shed theirs. So much so that one evening, after the Craven week, when Arthur Coventry came round my stables, he remarked when he looked at her, " Well, that's an ugly-looking beast : you won't do much good with her." He heard a good deal about this unfortunate remark of his after she had won the Oaks.

There was never any chance of having her ready to run before Epsom, and the present Lord Derby, who then managed his father's stable, will remember the first trial gallop I was able to give her, which was in the Two Thousand week, when she failed to stay, and was easily beaten by a useful old horse called Persinus. He was much disappointed at this, but I told him then that she would win the Oaks, as I knew the gallop would bring her on a great deal. Like most of Persimmon's stock, she wanted to be hard trained to be at her best.

But the Saturday before Epsom she showed herself in her true colours, when she came home twenty lengths in front of some useful horses. Danny Maher was away riding somewhere, and she was ridden by Kempton Cannon, who said he had never been on such a mare in his life.

With Danny Maher up, she started a hot favourite for the Oaks, and won in a canter. I think this race gave the late Lord Derby more pleasure than any of his victories. Keystone was the first classic winner of his own breeding, and he was able beforehand to tell all his friends to back her. The mare followed up her Epsom victory by winning the Coronation Stakes at Ascot in a canter with her penalty. On that day she was a great mare and she looked it.

She went to Goodwood to run for the Nassau Stakes. The summer had been so dry that even that glorious course was as hard as a brick, and having an efficient substitute in Glasconbury, a filly by Isinglass out of Canterbury Pilgrim, we did not run her. Glasconbury won, although she was 21 lb. behind Keystone.

I now had to train the mare for the St. Leger, and what a horrible time I did have, for I think it was the driest summer I have ever known. She was a big mare, and wanted a lot of work. Danny Maher loved her and rode her in nearly all her work. It was wonderful how smoothly he contrived to make horses gallop, and she arrived at Doncaster fit and well. But the course had not a blade of grass on it, and was in an awful state. Very different to what we find now, for I don't know any course that in my time has been so improved as Doncaster, which to-day is one of the best in England. The heat on the St. Leger day was tropical, which was bad for a mare, and Keystone felt it a good deal, and in the paddock was rather listless.

But Danny went out full of confidence, saying he would win " ten minutes," a favourite expression of his.

His description of the race afterwards was, " A bad start, a bad race and a bad finish." Keystone was favourite at five to four, and the Duke of Westminster's Troutbeck, with George Stern in the saddle, was second favourite at five to one. He was a beautiful little horse, had been third in the Derby, and had won eight races that year. Trained by Willie Waugh at Kingsclere, he looked a picture of condition, and bounded over the hard ground like a cricket ball. The start was a moderate one. George Stern got the best of it, and, jumping off in front, he made all the running, and won by a head from Prince William, Beppo being third, and Keystone fourth. The four horses passed the post almost in a line, heads just dividing the lot. In those days there was a very awkward bend in the course, and Keystone was badly placed coming to it. Just as Maher got out of his difficulties, Prince William rolled on to the mare and knocked her completely out of her stride. She was very unlucky to be beaten. Twelve days later in the Jockey Club Stakes she ran Beppo to a length, with a difference in weight of 16 lb. in his favour, and later at Sandown, in the Three-Year-Old Produce Stakes, then worth £5,000, she beat Prince William at even weights by six lengths, and she finished the season by winning a small race at the Liverpool Autumn Meeting.

The following year, as a four-year-old, although she looked well, she never showed any form, which has, I think, given Lord Derby a dislike to keeping any filly in training after three years. At the stud she was the dam of Archaic, second in the Derby, and Keysoe, winner of the St. Leger, and of Phalange.

George Stern, who rode Troutbeck, was a great jockey over a long course, and in this particular race he showed wonderful judgment and knowledge of pace, when he made all the running on a horse that really was not a true stayer. It must also be said that he rode a very rough race, and if Halsey, on the second, had objected, I think it was very likely that Stern would have been disqualified. But there is always a great feeling in England against any objection to a French horse and a French jockey when they come over.

The following year, as a matter of fact, George Stern did get disqualified in the race for the Ascot Cup, when he dead-heated on Eider with The White Knight. Here again he rode marvellously and nearly stole the race, but when he saw that he could not beat The White Knight he fairly went for him, and it was hundred to one against Eider when the objection was made.

In 1906, the year that Keystone won the Coronation Stakes at Ascot, that wonderful mare, Pretty Polly, met with her first and only defeat in England, when she was beaten for the Ascot Cup by Bachelor's Button. This was a source of great surprise and consternation to the general public, but there was one man who was not surprised, and that was Danny Maher, who rode Bachelor's Button.

Danny had ridden Pretty Polly in France, when she was a three-year-old, in the Prix du Conseil Municipal. She had started at two to one on, and had been beaten by a good French horse, Presto II, to whom she was giving 10lb. Many people who saw the race blamed the jockey, and said he had waited too long, etc. Mr. Gilpin was not one of these, but he thought that the journey had probably upset the mare. When Danny came back I asked him about the race. He was rather sore at the criticism of his riding, saying that he had no excuse, and that the mare was beaten on her merits. He said the course was very heavy, and as usual the pace very fast. For more than three parts of the journey he felt that he could do what he liked with the field, and that, when he first asked Pretty Polly to take her place to win the race, she responded readily, but then gradually she began to die away in his hands. Feeling this, like the good jockey he was, he sat as still as a mouse, hoping the other horse might crack, but that did not happen, and when finally he had to sit down to ride his mare there was nothing more left in her and she was beaten a length. Anyhow, from that moment he was certain that Pretty Polly, brilliant as she was, was not a true stayer.

The following year, as a four-year-old, she carried all before her, but Danny still stuck to his opinion, and said, " If I meet her in a two mile race, with a good horse, I shall beat her." Pretty Polly's last race as a four-year-old was for the Jockey Club Cup and Danny rode Bachelor's Button. Odds of five to one were laid on the mare in a field of four. I was on my hack, and watched them as they came to the T.Y.C. Post, which is about 5 furlongs from home. Bachelor's Button was in front of Pretty Polly, the other two were beaten off. The horse was running lazy in front, but, when Pretty Polly came alongside him and took a slight lead, he began to race in earnest, and he drew nearly level again, though it still looked fifty to one on the mare. About 100 yards from home Dillon just shook her up, and she won apparently easily by half a length. But after the race Danny came to me triumphant, saying, " What did I tell you, if I had only had something to help me I should have beaten her, for I am certain she was very tired." He added that, if these two met in the Ascot Cup the following year, Bachelor's Button would be certain to win. Sure enough, they were both entered for this race, and, when it came to the time, there were only five runners, Bachelor's Button, Cicero, Pretty Polly, and two other moderate horses. Danny was still confident that he would beat the mare, partly because he was convinced she did not stay, and partly because he did not think much of her jockey, Dillon. Odds of eleven to four were laid on her, and seven to one against Cicero and Bachelor's Button.

In spite of what I had been told, I could not bring myself to oppose Pretty Polly, and like nearly everyone on the course I wanted to see her win. But Danny proved right, the severe hill at the end of $2\frac{1}{2}$ miles was too much for her, and Bachelor's Button beat her just cleverly. He was a sterling good horse, especially at Ascot, but he was not a Persimmon, and if a real good jockey had been on Pretty Polly I think she might just have scrambled home.

Bachelor's Button would never do as much for other jockeys as he would for Maher, and he wanted a good galloping course. I remember Morny Cannon riding him at Stockton in a weight-for-age race they had one year, the Jubilee Cup. Danny was riding a big horse of Lord Derby's called His Majesty. He was receiving 11lb., and I did not think that was enough, but Maher said Bachelor's Button would never act on that cramped course, and again he was right, for His Majesty won, and Bachelor's Button was only fourth. I remember Danny won the last two races for us that day, each by a short head, and on each occasion he ought to have been second.

Lord Derby had another good three-year-old in 1906, Bridge of Canny, by Love Wisely. He won nine races that year, and was four times second, running fifteen times, and winning over £10,000 in stakes. He came out again the next year a real good horse, not a bit the worse for his hard season.

It would be difficult nowadays to find a good-class horse that could stand this amount of work and thrive on it. Curiously enough, Bridge of Canny as a two-year-old, was an excitable, nervous horse, and did not show his proper form. This was an instance of what I have said before, that Maher could make a moderate horse into a good one, for he always liked Bridge of Canny, and took an immense amount of trouble with him.

Glasconbury, the filly who won the Nassau Stakes, was another very stout one. As a three-year-old, at the First October Meeting at Newmarket, she happened to be in two races the same day, the Royal Stakes, a mile and a quarter, and the Newmarket Oaks, a mile and three quarters, so I thought I would try and win them both.

They were the first and the sixth race on the card. She won the Royal Stakes by five lengths. I then sent her to some stables at the Links Farm close by, on the

Cambridge road, and kept her there till it was time for the Newmarket Oaks.

The rule that horses must pass the Stands on the way to the Post had only just been brought in. We none of us remembered it, and Maher got on the mare at the stables, and took her straight to the Post, with the result that she had to come all the way back again to go down so as to go past the Stands. This meant that before starting for her second race she had gone nearly five miles without including the race she had already won.

She was rather an excitable mare, and she was pulling Danny about most of the time. I went down to the Post the last time with her myself. The jockey and the mare by this time were both so thoroughly upset that I would not have taken a hundred to one about them, and yet she made all the running, and won, after a very hard race, by half a length.

The next morning she came out as fresh as paint, not a bit the worse for her exertions. Unfortunately, later on, she broke her leg on the Limekilns, and had to be destroyed. She was an incalculable loss to Lord Derby's stud.

CHAPTER XXIII

LATER TRAINING DAYS—SWYNFORD'S ST. LEGER

In 1907 I had a very moderate lot of horses, and Lord Derby only won £13,000 in stakes. Keystone II had lost her form, and, if it had not been for gallant old Bridge of Canny, the season would have been disastrous. Amongst other races, he won a Liverpool Cup, the Queen's Prize, and the Great Yorkshire Handicap, carrying top weight on each occasion. He was also third for the Ascot Cup, and second for the Doncaster Cup. He was a loss to England, when, after a short time at the stud, he was sold for £10,000 to go to South America. In spite of his fine breeding, by Love Wisely out of Santa Brigida, and his great record as a consistent stayer, he met with little patronage from breeders in this country. He was the sire of a good horse in Cantilever, winner of the Jockey Club Stakes and the Cambridgeshire, who in turn sired that most genuine and honest stayer, Bracket, winner of the Cesarewitch. It is curious how everyone in this country laments the lack of stayers, and yet how they turn their backs on them when they are at the stud.

In this year, 1907, Lord Derby had only one two-year-old of any note, a big chestnut colt by Count Schomberg, called Cocksure II. This was a rattling good horse, although very backward, and he won three good races. I expected great things of him as a three-year-old, but owing to Lord Derby's death the following year all his engagements were void.

Lord Derby died on the Sunday before Ascot in 1908. His death was terribly sudden, but, if death can be beautiful, then his was so. He had been out for a walk on a lovely evening, at Hollwood, his place in Kent, of which he was very fond. He came in just before dinner, and had been telling Lady Derby of the beauty of the summer evening, and how he had enjoyed his walk. He sat back in his chair, and a moment afterwards was dead, a fitting end to a wonderful life of unselfishness. One of his principal objects was to make others happy, and in that he succeeded as few men have done. The family life at Knowsley was an extraordinarily happy one. Constance Lady Derby was really a wonderful woman, so full of fun and charm, and yet so direct and straight. Her many sons and one daughter simply adored her, and no wonder. Besides her other great qualities I think she was one of the bravest women I ever knew, physically and morally. Anything like humbug she detested, and she was extraordinarily quick at seeing through what was not genuine and sincere, and had little patience with that sort of thing.

At Knowsley, for Liverpool races, there would generally be a party of from thirty to forty people. A constant guest was Marcus Beresford, of whom Lady Derby was very fond; she always insisted on his playing cards at her table, and then the game would not be taken very seriously. All through the autumn and winter you would be sure of finding at Knowsley the most brilliant and interesting people of English Society, but whether they were Kings and Queens, Archbishops or Politicians, they would all laugh and be merry in that house.

Lord Derby had always expressed a wish that his racing stable should be carried on after his death, so, after a suitable time, his horses were leased to my brother Durham for the remainder of the season, and they did fairly well for him. Cocksure II won eight races, and started a hot favourite for the Cambridgeshire, with 8st. 5lb. on his three-year-old back. I think he would, in any ordinary season, have won it, but that year both the Cesarewitch and Cambridgeshire were run on ground like iron, and Cocksure, being a big horse, and rather straight in front, failed to act coming down the hill, although he finished fourth close up, and full of running. After Ascot of the following year, the present Lord Derby started racing again, and I soon discovered that everything was to go on in the same pleasant way as in his father's time. I had the same free hand ; the horses were allowed plenty of time, and there was the same kindness and forethought for his employees in the stable.

Father and son were very different in character, for the former was a man of very deliberate and quiet judgment, while the present Lord Derby is impulsive, and perhaps inclined to be hasty, but in their different ways they would both arrive at the same happy results.

In those days, both before and after he succeeded, Lord Derby was less immersed in public affairs, and was able to take a far more active part in the management of his horses than is the case to-day, and he and Lady Derby were very frequently down at Newmarket.

Lady Derby was a daughter of the late Duchess of Devonshire. She and her sister, the Duchess of Hamilton, were both fine riders, and devoted to hunting, and both extraordinarily good judges of any kind of horse. Lady Derby took the keenest interest in the Racing Stable, and especially in the Stud, and, when she set her affection on any particular yearling, I have seldom known her wrong. Owing to heavy death duties the first year or so the number of horses in training was considerably reduced, and Lord Wolverton, Lord D'Abernon, then Sir Edgar Vincent, and the late Mr. Arthur James joined the stable.

The year 1909 was a very bad one, and the horses were not of much account, but there was one amongst them which we thought would make a great name for himself, as indeed he did.

I think that if you could see most great race-horses three days after they were foaled you would say, if you were a fair judge of a horse, that they were likely to be something out of the common. In my last chapter I have told what a good foal Keystone II was, and in 1907 Canterbury Pilgrim dropped a magnificent brown colt by John o' Gaunt.

In those days I was more confident and optimistic than I am now, and I felt that this grand colt, with ancestors like Pilgrimage, Isinglass and La Fleche close up in his pedigree, would develop into a great horse. It was fortunate that I had this idea firmly rooted in my head, for a more disappointing horse in his early career was never foaled. As a yearling, Swynford, as they named him, grew into a great, plain, rather flat-sided colt, but he had a big, lean, game head, good legs and feet, and when he chose to extend himself he was a fine galloper. When he came into training he certainly was a very ugly customer. He had led the hard and simple life, running out in a paddock day and night, and had very little flesh on him. He was, as the expression goes, "all legs and wings," but when the breaking tackle was put on he soon showed that he was as strong as a bull, and full of courage, though at the same time very good-tempered.

Naturally, he was given plenty of time to develop, and it was not till July that he was ready to have a rough gallop.

Danny Maher and Fred Rickaby, who had often to ride him in his work, both had a tremendous opinion of him.

His first gallop was with a very smart sprinter of Lord Derby's called Well Done. I wanted to gallop him at 10 lb. with the old horse, but Danny Maher declared he would "eat him" if he did not beat Well Done at even weights, so they were tried like this. Swynford, like his dam, was a very hard puller, and, speedy as Well Done was, the two-year-old jumped off "like a whirlwind," and had him beaten in the first three furlongs. This pleased us greatly and it was decided that he should make his debut in the Exeter

Stakes at the First July Meeting at Newmarket. The race was six furlongs, which frightened me, but Danny said he would be able to drop him in behind and come with one run. Nothing of this sort happened, however, for, going out of the gate like a stone from a catapult, he took charge of Danny and ran himself to a standstill before he had gone five furlongs. I was never more disappointed in all my life.

After this he threw out the worst thoro' pin I ever saw. We had a great deal of trouble with it, and he did not run again as a two-year-old, which was probably a blessing in disguise. All the winter he did splendidly, and just before the Craven week the following year I was confident that I had a good horse. The first gallop I gave him was on the Limekilns, against some very moderate horses, at even weights, and I expected him to win it without an effort. But to my disgust, after making hot running for six furlongs, he stopped to nothing and began to roll about like a ship in distress. The worst of it was that he had done more work than any horse in my stable. I gave him another gallop about ten days later, with exactly the same result, but after both these gallops he came home quite pleased with himself, ate up and was ready for anything the next day. This gave me hopes that he might improve, and in spite of his bad performances I could not bring myself to believe that he was- really a bad horse. He had speed, and, bred as he was, how could it be possible that he would not stay? He was a delightful horse to train, a good doer in the stable, quiet and sensible out of it, and, although he would pull very hard when upsides with another horse, he would follow one at any pace you wanted.

Ten days before the Derby he, for the first time that year, put up a good gallop. Instead of stopping after six furlongs he galloped on remorselessly until the horses that were with him were all stone cold. So I told Lord Derby that if he liked to run the horse at Epsom he would not disgrace him. That year there were two real good three-year-old colts, Lord Rosebery's Neil Gow and Mr. Fairie's Lemberg. Neil Gow was a beautiful bloodlike chestnut horse by Marco out of Chelandry, impossible to fault except for his rather weak hocks. He had been a brilliant two-year-old, and had carried all before him, but he was a wayward, bad-tempered customer, and very troublesome at the gate. He had been beaten in both his first two races from getting badly off. Danny Maher had always ridden him, and was engaged to ride him as a three-year-old. Trained by Percy Peck at Exning, near Newmarket, he gave his trainer many anxious moments, for on some days he was almost unmanageable.

Lemberg, by Cyllene out of Galicia, trained by Alec Taylor, was half-brother to Bayardo. In many ways he was better-looking than that great horse, and showed more bloodlike quality. But, curiously enough, like Neil Gow, his weak spot was also in his hocks. He, too, had been a smashing good horse as a two-year-old, winning six races out of seven, his only defeat being in the Champagne Stakes, when he was a moderate third to Neil Gow. But it was evident that on this occasion he did not run up to his proper form.

His first appearance as a three-year-old was in the Two Thousand Guineas, whereas Neil Gow had already been out and had won the Craven Stakes in a canter by three lengths. The rivalry between these champions of Newmarket and the country stables reminded me of the old days of Minting and Ormonde.

There was a good field for the Two Thousand and no horses ever started for it in more beautiful condition than Lemberg and Neil Gow. Another lovely horse in the race was the American Whisk Broom, owned by Mr. H. Whitney and trained by Andrew Joyner.

I went some way down the course to see the race, and it was indeed one worth seeing. Coming into the dip, Lemberg, who was ridden by Dillon, and Neil Gow were close together on the Stand side, and after

THE HON. GEORGE LAMBTON AND THE LADS AT STANLEY HOUSE

Photo: Clarence Hailey

"DIADEM", WINNER OF THE 1000 GUINEAS, 1917, WITH
JOHN LAMBTON, AGE 7 YEARS, AND R. OSGOOD

DIADEM AND
STEPHEN DONOGHUE

From the painting by Lynwood Palmer

Whisk Broom had made a bold show they singled themselves out from the rest of the field, Lemberg with a trifling advantage. Then Danny sat down to ride with that confidence and determination that will not be beaten. Leaning over the rails close to the struggling pair I could see the jockeys' desperate faces, the horses with their ears flat back on their heads, both running as true as steel : it was a great sight. The last two hundred yards I looked at them from behind. Although being close together, neither horse swerved nor flinched. Dillon hit his horse oftener than Maher, but the latter, when he did use his whip, did so exactly at the right moment, and Neil Gow won by a short head. It was the riding that did it, though I must say that Dillon rode the race of his life that day, and it was hard lines for him and Lemberg to have Maher to beat. So fierce was the struggle that I remember wondering if either of the horses would ever forget the race.

I have lately heard and read that racing is no real test of the value of the thoroughbred horse, but where could you find any animal except a horse of the best English blood that could show the gameness and pluck of these two beautiful and high-strung horses, for later in the year they met again in the Eclipse Stakes, at the same weights, and with the same jockeys. I did not see the race, but after a magnificent struggle it ended in a dead-heat. There is a case of consistency for you !

But to return to Swynford and the Derby. Before that race Neil Gow had been giving Percy Peck a lot of trouble with one of his hocks, and was not at his best, so Lemberg started a hot favourite at seven to four. He won cleverly by a neck from Lord Jersey's Greenback. At one time during the race he had looked like winning in a canter, but in the last hundred yards I thought he was tiring pretty quickly. Swynford was again a disappointment, for he made no show, but there was a good excuse for him, as he was badly struck into. The skin was taken clean off the back of his leg from his hock to his fetlock joint, and it was the

T

nearest thing in the world that he was not ruined for life. I took him to the late Mr. John Coleman, the Epsom Veterinary Surgeon, who treated him with great skill, and soon had him quite all right again.

Swynford at this time had a very nasty habit of just brushing the inside of his off joint, which caused me a lot of anxiety. He had very big feet, and nothing we could do would stop this until I happened to mention it to Mr. Lynwood Palmer, the celebrated horse painter, who was at Newmarket just then. He said he thought he could stop it, although the treatment of the near foot would be very drastic. Lynwood Palmer is the cleverest man with a horse's foot I have ever come across, and, as he was confident that it could be done, I took the risk. It came off all right, and we had no further trouble. It was a curious thing to find an artist with this great knowledge and I asked him how he had acquired it. He told me that as a young man he had been horse-master to one of the biggest cab proprietors in New York. His salary depended on the work the horses did, and he found out that, when the horses went lame, in most cases it came from the foot.

Consequently he made a great study of this, and being a clever man, with the sensitive touch and fingers of an artist, he could use his knife on a horse's foot better than any man I have ever met. Ever since those days he has been in charge of that department in my stable.

So well did Swynford do in a gallop before Ascot that I told Lord Derby and his friends it would take Lemberg all his time to beat him in the St. James's Palace Stakes. But again he disappointed us, and finished a bad third, after rolling all over the course when he came round the turn. I felt a considerable fool after the race, and I think everyone gave up the horse except Frank Wootton, who was then Lord Derby's first jockey, and myself. We brought him out again for the Hardwicke Stakes on the Friday. He won cleverly, but I must own his performance was not very encouraging, for, although he was in receipt of a lot of weight, he only just got home, and my confidence in him was much shaken.

After Ascot he had a short rest, and then I started to train him for the Liverpool Summer Cup. So well did he go in his work that we set him a pretty hard task in his trial, making him give a stone to the useful three-year-old Decision, who had won the Ascot Derby and other good races. At last he did what was expected of him, for he galloped clean away from Decision and won by ten lengths. On this gallop the Liverpool Cup looked a certainty, but as usual there was one " if " in the proposition. He pulled so hard and carried his head so low that Frank Wootton was very doubtful whether he would get him round those sharp turns. In the race, as soon as the gate went up, he dashed off in front, and, coming to the canal turn, he was leading by ten lengths. Instead of going into the canal as we feared, he came round like a polo pony and won pulling up by a distance. Only once after this was he ever headed for a single stride in any race he ran for.

He did not run again before the St. Leger, and in his preparation for this race he seemed to go better in every gallop. He wore out nearly all the horses in my stable. With his enormous stride, and going very wide behind, he was not a very taking goer to look at. I told a friend of mine, Billy Keen, to back him for the St. Leger. He, thinking that I was probably prejudiced in my opinion, asked a trainer at Newmarket if he thought the horse had any chance of beating Lemberg. " Yes," was the reply, " he has a chance—about the same as my hack would have."

In the sale paddocks at Doncaster, the day before the St. Leger, I told Danny Maher, who was riding Lemberg, that I thought I should beat him. He scoffed at the idea, saying, " No doubt yours is a good horse but he is not the same class as Lemberg." Skeets Martin, who was with us, remarked, " Well, I've ridden one or two gallops behind Swynford, and I should not like to be the horse to follow him for a mile and three quarters at Doncaster, and you will be finding it out to-morrow!"

Having an idea that Lemberg was not a great stayer, I told Frank Wootton to make the pace as hot as he could from the start. In the race he had the field on the stretch in the first furlong. Coming to the Red House, Danny moved up on Lemberg, but whenever he got to Swynford's quarters the latter put in some of his great big strides and went away again. Two furlongs from home, Maher was following dead in his tracks. Although he was sitting still, so well did I know Danny's riding that I was certain his horse was tiring, and I said to Bob Vyner, who was beside me in the Stand, " I've got him, we shall win." Frank Wootton was but a boy at the time, riding 7st. 4lb., and by this time he was a passenger on Swynford, who was hanging away from the rails, where the Yorkshire crowd were shouting and waving their race cards according to their usual custom. There was plenty of room for Lemberg to come up on the inside had he been good enough, but he was not—his bolt was shot. As it was, Bronzino, a horse of Mr. Jimmy Rothschild's, came with a tremendous rush in the last hundred yards, nearly catching my horse on the post, but the head was the right way. You can see from the picture of the finish that the jockey was far more beat than the horse, but it was a marvellous performance for a boy of that weight to ride such a big, heavy horse at all. His father, Dick Wootton, told me that the night after the race Frank kept talking in his sleep, and crying out, " I won't let you up, Danny, you shan't get up."

My description of the race, I know, entirely differs from what was the general opinion. This was that Maher rode a shocking race, and ought to have won. I have heard it said, and often seen it in print, but I firmly believe my view to be the true one. I think there are very few people who realize when watching a race what a dangerous sign it is when at the critical moment a good jockey is to be seen sitting perfectly still. I have only seen it with really great jockeys, and I know that it generally means that their horse is dying away under them.

I remember, the day after, that Maher told me that Lemberg would never beat Swynford in any race of that distance, run at the pace the St. Leger was. In describing the race to me, he said, " When I first went up to Swynford, I did so easily, but he kept going away from me again, and each time I had to ask my horse to go after him the response was weaker, and, two furlongs from home, I knew that, unless an accident happened, he had me beat." He declared that a furlong from home there was room for him to come up on the inside of Swynford, as he was hanging away from the rails, but that Lemberg had not the effort left to take advantage of this. It was just such a race as Pretty Polly's in Paris, where Maher was also blamed, and defeat came from the same cause, that neither horse was a real, genuine stayer.

I have not spoken to Skeets Martin, Maher's great friend, on the subject for years, but I believe he would bear me out in this.

The performances of the two horses the following year bore out Maher's contention. In a slow-run race, the Coronation Cup at Epsom, Lemberg beat Swynford three parts of a length. Frank Wootton, for the first and last time, waited with the horse, instead of letting him stride along, which, in my opinion, lost him the race. They met twice afterwards, in the Princess of Wales Stakes, at Newmarket, and the Eclipse Stakes, at Sandown when Swynford made all the running and won easily.

Then came the tragedy which put an end to the racing career of this great horse. I was training him for the Jockey Club Stakes, and one September morning, two days before the race, we were out on the July Course. Curiously enough, that very morning, when riding out to exercise, Frank had said to me, " Nobody knows how good this horse is now ; I don't think there is anything he could not do, from five furlongs to five miles." Half an hour afterwards he smashed his fetlock joint to atoms, in a steady half-speed gallop. I shall never forget that morning. There were only two horses in the gallop, and they had to pass a haystack, which hid them from view for a moment or two. I watched them go behind it and then only one horse came on. I galloped straight down, and found Swynford standing on three legs. It was an hour and a half before we could get Mr. Livock, the veterinary surgeon, and an ambulance, and then it was nearly an hour before we could get the horse into it. The task of getting such a great big horse out of it on three legs seemed impossible, and it was a wonderful piece of work on the part of Mr. Livock to accomplish it. Personally I have never spent a worse day in my life.

Swynford was a marvellous patient, and thanks to this, and chiefly to Livock's wonderful skill and care, he was saved for the Stud.

CHAPTER XXIV

STEDFAST AND KING WILLIAM

In 1910, the year of Swynford's St. Leger, Lord Derby had two very promising two-year-olds in King William, a bay colt by William the Third out of Glasalt, and Stedfast by Chaucer out of Be Sure.

King William, half-brother to a good stayer in Glacis, who had won the Chester Cup, was a big lengthy bay with plenty of quality. On his first appearance he ran second for the Gimcrack, and, after running very well in the Middle Park Plate, dead-heated for the Dewhurst Plate, and should have won it outright, but for crossing his legs at the start, coming on to his knees and losing a lot of ground.

Stedfast was a magnificent chestnut horse, half-brother to Cocksure. How the little pony Chaucer could have sired such a big colt was wonderful. As a foal he was most unattractive, back at his knees and with his hind legs in another parish. But his grand head and his beautiful dark chestnut coat ticked with grey hairs gave him an air of distinction. Very backward in his early days, as a two-year-old he did not make his debut until the First October Meeting at Newmarket, when, after beginning very slowly, he finished a good third. This race brought him on tremendously, and he then won his next three races, his fine action attracting a good deal of attention.

As a two-year-old, and in his early training as a three-year-old, he was very easily upset in his work, and I was not at all sure which way his temper would go. He first came out that year in the Union Jack Stakes, at Liverpool. He was a long time settling down in the race, but, patiently handled by Frank Wootton, he put in some real good work at the finish, and, although he was only third, beaten two lengths from Seaforth and Athelstan, it was plain to everyone that these horses would never beat him again. In his next race he was second to Sunstar for the Two Thousand Guineas, after getting off very moderately.

All through the spring he and King William had been doing their work together, and King William appeared to go the better of the two, but he met with an accident, and was not able to run for the Two Thousand Guineas or the Newmarket Stakes. Ten days before the Derby, however, he was again going in great style. We had intended to try the two horses together, but just before the day of the gallop Stedfast overreached himself badly as he was galloping up the Cambridge Hill on the Moss Litter track. Fortunately, we had some other useful horses in the stable, amongst them Persephone, a three-year-old filly, who had been third to Sunstar in the Newmarket Stakes, beaten two lengths, so we were able to give King William a good trial. He won the gallop much more easily than I had even hoped for, and I certainly thought that he accomplished more than Stedfast could have done. However, Frank Wootton, who was our first jockey, was given his choice of the two horses in the Derby, and could not make up his mind which he would ride. He wanted me to decide, but I told him that he ought to be the best judge, as he was always on their backs. Finally he elected to ride King William, and I certainly thought he had chosen the right one. We both of us had an idea that Stedfast might not act on the Epsom course. Fred Lynham was engaged for him, a very fine horseman, and a good jockey with the best of hands, which was important for Stedfast. On the Saturday before the Derby, so well did both horses go that I do not think either jockey would have changed mounts. On the morning of the race, after their canter, I walked them both down the course, past the Stands, with the jockeys riding. King William behaved like a perfect gentleman, calm and cool, while Stedfast was considerably on his toes, and sweating. Frank Wootton's confidence rose high, and so did mine, as my only fear had been that King William would not stand the noise and racket of Epsom.

In the race King William drew a good place, and Stedfast the extreme outside of a field of twenty-six. There was a big and noisy crowd of people on the rails by the start: Stedfast got terribly upset, and when the gate went up he whipped round, and was left at least a hundred yards. He got on terms with the rearguard of the field at the top of the hill just before the descent to Tattenham Corner. Lynham, considering it useless to try and thread his way through such a mass of horses, took him to the extreme outside, so that he could get a clear run. He made up an extraordinary amount of ground, and finished second to Sunstar, beaten two lengths, with the third four lengths behind.

King William, meantime, had got off well, and ran a brute as he did on many occasions afterwards. I was greatly disappointed in him.

Stedfast was not beaten again that year. He won eight races, including the Prince of Wales Stakes and the St. James's Palace Stakes at Ascot, the Jockey Club Stakes and the Newbury Stakes, where he beat Prince Palatine, winner of the St. Leger. These two horses were constant opponents, and there was never much between them. Prince Palatine beat his rival a short head for the Eclipse Stakes, and Stedfast beat the Prince for the Coronation Cup, but certainly Prince Palatine was the best when it came to racing over two miles or more. Frank O'Neill, who generally rode him, told me that over a distance he was the best horse he had ever ridden: and what a fine jockey O'Neill has always been, such strength, and such a cool head.

Prince Palatine was not quite a taking horse in appearance. He was a shocking bad walker, and always had a very untidy mane and tail, but that he was a smashing good horse over two miles I am certain.

His last race at Goodwood for the Cup was a painful sight which I shall never forget. There is no doubt the horse was quite unfit to run as he had been suffering from foot trouble for some time. A mile from home he was in distress, but gallantly he struggled on, and opposite the Stands made a supreme effort. For a moment it looked as if he would overcome his difficulties, but then he staggered from one side to another, and nearly fell from sheer exhaustion. I remember Richard Wootton telling me that he had seen horses give that stagger in Australia where they ran races in heats, and that nine times out of ten it meant death from a strained heart. I have no doubt that Prince Palatine broke his heart in that race, and that this is the reason he was such a failure at the Stud.

Stedfast won over £30,000 in stakes and second money. He also ran second for the Derby, the Two Thousand, the Ascot Cup, the Eclipse Stakes, and the Jockey Club Stakes. Few horses have such a record. At the beginning of his career he was very easily upset, and irritable in his work, but when he gained his proper strength all that left him, and a more beautiful-tempered horse, or a gamer one, never lived. When he went to the Stud he was overshadowed by Swynford and Chaucer, and was not given a really good chance. In spite of that he has sired some good horses and an Oaks winner, but his stock must be given time to find themselves.

Few trainers, I think, have been more criticized than I was after that Derby. What a d——d fool I was supposed to be, not to find out which was my best horse! I must say, at that time, I often wished King William had never been foaled, although he did win one or two good races, amongst them the Ascot Derby. That was in the same week that Stedfast won the Prince of Wales Stakes and the St. James's Palace Stakes, Swynford the Hardwicke Stakes, and Hair Trigger II was beaten a short head for the Coronation Stakes, a good Ascot!

Before the First July Week that year I tried those three horses at weight for age over the last mile and a half of the Cesarewitch course.

    Swynford - - Lynham
    King William - D. Maher
    Stedfast - - F. Rickaby
    Decision - - —

Swynford won cleverly by a length, two lengths between second and third. Decision, a useful horse, he had been beaten a head for the Ascot High-Weight Handicap with top weight, with a "postage stamp" on his back, was beaten off. These were the three best horses I have ever trained, although King William never produced his form on a race-course. After the gallop Danny said to me, King William, if he got confidence, would be as good as Swynford, and a fortnight later he rode him in the Princess of Wales Stakes at Newmarket, when he finished a good third to Swynford and Lemberg, but he unmistakably "turned it up" when the pinch came. At that time Frank Wootton was first jockey to Lord Derby, and at the very top of his form. He was a great jockey: all horses or courses were alike to him, I have never known a jockey with fewer fads and dislikes, and he seldom came back with an excuse after a race. When he was beat it was because the horse was not good enough. He and Danny Maher were great rivals and there was not much love lost between them, but I am bound to say that it was chiefly Maher's fault, for Frank Wootton was always a good-natured, easy-going boy when off a horse : but in a race like all good jockeys he was quick to take advantage of anybody or anything. I think he had a cooler head than Danny, who had a very quick temper, and in a big field of horses he was perhaps a little better at overcoming difficulties, but at Newmarket I think that Danny was the better.

Richard Wootton, the father of Frank and Stanley, was a wonderful tutor of jockeys : he always taught his boys that they must go the shortest way, and if they were seen on the outside round a turn he did not forget to tell them what he thought about it; the consequence of this was that in their anxiety to escape his wrath they were at times a bit rough in their methods to get on the rails or in forcing their way through. This led to objections and complaints to the Wootton boys, who got rather a bad name in consequence. Dick Wootton, who was a very excitable man, on these occasions invariably lost his head, and would say or do anything for the moment, which generally made matters worse, but his temper did not last long, and although he would vow eternal war against someone it would soon blow over. He was devoted to his boys and most intensely proud of them and could not hear a word said against them without taking up the cudgels. There was nothing petty or mean about Richard Wootton. I knew him well : he had his faults but he was a warm-hearted, generous man, and a good sportsman. He was a very fine judge of a horse, and if I was thinking of buying a yearling I always liked to get his opinion of it. He was a man who never said things to please people, but exactly what he thought, which does not tend towards popularity.

Stanley Wootton, who had a most gallant record in the War and now trains at Treadwell House, was also a fine jockey, and in a long race was quite as good as Frank.

In 1912 young Rickaby became first jockey to my stable, although Frank still rode some of the big horses like Stedfast when the weight permitted.

Freddie Rickaby, son of my old jockey, was as faithful a servant and an even better jockey than his father, he was just at his best when the War claimed him. I don't think I ever knew a jockey so universally respected and liked by owners, trainers, and by those of his own profession, and so it was in the War. He joined the Tank Squadron, and his commander told me that he was the most gallant and orderly little fellow in his command, and set a good example to everyone, not only when fighting, but when in camp : towards the end of the War he had the opportunity of coming home, but he was determined to see it out, and refused : he was killed in one of the last actions that were fought. The Turf could ill afford to lose a jockey of his character and ability, and he had a great career before him. He won the One Thousand three years in succession, and the Oaks on Jest.

CHAPTER XXV

DIADEM

I HAD not intended in this book to write much about racing of more recent days, but I must make an exception in the case of Diadem, the sweetest and most gallant little mare that ever was seen on a race-course.

A chestnut filly by Orby out of Donnetta, she was bred by Lord D'Abernon, who, as Sir Edgar Vincent, had raced for many years, and joined my stable after the late Lord Derby died. He is one of the cleverest men I have ever met racing. Diadem's dam, Donnetta, had a distinguished career on the Turf, and won Sir Edgar many big races. She ran till she was eight years old. She is an example of my theory that a strenuous career on the course does not necessarily injure a mare for the Stud, for her second foal, Don Reynaldo, by St. Frusquin, after running second for the Prince of Wales Stakes at Ascot, was sold for a good price to go to Australia. She then threw a good colt to Orby in Diadumenos, winner of many races, including the Jubilee and the Liverpool Cup ; he was only beaten a head for the Cambridgeshire. She also bred two useful winners in Pharpar and Dionysos, the brilliant Diadem and Diophon, winner of the Middle Park Plate, and at twenty-three years of age foaled a lovely filly by Grand Parade.

When Diadem was a yearling Lord D'Abernon told me that she was the best he had ever bred, but I am bound to say that when she first came to me I was rather disappointed. She was a small dark chestnut filly, rather light of bone, with a light neck and apparently without much energy, but she had a beautiful intelligent head and did everything that was asked of her without any fuss or bother. Still I could not see where her great excellence was to come from. However, Lord D'Abernon was such a fine judge of a race-horse that I took more than the ordinary interest in her. Through the winter and spring she did her work well without showing any particular merit.

Being late in shedding her winter coat and rather a shy feeder, her owner decided not to run her before the Coventry Stakes, which race, owing to the War, was run at Newmarket that year. Ten days before the race I gave her a rough gallop, and for the first time she showed a glimpse of that wonderful dash and speed for which she was afterwards so famous. This gave me great hopes that she would win, but when she appeared in the Paddock she looked so listless and so small that I began to lose confidence, and when she cantered down to the Post she appeared not to be able to move at all. I then felt certain that she must have gone amiss, and wished she were back in the stable. I don't think I was ever more surprised in my life when, after standing as quiet as a sheep at the Post, she jumped off like a flash, and settled her field in two furlongs. That was Diadem; she seemed to keep every ounce of energy in her little frame for the supreme moment. Her listless walk in the Paddock and her wretched action in going to the Post often got us a point or two better odds against her. Martin, who rode her, said to me after the race, " If the others are worth a shilling this is the best mare I ever rode in my life."

Owing to the War, there was very little racing that year, so Diadem had no opportunity of making a great name for herself as a two-year-old, but she won four races out of five, and when beaten by Dansellon in the Hopeful Stakes she was giving him 9 lb., and was badly interfered with at the start.

As a three-year-old, her first race was for the One Thousand Guineas, which she won cleverly from Sunny Jane, in spite of being badly amiss from sexual causes. The same week the Two Thousand had been won by

Gay Crusader. He had only just scrambled home from his stable companion, Magpie, and in the Craven week he had run second to Lord Derby's Coq d'Or in the Column Produce Stakes. He was certainly giving 9 lb. but Coq d'Or was nothing more than a useful horse, although as a two-year-old he had beaten Gay Crusader in the Criterion (the only two occasions on which this great horse was beaten).

These performances did not give Lord D'Abernon and myself an exalted opinion of Gay Crusader, so it was decided that, instead of waiting for the Oaks, Diadem was to run for the Derby. Coq d'Or, having been sold to go to Australia, I had nothing in my stable capable of extending the mare in her work. On the day of the race, we were rather afraid of that extra half-mile, and were more full of hope than of confidence, but when we saw Gay Crusader in the Paddock even that hope went. I have never seen such an extraordinary improvement in so short a time ; he was an altogether different horse to the one we had seen in the Two Thousand. If at so late an hour it had been possible to have withdrawn Diadem, Lord D'Abernon would have done so, but she had been well backed by the public, so it was out of the question. There had been a lot of rain and the July Course was holding, and not suitable to the mare. Two furlongs from home her fate was sealed, Gay Crusader winning easily. Her jockey, Rickaby, had eased her the moment she had tired, so she did not get a hard race, and she was to come out again for the Oaks provided she was all right. Personally, I did not like the idea at all, but as she never left an oat, and seemed quite contented she had to run. It never stopped raining that week, and by the Friday (Oaks Day) the course was a sea of mud, but, in spite of this, so well had she run in the Derby that she started a hot favourite. In the Dip, she and her old opponent, Sunny Jane, singled themselves out, but by this time all Diadem's speed had gone, and nothing but her great heart enabled her to hang on. After a ding-dong struggle she was beaten

THE EARL OF DURHAM, K.G.

MAJOR GENERAL THE
HON. SIR WILLIAM
LAMBTON, K.C.B., D.S.O.

THE HON. MRS. GEORGE LAMBTON AND
HER SECOND SON EDWARD GEORGE

half a length. I went home a miserable man, thinking to myself she would never get over these two races, and I am sure that not one filly in a million would ever have done so, but after a good rest she came out in the Autumn as good as ever.

After her three-year-old career, Donoghue was associated with most of her triumphs, and a perfect combination they made. Stephen is a great lover of horses, but I am sure Diadem held first place in his affections and she thoroughly reciprocated it. I have seen her after a hard race, as he unsaddled her, turn round and rub her nose against his hands, more like a dog than a horse. Win or lose you could not have made Stephen hit her for anything in the world.

One of her greatest performances was winning the Salford Borough Handicap at Manchester, and on this occasion she was ridden by Carslake. Many great races has Carslake ridden for me, but he fairly excelled himself then, carrying 9 st. 12 lb., giving lumps of weight away to a smart field, including Irish Elegance, to whom she was giving 2 stone; she won in the last few strides by a neck. The pace was so tremendous that even with her speed she was on the stretch all the way; she was a tired mare a hundred yards from home, and Carslake fairly lifted her past the Post. Although he had never hit her, she had given every ounce that was in her. When he had taken off the saddle he looked at her as she stood, every nerve and muscle quivering, and said in his quiet way, " What a wonder, but how does she do it ? " She took some time to get over this race, but after a month's run in the Paddock she was as full of heart and dash as ever. Whenever she had a hard race I always turned her out in the Paddock for about three hours every morning.

Lord D'Abernon has been blamed for keeping her in training so long, and even accused of racing her commercially. There was never a more untrue or unjust accusation. There was little for her to win in stakes in those days, and he rarely, if ever, bets; whereas, if he had sent her to the Stud early in her career, her yearlings would have commanded a huge price at the Doncaster Sales. What he felt was this : He would never again have such a mare in his life, and, as long as she kept her form and her love of racing, he would keep her in training to have the joy of seeing her run. My instructions were that at the least sign of deterioration I was to send her home.

As a six-year-old she ran in twelve races, winning seven and being second in the other five, always carrying welter weights. Having won the Rous Memorial two years running, she was to try and win it for the third time, when seven years old, and then go out of training.

I had some trouble with her near fore-joint after she had run at Epsom, where she had made a gallant fight, carrying 10 stone. This had been got over, but that year the going at Ascot was terribly hard, and I had some doubts about running her. However, she moved so freely and well, the morning before the race, that I told Lord D'Abernon that she could run and would win. Starting with three to one laid on her she was beaten easily by Monarch, and pulled up very sore, not on the leg that had been giving the trouble, but, as is so often the case, saving that one had put too much pressure on the other.

I don't think I have ever felt a defeat more, for not only was my favourite beaten, but I had let her owner down badly. Tragedy as it was to him, he had not a word of reproach for me, although I deserved it. A curious thing happened in connection with this race. After Diadem's first victory Lord D'Abernon had given my wife a very pretty brooch with the mare's name in diamonds. She, like the rest of us, was devoted to Diadem, and always wore it. On going into the Paddock to see the mare saddled, she suddenly realized that the brooch was gone ; she never told me at the time as she thought it was such a bad omen, and so it was. It never was found.

In her career Diadem ran in thirty-nine races, won twenty-four, was second eight times, three times third, and four times unplaced. She kept her placid nature and her grand courage to the end. On the very day that I write this, I have seen a filly foal two days old, which is a racing machine already, by Phalaris out of Diadem, and with the same beautiful intelligent head as her dam. Although Phalaris and Diadem were in training at the same period, they never ran against each other. I once tried them at even weights over half a mile. It was a wonderful race all the way, but I gave it to the mare by a nose.

There were some good jockeys associated with Diadem, and it was greatly owing to their beautiful riding that she was able to race, for six seasons, and still love the game: Martin, Rickaby, Carslake, and Donoghue.

I think Carslake is one of the strongest finishers I have ever seen, and he can get more out of a big lurching horse than any jockey riding in these days.

I have heard people say that he does not like Epsom, and he certainly has not had much luck there, but he would be quite good enough for me if I had the horse. The fact is, he has continually ridden horses that either have no chance or are entirely unsuited to the course. I remember hearing him greatly criticized when he rode Furore in the Great Metropolitan for lying out of his ground; his critic quite ignored the fact that Furore on any course in any race was always tailed off in the first half of a race, and those who backed him at Epsom were fools, and there must have been many, for he started favourite.

But Diadem's favourite jockey was Donoghue, who with his beautiful hands and his tender treatment of a horse, combined with his marvellous dash and nerve, has always been a pleasure to watch. Carslake said to me once, "Stephen can find out more about what is left in his horse with his little finger than most men with their legs and whip." This delicacy of riding has often brought suspicion on Donoghue without the slightest cause for it.

CHAPTER XXVI

RACING AND THE WAR—HORATIO BOTTOMLEY

RACING for a short time was stopped during the War. The reason for this was simple ; a certain amount of sentimentalists, a few politicians in high places, who were supremely ignorant on racing matters, combined with the Anti-Gambling League and those few people who are against all sport, got up a cry against the continuation of racing. For a time they had it all their own way. The racing community, who knew that if racing was once stopped, the horse-breeding industry of Great Britain would receive a blow from which it would take years to recover, never thought for one moment that the authorities would do anything so foolish or shortsighted and went quietly about their business, whilst all the talking and writing was done on one side. So when it was announced after one of the Newmarket Meetings that there was to be no more racing till the end of the War there was general consternation. The reason given by the Government was "That it was against public opinion that racing should be continued." They could not say that the continuation of racing was in any way prejudical to the conduct of the War, for the Racing World had been as closely combed as any other, and the Stables were run by men over the age for the Army, by young boys and women. My youngest brother Francis Lambton who had been training for three or four years most successfully, although he was well over forty and had no military training, joined the Blues as a lieutenant in 1914 and was killed in the first months of the War in Belgium.

The Stewards of the Jockey Club were in a very unpleasant position, as any strong move on their part savoured of unpatriotism, and although they remonstrated with the Government there was nothing for them to do but accept the verdict and close down. Fortunately, there were many of us who knew that so far from doing any good to the country this action was really doing great harm. It threw more people into unemployment, it deprived the public of a recreation that for the moment took their minds off the horrors of war, and it would also destroy the one industry in which Great Britain was really supreme. The trouble lay in the fact that many of the politicians looked upon racing only as a sport, and they could not, and would not, understand that it was a great industry by which thousands of people were employed, and in which thousands had invested their money in the same way as in stocks and shares, or Government securities. It was difficult to get anyone to stand up and take the odium that would be thrown at him as being a man so lost to all sense of decency that he could give his mind to horse racing while his country was in the throes of such a desperate struggle.

My brother, Durham, although he never himself set foot on a race-course during the War, wrote a letter to the *Times* setting forth plainly the reasons for continuing racing, and this carried great weight and had much to do with changing public opinion. But it had no effect on the Government, and pressure had to be brought to bear on them from a different quarter. The Bloodstock Breeders' Association, of which Lord D'Abernon was chairman, and the Owners and Trainers' Association, of which I was chairman, got to work, and eventually the latter organized a campaign for holding public meetings all over England showing the disastrous effect the complete stoppage of racing would have on the Horse Breeding industry, and proving that public opinion was not against the holding of race meetings. We had the help of one man who at that time carried great weight and had considerable influence, Horatio Bottomley. He was the editor of *John Bull*, certainly one of the most patriotic papers, and one of the Government's staunchest supporters in its conduct of the War.

I had known Bottomley but slightly before this time, but for about six weeks I saw a great deal of him as I was in the chair at all his meetings. He was a most remarkable man, and his energy and power of work was amazing. Our campaign was a great success wherever we went, and I remember well, one afternoon shortly after a meeting at the Queen's Hall, Lloyd George telephoning to Bottomley, "You can have your racing if you can arrange matters with the railway companies," for by this time the question of transport was one of great difficulty. Here we had a great friend in Sir Herbert Walker, who was chairman of all the South Coast Railways, and he did all in his power to help us. The difficulties were immense, and the racing public have never known what a debt of gratitude they owe to Mr. T. A. Edge, the secretary of the Race-horse Owners' Association, for I am certain without his untiring energy and work we could never have overcome those difficulties, there would have been no racing, and the Horse Breeding industry would have been in a very different state to what it is now. Another man who put his back into the struggle was Mr. Batty Smith, the editor of the *Sportsman*. He was at times for more vigorous methods than those which we employed, and occasionally did not see eye to eye with the Stewards of the Jockey Club, but he always stuck to the ship and was at heart a staunch supporter of the Club and its ruling. Lord Jersey was then Senior Steward, and if it had not been for his tact and steady common-sense, and above all for his great character of a straight English gentleman, the ship might have gone on the rocks in that time of the great world-struggle.

Jersey was one of those men that the more you knew him the better you liked him. As a young man he had been a very fine gambler. He would stand to win or lose a very big stake with marvellous coolness, and his judgment was always good. When he grew older he dropped all that, and became a great figure in the Jockey Club. He was the greatest loss to the Turf and to his many friends when he died.

My readers will remember the famous Bottomley case as one of the greatest sensations of recent times. Poor Bottomley : I could not help being sorry for him when the crash came, and he was sentenced to a long term of imprisonment, although it is not possible to find excuses for him. But I do not believe that he deliberately laid himself out to rob and defraud people, but he had so many irons in the fire, his brain was so full of innumerable schemes and plans, his ideas were so large that no one man could carry them out. Although he prided himself on being a great financier, I believe him to have been one of the worst. I remember one of his secretaries saying to me, " Oh, the Guv'nor is a child about money, he never has any and never will have any."

Anyhow, I shall always think well of Bottomley for one thing, his Patriotism, which I am convinced was real and genuine. He loved England and Englishmen, and in the darkest days of that War he never lost heart. His paper, *John Bull*, always did its best to cheer people and keep them from being despondent. Bottomley with all his cleverness and with his great gift of speaking (he had a most delightful voice) was in some ways as simple as a child. He was very vain, loved flattery and the applause of the mob. About racing matters, although he had a large stud of very bad horses, he was supremely ignorant and lost heavily. When he won the Cesarewitch with Wargrave, on paper he won a big stake, but I fancy most of it went in paying old debts.

One of the arguments that was used by those who thought racing should stop was that the men who were fighting in France were much against its continuance. I believe this to have been an absolute fallacy. I certainly never came across one soldier, whether officer or private, who had that opinion, and on the one occasion when I went to France during the War I was surprised at the interest that was taken in it. I had several opportunities of going to France, but I had a strong feeling against civilians going over unless they had important business. But when I heard that my brother, General William Lambton, had been terribly injured by his horse falling with him, and that his life was in great danger, I was determined to get to him as soon as possible. Fond as I was of all my brothers, he had always been my favourite. By the help of the late General Cowans, who, though he was perhaps one of the hardest-worked men in the British Army, could always find time to do a good turn to a friend, I was able to accompany Lord Durham when he went out. They had not been able to move my brother to the Base, and he was still at the Clearing Station close to Arras. When we arrived there, he was alive but completely paralysed, in fact he had practically broken his neck. The head surgeon told us that the case was as serious as it could be and that only his pluck would pull him through. He added that he had better hopes since the morning as Billy's language had been so very bad! Pluck did pull him through, as it also did through three years when he was such a cripple that I sometimes wondered if it would have been better for him to have been killed outright, but he eventually made a wonderful recovery, though he had to give up the profession which he loved. At the beginning of the War he went out with Sir John French as his Military Secretary, but at the time of his accident he was commanding the 4th Division, having done so all through the Campaign of the Somme, and was just about to get an Army Corps.

Before I had been in the camp a couple of days I found everyone, Doctors, Officers, Tommies, Nurses, all talking to me about racing, and there, close up to the firing line, in a camp full of wounded, racing and the sporting papers were studied with the greatest interest by all ranks. That little glimpse of War I am thankful to have had. I could never have believed there could be such fine spirit, such untiring devotion to duty if I had not seen it myself, and, incidentally, I met and got to know such splendid fellows.

As a rule, about ten o'clock at night things became fairly quiet in the camp, and the hard-worked doctors drifted into the mess tent where they had made us their guests. Then out would come a roulette board, and for an hour or so they would forget all the horrors of War. I shall always remember those evenings and the men who sat round that table. They told me they could never have got through the strain of their life without this hour's relaxation. I am glad to say since the War I have met one or two of these friends of mine occasionally on a race-course.

I went once more to France after the Armistice with Jack Cowans and a great friend of mine, Evelyn Fitz-Gerald, and I had a wonderful time.

Jack Cowans was a most lovable man, his capacity for work was astounding, yet at any moment he could throw it off and enjoy the frivolities of life like a schoolboy. His work as Quartermaster-General to the British Army was one of the great features of the War, and I do not believe that he ever got half the recognition and honour that should have been his. Nothing could upset him, and, however gloomy and disastrous affairs might be, he faced them with a cheerful courage and determination to carry on to success.

I remember once I was telegraphed for to come up to the War Office on some business late in the afternoon. Owing to a thick fog I did not arrive in London till midnight. I thought I had better go there and explain, but when I got there the whole place was in darkness, and the hall porter told me that everyone except General Cowans had left. And there I found him still at work alone in his room.

After the War it took some time for racing to get into full swing again, but it did so, and I think now the Turf has never been in a more prosperous and healthy state.

When I began to write these memories I did not intend to touch upon such very recent times as I have done in these latter chapters, for, though I have trained some good horses and had many good friends in the later years of my life, of these I cannot write to-day.

On looking back, I sometimes wonder whether if I began life again I should take up the profession of a trainer of race-horses. It has many advantages, but it also has many drawbacks. With a large stable of horses there is very little time or leisure for other things; your horses occupy your thoughts to the exclusion of everything else, and the man who is not always thinking about them is not usually much good at his job. I remember once a long time ago some trainer being discussed and making the remark, " Oh you can wipe him out, he has just been married." I was much chaffed by my friends about this when at a future date I had cause to alter this opinion and was married myself. I found that by so doing the rough passages of life were made smooth, and the pleasant ones delightful. Certainly without the help of my wife this book, whether for good or for bad, would never have seen the light, and it is to her that I dedicate its pages.

INDEX

	PAGE
"Abbesse de Jouarre"	186, 187
"Abbot, The,"	37
Abington, Mr. *See* Baird	
Adams, Jimmy	26, 155-6
"Aida"	266
"Albert Cecil"	34
Alderson, General	270
"Alice Hawthorn"	238
Alington, Lord	46, 52, 190, 192, 231
Allison, William	201, 269
"Altiora"	242
"Altmark"	242-45
American style of riding	241-2
"Andrea Ferrara"	256
Apperley, Newton	14
"Aragon"	77
"Archaic"	278
Archer, Charles	45, 46
Archer, Fred	27, 32, 36-51, 55-59, 74, 76, 78, 79, 86-93, 107, 111-17, 120-24, 128, 130-32, 147, 156, 161, 188, 215, 232, 247, 251
"Archer's Mixture"	41
"Ard Patrick"	260, 268, 269
Astley, Sir John	23, 47-50, 84, 106, 155-6
"Athelstan"	296
"Ayrshire"	174, 175, 217
"Bachelor's Button"	279, 281
Baird, Abington	26, 28, 143, 181-4, 259
—— Douglas	213
Baltazzi Brothers	98
"Banstead"	198
Barber, Captain Lee	26, 73-4, 167
"Barcaldine"	106, 107, 209
Barclay, H. T.	26, 119, 120
"Bard, The"	110, 111, 114, 116, 117, 119, 121, 225
Barker, Harry	203, 204
Barrett, Fred	21, 86
Barrett, George	115, 124, 146, 150, 192, 196, 203, 244
Barrington, Charles	20
Bates, Fred	53, 75, 79, 80
Batthyany, Prince	109
"Bayardo"	288
"Be Sure"	295
Beaconsfield, Earl of	226
Beasley, Harry	152, 154, 163, 179
—— Tommy	167, 170, 178
—— Willie	164
Beasley Brothers	26
Beatty, Major Charles	229, 269, 270
Beaufort, Duke of	54, 104, 121
"Bellatrix"	175, 176
"Bellona"	140-3, 168
Belmont, Mr.	260
"Ben Battle"	85, 119, 175
"Bend Or"	50, 51, 191
"Bendigo"	87, 88, 116, 119, 120
"Beppo"	278
Beresford, Lord Charles	240
Beresford, Lord Marcus	26, 29, 44, 60, 93, 99, 104, 132, 146, 192, 194, 224, 227-9, 240, 284
Beresford, Lord William	28, 240, 242-3, 245, 247, 251
"Bevil"	219
Bevill, W.	26
Bewicke, Percy	26, 143, 200, 249
"Binfield"	81
"Birch Rod"	220, 221
Bismarck, Prince	226
Blackwell, George	140, 205, 266-7
Blanc, M.	195

	PAGE
"Blue Bonnet"	228
"Bobette"	248
"Bolero"	171, 173
"Bonny Jean"	210
"Borneo"	86
Bottomley, Horatio	310-11
Bourke, Algy	58, 59
Bowes, Mr.	112
Bowling, Captain	45
Brabazon, General	134
"Bracket"	283
Bradford, Lord	44, 52, 56
Bragge, Harry	118
"Braw Lass"	112, 113, 114
Bremond, M. de	189
Brett, Reggie. *See* Esher, Lord	
"Briar Root"	174
"Bridge of Canny"	281, 283
Bridge (game)	157
Britannia, yacht	179
"Broad Corrie"	221
Brocklehurst, Arthur	26
Brockton, W.	26
Broeck, Ten	132, 250
"Bronzino"	292
Brown, Tom	120
"Bruce"	56, 57
Bruckshaw, Tom	76
"Bullingdon"	129, 207
Bullock, jockey	37
"Burgomaster"	21
Cadogan, Lord	52, 144, 235
—— Lady	52
Calder, jockey	124
Calthorpe, Lord	54, 174, 193
Cannon, Joe	42, 55, 57, 88, 94, 120, 135, 137-41, 143-49, 151, 181-84, 198, 202, 215, 259
Cannon, Kempton	230, 240, 277
Cannon, Mornington	156, 189-90, 203-4, 208, 213, 219-21, 270, 271, 281
Cannon, Tom	36, 37, 42-3, 50-1, 56-7, 85, 88, 122, 156-60, 188, 200, 223, 236
"Canterbury Pilgrim"	109, 126, 221, 233-9, 263-4, 277, 281, 286
"Cantilever"	283
Cantiniere	55
"Captain, The"	54, 153-4
Cardross, Lord	89
Carew, General Sir Reginald Pole	66
"Carine"	56
"Carlton"	110, 122-4, 244
Carmarthen, Lord	33
Carslake, jockey	37, 116, 305, 307
Castlereaghs	52, 64
"Cathedral"	25
"Cetewayo"	91
Chaine, Mrs.	131
"Chancellor"	165
"Chancery"	154
Chaplin, Henry	129, 221
Chaplin, Lord	133-4
"Chaucer"	126, 238, 264-6, 273, 295, 298
"Cheers"	256
"Chelandry"	210, 288
"Chesterfield"	76
Chetwynd, Sir George	52, 83, 100-104
Childs	26, 34, 37, 60
Childwick, Mr. *See* Maple, Sir John Blundell	
"Chippendale"	44, 52
"Chiselhampton"	221, 248
Cholmondeley, Lord	26
Churchill, Lord Randolph	18-80
"Cicero"	215

315

INDEX

"Claribel" - 83, 84
Clayton, Edward - 63
Clifford, Lord and Lady de - 83
Clitheroe, Colonel - 136
"Cloister" - 61–63, 178–79
"Cob, The" - 110
"Cocksure" - 283–5, 295
Coleman, John - 290
Colling, Bob - 35
"Comeaway" - 178, 179
"Comfrey" - 240
"Common" - 52, 192–196
Constable - 36
Cookson, J. B. - 53, 76, 80
Coombe, R. H. - 88
Cooper, Arthur - 32–34
Cooper, Sir Daniel - 205, 217, 267
Cooper, Percy - 93
—— Mrs. - 93
"Coq d'Or" - 304
Corlett, John - 181, 182
Corns, Tom - 81, 262
"Corrie Roy" - 100, 101
"Count Schomberg" - 283
Coventry, Arthur 23, 26–30, 89, 108, 119, 122, 152, 156–57, 169, 190, 213, 276
Coventry, Lord and Lady - 54
Cowans, General - 312–3
Cox, Fairie - 217
Craven, W. G. - 53
Crawford, Mr. - 124
Crawley, Eustace - 198
Crawshaw, Mr. - 26
"Cream Cheese" - 33
"Cremorne" - 55
"Crestfallen" - 239
"Crowberry" - 174
"Cruiser Arc" - 178, 179
Cunningham, Charlie 25, 26, 143, 167, 177–81, 254
Cuthbert, Harry - 251
"Cyllene" - 288
"Cypria" - 149

D'Abernon, Lord - 285, 302–306
Daily Telegraph - 180
Dalgleish, Jerry - 21
"Damsel II" - 254
"Dansellon" - 303
Darling, Sam - 229, 260, 273
Davies, Gwyn - 26
Davis, Joe - 93
Dawson, George - 52
Dawson, John - 45, 109, 112–13
Dawson, Mat 38–40, 41, 44–45, 52, 57–58, 91, 109, 111, 113–15, 118, 140–41, 144, 205–10, 238
Day, Mr. Mat Dawson's secretary - 40
Day, William, trainer - 52, 260–2
De Clifford, Lord and Lady - 83
De Walden, Lord Howard - 269
"Decision" - 291, 299
Derby, Lady - 239, 284
Derby, Lord 126, 215–7, 221, 233, 236–37, 239, 242, 263, 271, 273, 275, 277–78, 282–85, 287, 290, 295, 299. *See also* Stanley, Lord
Devonshire, Duke and Duchess of - 53
"Devotion" - 55
"Dexterity" - 84
"Diadem" - 116, 238, 302–307
"Diadumenos" - 238, 302
"Diana" - 197, 198
Dillon, jockey - 288–89
"Dingle Bay" - 217–219
"Dionysos" - 302
"Diophon" - 238, 302
Dixie, Sir Beaumont - 262
"Dog Fox" - 152
Dollery, jockey - 165
"Dolores" - 239

"Domino" - 43
"Don Juan" - 53, 108
"Don Reynaldo" - 302
"Donnetta" - 238, 302
Donoghue, Stephen - 42, 74, 215, 305, 307
"Donovan" - 84
Doping of race-horses - 252–7
"Downpatrick" - 152
"Draycot" - 131
Drewett, Mrs. - 49
Du Bos, A. - 174
Dudley, Georgina, Lady - 173
Durham, Lord 13, 53, 76, 88, 94, 97, 103–4, 135, 143, 150, 157, 165, 175, 202, 213, 215, 255, 284, 309, 312
"Durham" - 25
"Dutch Oven" - 54–58, 208
"Dutch Skater" - 55

"Eager" - 253
"East Sheen" - 221, 254
"Eastern Emperor" - 88
"Eastern Empress" - 84
"Eau de Vie" - 155
"Echo" - 76
"Edelweiss" - 44
Edge, T. A. - 310
Edward VII 47, 90, 190, 192, 223–24, 226, 228, 235–36
"Eider" - 279
"Ejector" - 203
Ellesmere, Lord - 45–46, 161
"Ellis, Mr." *See* Morbey, Charles
"Elzevir" - 54
"Emin" - 202
Enoch, Joe - 53
"Entebbe" - 264
"Equator" - 264
Escott, Harry - 28
"Esher, Lord" - 201, 202, 212, 217
"Eunuch" - 132

Fagan, jockey - 76
Fairie, Mr. - 288
Faithful, Mr., crammer - 20–21
Falmouth, Lord 38–41, 55, 58, 188, 238, 267
Farquhar, Sir Horace 221, 243–45, 247, 254
Farquhar, Lord - 64, 100
"Father O'Flynn" - 30, 31
"Favo" - 252
Fenwick, Noel - 39, 40
Fernandez, solicitor - 117
"Fierté" - 172
Fisher, Bobby - 33
Fisher, Captain - 198
Fitzgerald, Evelyn - 313
"Flare Up" - 234–236
"Florence" - 147
"Flotsam" - 262
"Flying Fox" - 189–192
"Folkestone" - 255
Forbes, Lady Helen - 173
Ford, William - 93
Fordham, George 17, 36, 42, 49–50, 53, 55, 79, 84, 130, 231–32
Forester, Col. Henry - 52
"Fortissimo" - 79
"Foxhall" - 50, 260, 262
"Franciscan" - 144, 145, 198
"Freeny" - 166
French, Earl - 312
"Frigate" - 152, 153, 163–67, 178
"Fright" - 221
"Fugleman" - 202
"Fullerton" - 110
"Fulmen" - 107
"Furore" - 307

"Galicia" - 288
"Galliard" - 43, 46

INDEX

	PAGE
"Galloper Light"	230
"Galopin"	110, 193
"Galtee More"	103
Gambling	20
"Gamecock"	29, 61, 152–53, 163, 168, 178–9
"Gay Crusader"	304
"Gay Gordon"	265
"Gay Hermit"	110, 112
"Geheimness"	54, 55, 57, 58
"General Peace"	249
"General Scott"	261
George V	192
George, David Lloyd	310
Gerard, Lord	46, 54
Giles, Jockey	113
Gilpin, Mr.	279
"Glacis"	101, 295
Gladstone, William Ewart	15
"Glare"	205
"Glasalt"	295
"Glasconbury"	277, 281–2
"Glendale"	168
"Glengarry"	17
"Glenhill"	90
"Glenthorpe"	168–69
Goater, James, Jockey	18, 36
Goater, William, trainer	21, 53
"Gold"	54
"Gold Riach"	266
"Golden Rule"	221, 243
"Goldfield"	43, 46
Golding	43, 92, 157, 258
Goodlake, General	23
Gordon, Lord Douglas	21
"Gouverneur"	194, 195
"Grand Parade"	302
Green, Tom, of Beverley	23, 53, 71–73, 75, 77, 80–83, 90–91, 214
"Greenback"	289
Greenwood, Charles	180
Gregory, bookmaker	84
Gretton, Mr.	190
"Grey Tick"	270
"Greywell"	217
Griffiths	44, 233
Grosvenors	54
Gubbins, Mr.	103, 154, 260
Guest, Montague	18
"Gulistan"	237
Gurry, Martin	111, 114, 116
Gutteridge, Tom	32
"Hackness"	107, 108
"Hagioscope"	44
"Hair Trigger II"	298
Hall, Harry	75
Halsey	139, 278
Hamilton, Duke of	40, 84, 117, 154
Hamilton, General Bruce	66
Hammond, Jack	87, 147, 148
"Hampton"	45, 205
"Handspike"	246
"Hardrada"	27
Hardy, jockey	268
Hartigan, Frank and Hubert	68–9
Hartington, Lord	53
Hartopp	70, 135, 139, 145–7, 150
"Harvester"	147
Hastings, Lord	52
Hayhoe, trainer	53, 223–25, 229
"Hazeldean"	55
"Hazelhatch"	221
"Heresy"	193
"Hermit"	55, 56, 129–30, 133, 262
Herring, George	129
"Hettie Sorrel"	212, 213, 217
Hibbert, Charles	149, 167
"Hidden Mystery"	169
Higgins, Harry V.	104
"Highland Chief"	45, 46
"Hippia"	55

	PAGE
Hirsch, Baron	190–92, 208
"His Majesty"	281
Hobson, Teddy	142
"Hollington"	198–200
Holman, J.	26
"Holocaust"	189, 190
Horses with prick ears	138
Houldsworth, Mr.	17
Howett	167
Huggins, J.	240–42, 246, 250, 253, 260
"Humewood"	127, 158, 166
Humphreys, trainer	112
Hungerford, Harry	52, 65, 70, 73, 85–88, 94, 152, 166
Hunt	26
Huxtable, jockey	126
I'Anson, Robert	26, 34, 53, 75, 80
"Ilex"	139, 178–9
"Illuminata"	205
"Irma"	82
"Irish Elegance"	305
"Iroquois"	250
"Isinglass"	127–29, 184, 203, 204, 207, 277, 281, 286
"Ismail Pasha"	94
"Isonomy"	37, 132, 174, 217, 250
"Jack Frost"	147
"Jacobite"	112
James, Arthur	285
Jameson, Willie	179
"Janissary"	275
Jardine, D. J.	178
Jardine, Sir Robert	53, 79–80
Jarvis, William	204
"Jeddah"	126, 243
Jenkins, Lady Caroline	63
Jenkins	32, 33, 61–64, 162–63, 165, 167, 171
Jennings, Tom, trainer	18, 53, 149, 262
Jersey, Lord	289, 310–11
"Jest"	301
Jewitt, trainer	26, 54, 127–29
Jockeys and smoking	214–5
Jockeys, old and new	214–5
Jockeys, present-day	74–75
John Bull	310–11
"John o' Gaunt"	238, 286
"Johnny Longtail"	165, 166
Johnstone, Sir Frederick	46, 52, 185, 187, 190, 192
Johnstone, Major Hope	129
Johnstone, Wenty Hope	25, 26
"Jolly Sir John"	152
Jones, John	26
Jones, Oliver	68, 169
Jones, Wengy	169
Jones, jockey	192
Jousiffe	193-94
Joyner, Andrew	250, 253, 288
Kavanagh, General	66
Keaner, Mr.	14
Keen, Billy	291
Keene, Mr.	260
"Kermesse"	54, 55, 57
"Keysoe"	278
"Keystone"	275–79, 283, 286
"Kilwarlin"	127, 166
"Kilworth"	65, 152
"King of Diamonds"	144, 259
King William	295–9
"Kingsclere"	57
Kinsky, Count	26, 33, 61, 62, 64–67, 85, 134–6, 152, 153, 173, 217
Kirby, jockey	162
"Kirconnel"	209, 210
"Kisber"	98
"Knight of the Thistle"	54, 247
"La Flèche"	191–2, 286

INDEX

	PAGE
"Labrador"	227
Lacy, Mr.	186
"Ladas"	39, 129, 205-210
Lambton, Colonel Charles	197, 246
Lambton, F. W.	76
Lambton, Francis	308
Lambton, Freddy	15, 53
Lambton, Hon. George	
—— accident on "Hollington"	199-200
—— boyhood	13-14
—— buys his first race-horse	21
—— goes to Eton	16
—— —— Trinity College, Cambridge	19
—— marriage	314
—— opinion of "St. Simon"	109
—— real start as a jockey	152
—— rides for Tom Cannon	156
—— rides his first winner	23
—— school at Winchester and Brighton	15-16
—— stables burnt	273
—— starts as a trainer	201-202
—— —— for Derby stable	215
—— writes for *St. Stephen's Review*	201
Many references throughout the book.	
Lambton, General William	312
Lane, jockey	267
Lansdowne, Lord	98
Lascelles, Lord	52
Lathom, Mr.	198
"Laveno"	208
Lebaudy, M.	258
"Le Nord"	194
"Le Sancy"	175
Leader, Tom	136
Lee, Billy, headmaster at Brighton	16
Lee, Fred V.	252-3
Lefevre, Mr.	262
Lehndorff, Count	221-2
Leigh, Mr. "Bunny"	54, 138
"Lemberg"	288-93, 299
Lewis, Sir George	103
Lewis, Sam	95-101, 173
Lewis, Mrs. Sam	100
"Lily Agnes"	118, 238
Linde, H. E.	152, 154, 163
"Lioness"	65, 152
Livock, Mr.	273, 294
Loates, Sam	210, 245, 249
Loates, Tommy	149, 203-4, 208, 214, 223, 225
"Lock and Key"	275
Loeffler, horse dentist	175, 176, 192
Londonderry, Lady	53, 64
Londonderry, Lord	14, 197
Lonsdale, Lord	70
"Lord Beaconsfield"	159
Lorillard, P.	240, 250-51
"Love Wisely"	224, 281, 283
"Loved One"	110
"Lowland Chief"	46
"Lowlander"	136
"Lown, The"	136, 137
Lowther, James	53, 76
"Lucerne"	106
Luke, jockey	120
Lund, Charles	75, 76, 82
Lurgan, Lord	52, 70, 72, 89, 159, 160
Lushington, Tommy	218
Lynham, Fred	296-7, 299
McCalmont	54, 269, 270
McGeorge	29, 108
Machell, Captain	48, 54, 84, 125-27, 129-31, 133, 135, 136, 138, 146, 165, 176
McQueen, Professor	273
"Madcap"	146, 147
Madden, jockey	268
"Magpie"	304
Maher, Danny	213, 215, 257, 264-68, 271-72, 276-82, 286-93, 299
"Maid of the Mist"	198
Mainwaring, Reggie	125

	PAGE
Manser, W. H.	93, 94
"Manton, Mr." *See* Montrose, Duchess of	
Maple, Sir J. Blundell	91, 112
"Marcian"	118, 242
"Marco"	288
"Marden"	217
"Marie Stuart"	234
Marlborough, Duchess of	240
Marriott, Cecil	274
Marsh, Dick	26, 152-55, 178, 192, 223-29, 275
Martin, Johnny	71, 72, 268, 272, 303, 307
Martin, "Skeets"	260, 267, 275-6, 291, 293
"Martini"	84
"Martyr, The"	21
"Matchbox"	206, 208
"Matchmaker"	52
Mawson, jockey	164
Maynard, Anthony	13
"Mazagam"	213-14
"Meddler"	183
"Melange"	221, 240
"Melton"	122, 123
"Memoir"	193-95
"Mephisto"	110
"Mercutio"	149
Merry, Archie	193
Merry, Charlie	77
"Merry Maiden"	167
Meux, Admiral Sir Hedworth	90, 91-3
Middleton, "Bay"	25, 26
Middleton, Lord	26
"Midshipmite"	61, 198
"Miguel"	33
Miller, Sir James	266-7
Miller, T. B.	143
Milner, Dudley	76
Milner, Harry	157
"Mimi"	39, 40
"Minoru"	149, 226
'Mintagon"	80
"Minthe"	118
"Minting"	39, 110-21, 217, 288
"Miss Foote"	193
"Miss Jummy"	110, 117-18
Mitchell, "Mike"	16
"Modwena"	110
Molyneux, Lord	202-4
"Monarch"	306
Moncrieff, Ronnie	156, 170-73
Montague, Lord Charles	256
Montrose, Duchess of ("Mr. Manton")	44, 54-55, 100, 121, 124-26, 233
Montrose, Duke of	76
Moore, Garrett	67, 68, 165, 170, 193-95
Moore, John H.	68
Moore, Willie	26, 67, 68, 165, 169
Morbey, Charles	149-50, 237, 250, 275
Mordan, Sammy	56
Mordaunt, Lady	173
Morgan, Harry	84
Morris	87
Morton, Charles	183, 259
"Mosquito"	202
"Mowerina"	84, 110, 193
Murrietta, C. and F.	135, 136, 145
"Nameless"	55
"Narcissa"	57
"Neil Gow"	210, 288-9
"Nellie"	54-58
"New Oswestry"	63
Newman, Bill	248
Nightingall, Arthur	199
"Nimble"	231
"Nina"	146
"Nouveau Riche"	221, 244-5
"Novice"	244
"Oberon"	28, 110
"Ocean Wave"	200, 239

INDEX

	PAGE
"Old Joe"	162, 163
"Oleander"	217, 218
Oliphant, General	206
O'Neill, Frank, jockey	297
"Orangepeel"	202
"Orby"	302
"Orme"	191, 192
"Ormerod"	200, 201
"Ormonde"	109–11, 114–16, 119–21, 191, 225, 228, 238, 288
"Orwell"	194
Osborne, John	36, 58, 78–79
Osborne Brothers	75–76
"Outsider"	265
Owen, Hugh	26, 29, 108
Owen, Roddy	26, 29–31, 33, 61, 62, 145, 152, 170, 171, 178–80, 198, 200
Paget, Gerald	251
Palmer, Lynwood	290
"Pampero"	203
"Pan"	138, 139
"Papyrus"	88, 204
"Paragon"	268
"Parasang"	170–2
"Paris III"	237
Parker, Townley	168, 169
"Parole"	250
"Passaic"	78, 79
Peck, Percy	288–89
Peck, Robert	106–9, 111–12, 114, 116, 131, 233
"Peppermint"	58
Perkins, Charles	25, 53, 76, 80
"Persephone"	296
"Persimmon"	207, 223–28, 235, 237–8, 275, 277
"Persinus"	276
Persse, Atty	91
"Perth"	189
"Peter"	47–49, 106, 212
"Phalange"	278
"Phalaris"	307
"Phantom"	141, 142
"Pharos"	204
"Pharpar"	302
"Pilgrimage"	126, 233, 286
Pincus, Jacob	251
Pink Eye illness	265, 271, 273
"Plaisanterie"	86, 87, 120
"Playfair"	164
"Playful"	159, 160
"Polariscope"	73
"Polemic"	158
"Pompeia"	23
Porter, John	54–56, 110, 114–15, 189–92
Portland, Duke of	39, 52, 88, 91, 110, 129, 193, 195
Potocki, Count	110
"Presto II"	279
"Pretty Polly"	279–81, 293
Price, Peter	150
Prick-eared horses	138
Prince, J.	26
"Prince Palatine"	297–8
"Prince Simon"	258–9
"Prince William"	278
Pritchard, Ted	93
"Privateer"	78, 79
Prize-fighting	183
"Propeller"	217
"Pudding"	23–24
"Quack"	221
"Queen Bee"	131
"Queen's Journal"	101
"Quick Lime"	56
"Quintessence"	267, 268
Racing, North Country	75
—— South Country	75
Racing during the War	308–12

	PAGE
"Raeburn"	129
"Ravensbury"	128, 203, 204
"Red Eyes"	149, 150
"Red Hussar"	152
Redfern, Mr.	101
"Redpath"	29, 152, 162
Reeves, John	67
"Regal"	135
Reiff Brothers, jockeys	252
"Retreat"	52
"Reveller"	79
"Révèrend"	39, 40
Rhodes, Colonel Frank	30
Rickaby, Fred	86, 175, 187, 203, 212–14, 218–19, 235–37, 239, 242, 245, 248, 266, 271, 286, 300, 304, 307
"Ringlet"	164–66
"Riversdale"	117
"Robert the Devil"	50, 51
Robinson	175–6, 227, 243
"Rock Sand"	126, 221, 267–71
Rodd, Sir J. Rennell	31
Rodney, Lord	127, 158, 165
"Roquebrune"	267
"Roquefort"	32–34, 94, 152–53, 160, 126, 221, 163–64, 168, 178–7
Rosebery, Lord	32, 39, 55, 57, 135, 205–7, 209–11, 225, 288
"Rosemount"	72
"Rosicrucian"	55
"Rossiter"	50
Rothschild, James de	167, 292
Rothschild, Leopold de	53, 55, 103, 215, 219, 223–25, 227, 229, 230–32, 237
"Roundshot"	88–91
"Royal Flush"	252–3
Russell, Lord	99, 103–5
"Ruy Lopez"	256
Ryan, James, trainer	17–18, 151
Sadler, Alfred	83–86, 88, 90, 135, 152, 175, 239
"Sailor Prince"	123
"Sainfoin"	194, 267
"St. Amant"	230
"St. Blaise"	46, 52, 193
"St. Cloud"	240–41
"St. Frusquin"	223–27, 230, 302
"St. Gatien"	87, 119, 120, 147
"St. Julian"	21
"St. Marguerite"	54–57, 174
"St. Mirin"	110, 121–24, 131
"St. Serf"	264
"St. Simon"	109, 110, 193, 228, 238, 262–64
St. Stephen's Review	201
"St. Victorine"	264
Sanderson, trainer	44, 76
"Santa Brigida"	213, 283
"Saraband"	110, 112–15
Sassoon, Arthur	53
"Satellite"	33, 90
"Savoyard"	159, 162–65, 167–69
"Sceptre"	191, 265, 268–70
'Schomberg"	243
Schroeder, Baron	162, 163
Scott, John	216
"Sea Breeze"	174–76
"Seaforth"	296
"Seakale"	217
Seaton	86, 87
"Seclusion"	275
"See Saw"	56
Sefton, Lord	202
"Semolina"	193
Sensier, Billy	26, 60–61, 154
Sharpe, Harry	220, 237, 258
"Sheridan"	202
Sherrard, trainer	52, 100–101, 103
Sherwood, Bob	185, 187–88
"Shotover"	54, 56–58, 191
"Shrine"	157

INDEX

	PAGE
"Sidthorpe"	154
"Silurian"	101
"Silver Sea"	142
Sims, American jockey	241
"Sir Hugo"	52
"Sir Martin"	149
"Sir Visto"	39, 209–10, 227
Skelton, Tom	26, 29, 162–67
"Skopos"	214
Sloan, Tod	189, 190, 214, 240–48, 251, 266
Sly	65, 66
Smith, Batty	310
Smith, Captain "Doggy"	26, 64
Smoking and jockeys	214–5
"Snaplock"	259
Snowden, Jim, jockey	27, 36, 42, 76–78, 81
"Solaro"	217
Soltykoff, Prince	53
"Somers, Mr." *See* Somerset, Lord Edward
Somerset, Lord Edward	122–124
"Speculum"	73
Spence, Tom	25, 26, 71, 72, 177
Sporting Times	181
Sportsman	201, 269, 310
"Springfield"	18
Stag-hunting	232
Stamford, Lord	55
Stanley, Lady Alice	239
Stanley, Lord	213, 233, 243
See also Derby, Lord
"Stedfast"	295–300
Stern, George	278, 279
Stevens, W. G.	123
Stokes, Mr., horse dealer	30
"Stuart"	174
"Sunny Jane"	303, 304
"Sunstar"	296–7
"Surefoot"	193–95
"Suspender"	54
"Sweetbread"	46, 54
"Swynford"	126, 238, 286–87, 289–94, 298–99
Taylor, Alec	54, 121–23, 126, 137, 166, 269, 288
"Tetrarch"	175
"Tetratema"	116
"Thais"	224, 235–36
"Thebais"	88
Thirlwell, Dan	26, 153–55, 160
Thompson, George	25, 27, 119
"Thormanby"	238
"Thornfield"	155
Throckmorton, Sir William	141
"Throstle"	208
"Throwaway"	21
"Tom Jones"	33
"Tommy Tittlemouse," Archer's last mount	132
"Tenans"	120
"Toxophilite"	88
"Tracery"	88
"Tristan"	106, 233, 239, 260, 262, 263
"Tristram"	50
"Troutbeck"	278
"Turco"	67
Tuyll, Baron Max de	135, 168, 171, 173
"Usna"	163, 164
"Valour"	48, 106, 128
Vane-Tempest, Lord Herbert	157
"Vedas"	274
"Velasquez"	210
"Velocity"	265–6

	PAGE
"Venus's Looking Glass"	212
"Verneuil"	18
"Vibration"	84
Victoria, Queen	227
"Victorious"	276
Vincent, Sir Edgar. *See* D'Abernon, Lord
"Volodyovski"	252, 276
"Voluptuary"	32, 33, 168, 178
Vyner	44, 53, 76, 111, 115, 117–19, 174, 292
Wadlow	44, 52
Walden, Lord Howard de	269
Walker, Sir Herbert	310
Waller	26, 143
"Wallenstein"	106
Wallis, Rev. Colville	125
Ward, Bobby	156
Wargrave	311
Warre, Edmund, head master at Eton	16
Watson, Anthony	229
Watson, John	229
Watts, Jack	28, 36, 77, 89, 112, 115, 117, 192, 206, 208, 220, 221, 223, 225, 226, 259
Waugh, Charles	274
Waugh, W.	278
Weatherby, Edward	108
Webb, Fred	36, 42, 46, 54
Welden, jockey	76
"Well Done"	286
Wemyss, Lord	14
Westminster, Duke of	54, 56, 110, 188–91
Westminster, Lord	23
"Westwood"	43, 92
Wheatley, jockey	276
"Whisk Broom"	288–9
Whitaker, Captain A. E.	144, 198, 200
White, Tiny	205
"White Ant"	264
"White Knight"	279
Whitney	80, 250–52, 260, 288
"Why Not"	167, 178, 200, 201
Wickham, Major	146
"William the Silent"	181, 182
"William the Third"	295
Williams, General Owen	52, 104–5, 111, 116
Williams, Mr. and Mrs.	83
Williamson, George	180, 199
Willoughby, Sir John	54
Wilson	26, 31–34, 94, 152–53, 160, 167, 179, 215
Winans, Mr.	149
"Windsor"	47
"Winkfield's Pride"	227
"Winslow"	33
"Wisdom"	193
Wishard, American trainer	252–3
Wolverton, Lord	285
Wood, Charles	36, 42, 44, 46, 48, 49, 87, 101, 103, 104, 113, 116, 131
Wood, Sir Evelyn	31
Wood, Lindsay	14
Woodburn	122–24
Woodlands, Teddy	139
Wootton, Frank	213, 252, 271, 290–93, 296, 297, 299–300
Wootton, Richard	292, 298, 299, 300
Wootton, Stanley	300
"Xema"	85–88
Yates, Arthur	60, 61
Young, Mr.	274
Zetland, Lord	27, 53, 76, 78
"Zinfandel"	269, 270
"Zoedone"	33, 63, 152–53